George Sear's Norfolk

as told to

Antony King-Deacon

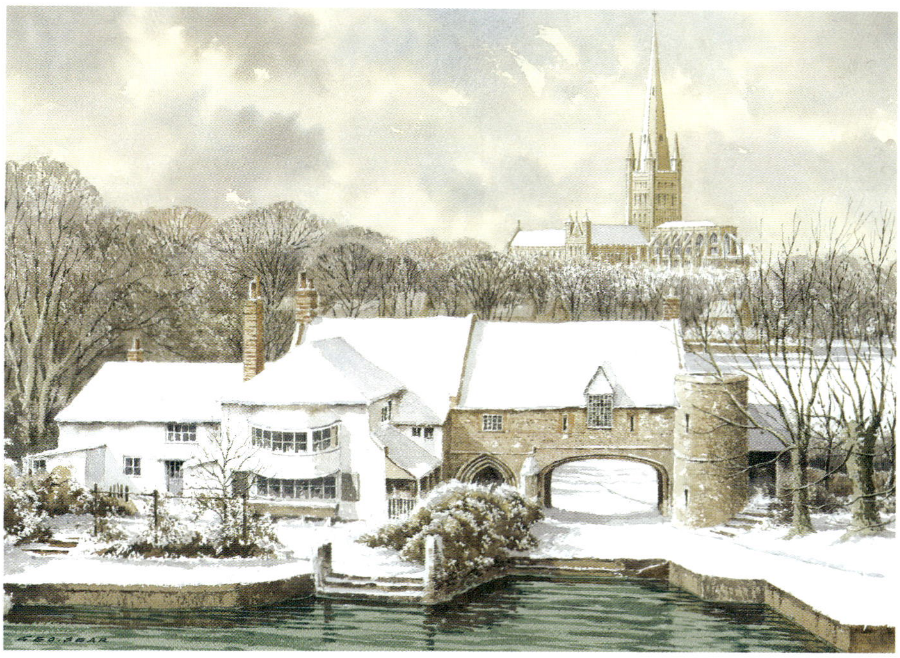

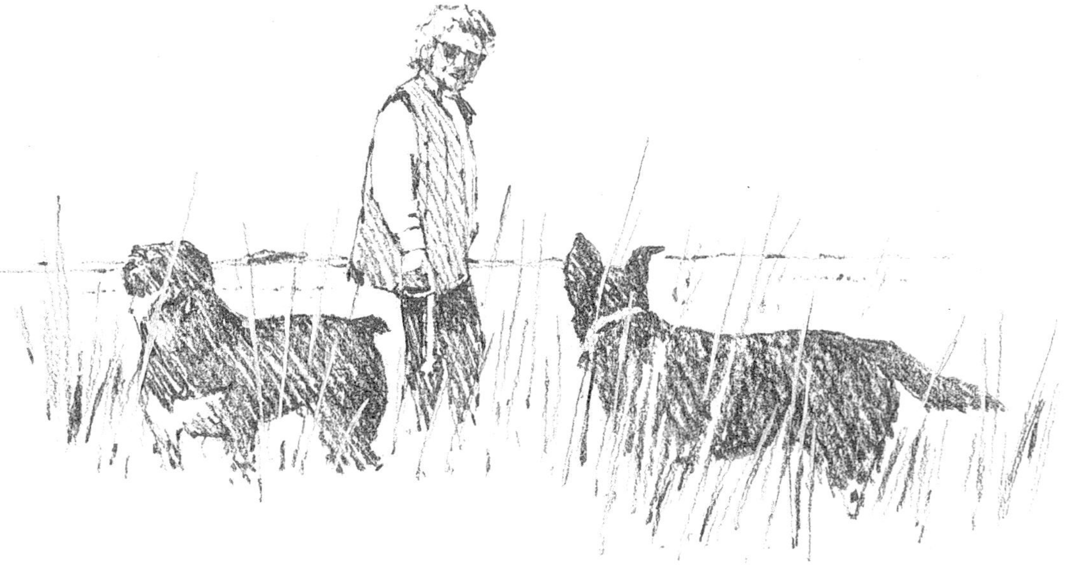

Dedicated to my wife Maureen

George Sear's Norfolk

as told to

Antony King-Deacon

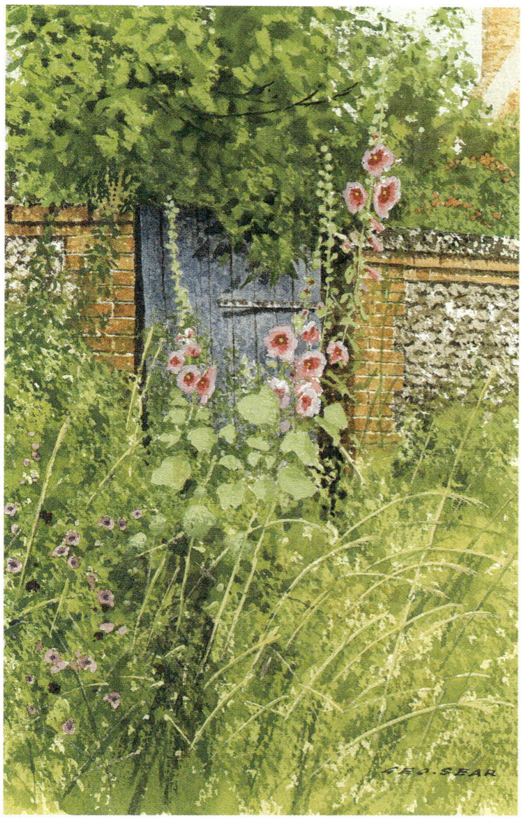

Barnwell's Timescape Publishing

Acknowledgements

To Michael and Teresa Hill of Picturecraft of Holt and our close relationship over the past two decades, both in business and as friends, where two years ago I met Antony.

I would like to thank Antony King-Deacon for his invaluable contribution and his patience and encouragement in the production of this book.

Ernie A. Janes, Photographer and Nick Hall Images, Photographer, for their expertise.

I would also like to thank all my patrons for their help and willingness to allow their paintings to be included in this book, some going back fifteen years.

First published August 2000 by
Barnwell's Timescape Publishing
Hall Lane
North Walsham
Norfolk
NR28 9DT

Second Impression September 2001

ISBN 0-9531851-4-1

Produced and printed in England by
Barnwell's Print Ltd
Barnwell's Printing Works
Penfold Street
Aylsham
Norfolk
NR11 6ET

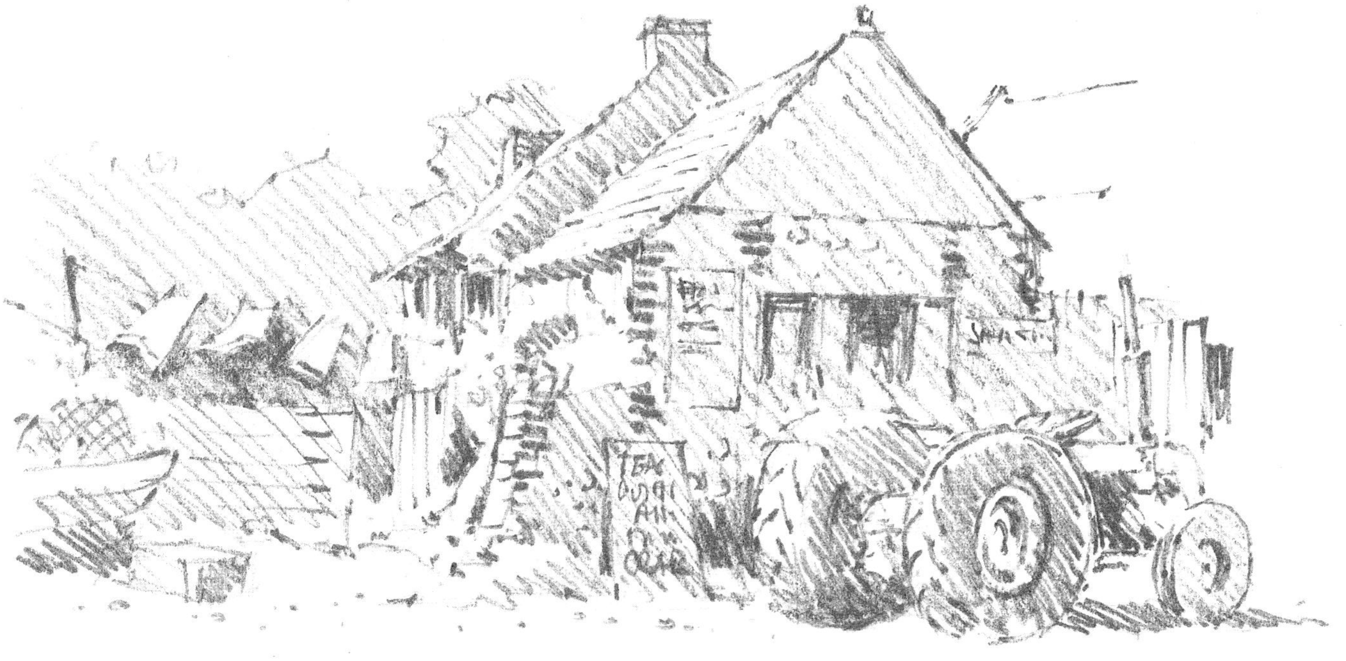

Contents

Introduction

George Sear doesn't strike you as an artist. But then, what should an artist look like; pale, tortured, haunted, thin from starvation in his garret? What does strike you about George is that he is large, big of spirit, comely of frame, enormous of fun. A man from whom you would not hesitate to buy a used car. Indeed, he is the artist as businessman. Those who buy his work are not, to him, clients but customers, many of whom become treasured friends.

The expression 'in your face' might have been coined to describe George's attitude towards his world. Certainly you get what you see with him. Bluff, candid and straightforward he is. But although he must don the motley of the showman, the extrovert, his heart is not in it. In the minutes prior to the preview evening of his one-man show each August at the Picturecraft Gallery in Holt he is a perspiring, nervous, fidgeting self-doubter. He has never taken his talent nor his customers for granted. Every work is an achievement won, every sale is as his first.

Our idea of making this book together was that George wanted to share the experiences he had during the painting of these pictures. Usually the artist is content to allow them to speak for themselves, to stand the scrutiny of prospective customers.

A strange meeting, then, there is between George and myself. I am a professional garden writer. Paintings are flat, one-dimensional - though according to the degree of magic can become three dimensions. Gardens, however, have six dimensions; the three that you see, yes, but also the senses of touch, smell and sound. Yet I can touch, smell and hear what George captures on paper or canvas. For me the marshes and fingering creaks along the north coast of Norfolk sing in his hands. So it was a marriage of the senses he and I enjoyed from the outset of our journey together. As George told me his stories I winkled out their essences and tried to distil them.

All of which is as nothing without Maureen. Theirs is a partnership, a love that those who pass near can warm their lives upon, as at a glowing fire. Maureen is stability, calmness and wisdom. The watcher in the wings, the home to return to and the guide through the storm, though one suspects that turbulence dare not spread beyond the mat at the door. Maureen is, in a word, the rock upon which George has built his life. Those who love his work should be grateful to her.

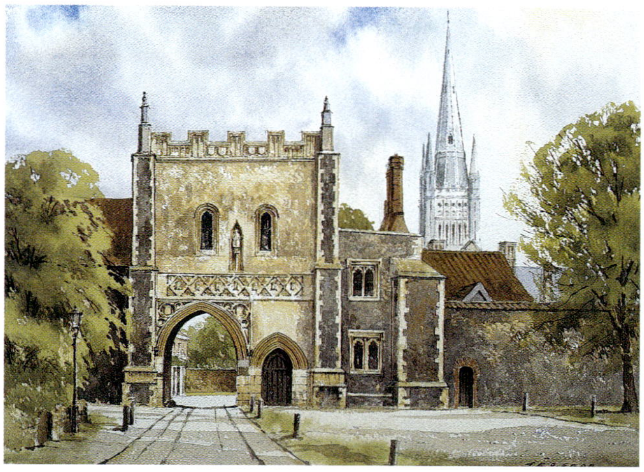

Preface

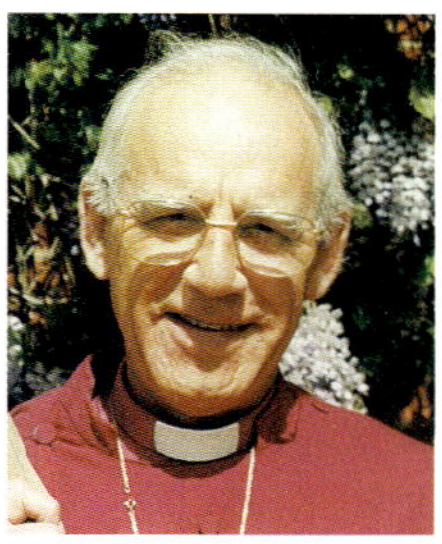

Perhaps more than any other county in England, Norfolk has attracted artists like a magnet through the ages. It has neither the spectacular vistas of the Lake District nor the dramatic coastal scenery of Devon and Cornwall, but it has something special that almost defies description.

There is a quality of light in this part of East Anglia and a subtlety of landscape, that both draws artists to it and inspires them.

It is a landscape punctuated by medieval churches, rooted in the soil like trees and as much part of the Norfolk scene as the water, cornfields and great skies that are present everywhere.

George Sear, like many great artists before him, has been inspired by the landscape we love and this book contains a variety of his skillful and deeply felt impressions. But unlike most artists, he has also recorded encounters with people he has met on his painting expeditions.

For those of us who have had the privilege of working with the people of Norfolk, they are as endlessly fascinating, locals and visitors alike, as the painterly landscape. This is why this book is so rare among reproductions of artists' work. Unusually, his ear is as acutely sensitive as his eye and this provides his readers with a book of absorbing interest.

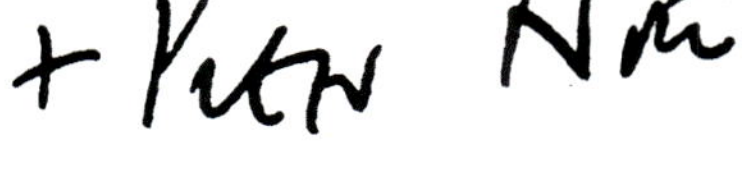

Peter Nott
Bishop of Norwich 1985 - 1999

'Norfolk was rousing my soul.'

Wiveton

They say that being a painter must be a solitary life. Well, it is and it isn't. Often I spend the whole day alone on the marshes or on the bank of a river or on the edge of a field of corn that is bloodied with poppies. Sometimes, sitting at my easel, people pass by. And sometimes they won't go away. But generally they do.

Many years ago, when I first started to paint the Norfolk landscape, when it had seeped into my psyche and haunted me, drawing me on to newer and more intimate aspects of its nature, I set about painting the church at Wiveton.

It was early spring, the middle of March perhaps, and the willows beside the slow-running Glaven were grey with buds. I sat on the river's gentle bank looking towards the bridge with the church behind. The breeze scudded the white cotton wool clouds quickly across the sky. The fitful sun was warm when it touched the skin.

The painting was going well. Norfolk was rousing my soul. I felt a strong sense of being at peace with nature, with the world.

Then I noticed two boys approaching from the village on their bicycles. Eleven or twelve, they were obviously friends. They stopped in the middle of the bridge, as lads do, and started to throw pebbles down into the river, as lads aimlessly do. Then I heard one of them say:

'Look, there's an artist.'

'So what?' said his friend.

'Let's go down and see what he's up to.'

'Nah,' said the other.

'Come on.'

'Nah. There'll be hundreds here soon. My dad says they come in with the cuckoos.'

Thus the quality of my relationship with the people on the landscape of Norfolk was established. We knew for ever who we were.

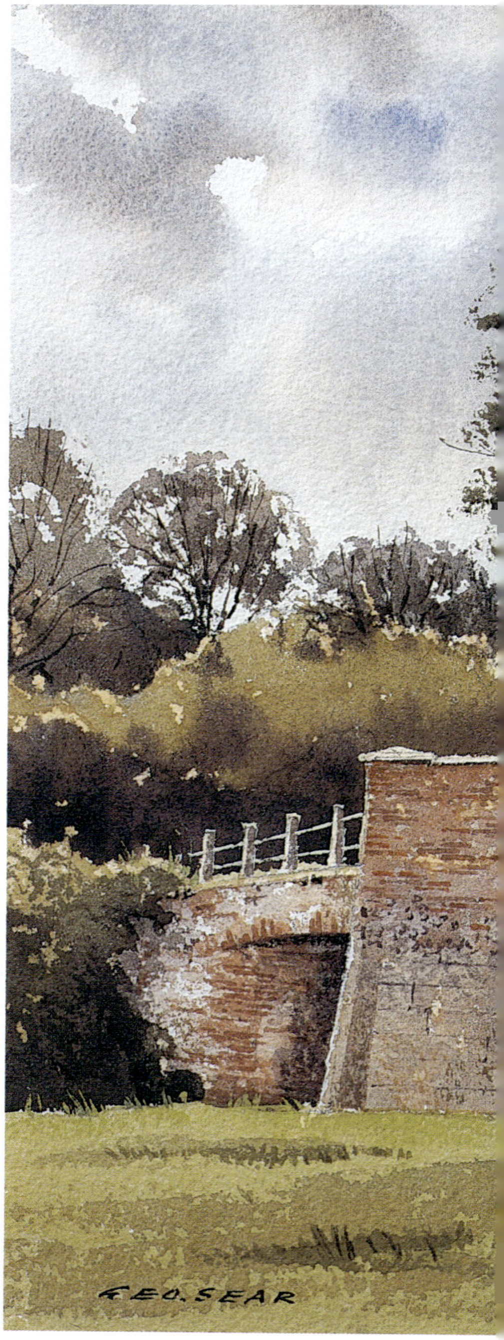

Bridge over the Glaven, Wiveton.

Fact File

Paint the picture in your mind before you begin. A few minutes thought before you start may enable you to move a few yards to a better view point.
This subject caught my eye, as having a rising focal point, from marsh, to bridge, then to the church. I placed the church just right of centre, and the tall willows stop the eye from moving off and also help to balance the group of trees above the bridge on the left. I positioned the boys so as to silhouette against the light sky.
With the darting cloud shadows dancing across the face of the tower, use counter-change to get a darker cloud behind the top of the tower for maximum impact, and a small patch of blue at the top left of centre, indicates more settled weather later. Be aware that the bridge has been repaired on many occasions, and also note the stone and brick patterns mingle. And don't over do the detail in the cobbled stones.
The paper used is Whatman 200 lb. Rough. I stretched it onto my board, I prefer it this way.

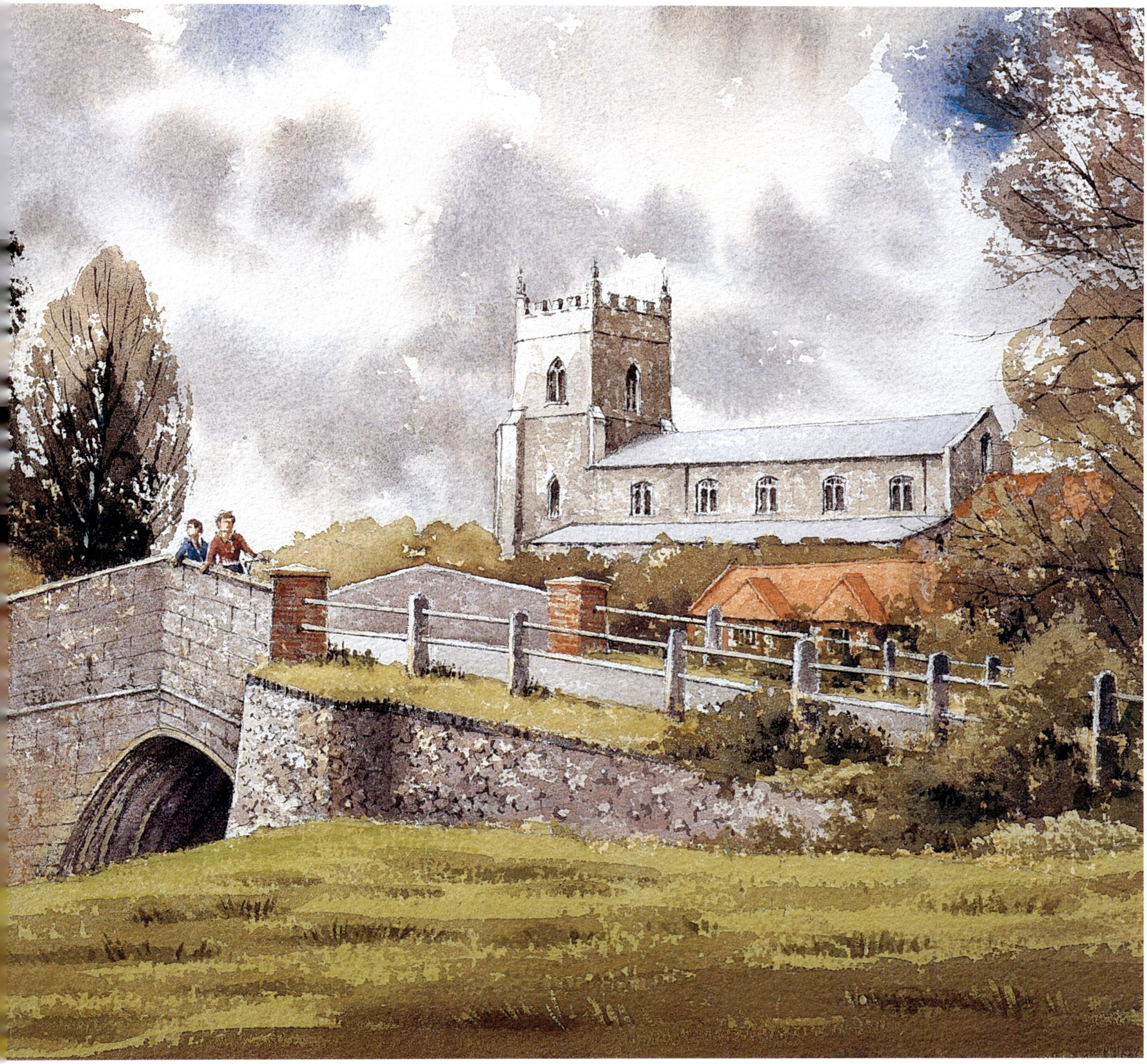

'Water-meadows fascinate me . . .'

Castle Acre

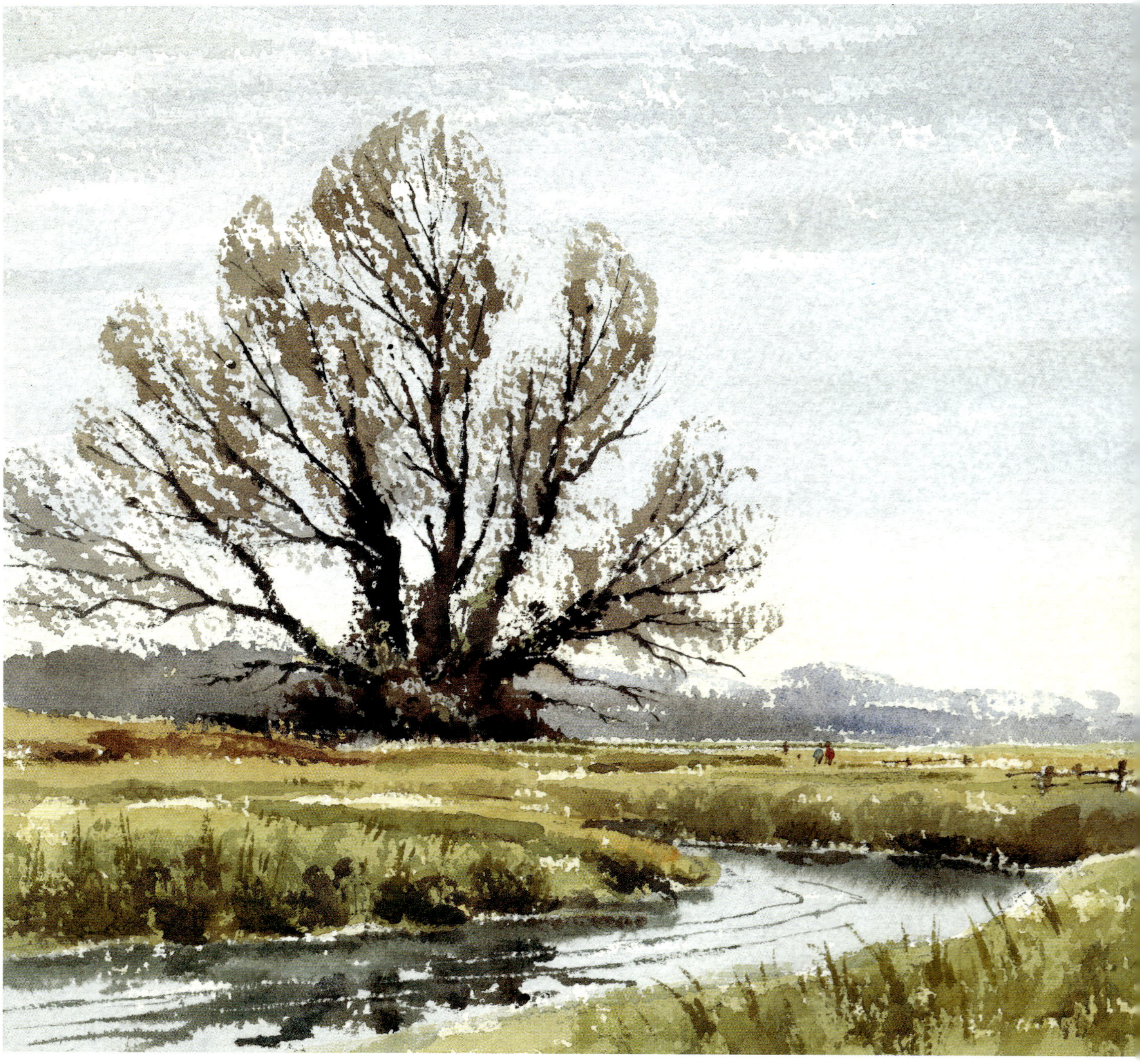

Fact File

Very little was needed to draw in this picture. Just a horizon line, the general position of the main tree and the curve of the river.
Make sure the sky is dry before dry brushing in the large old willow tree and notice the reflections of the far bank which were added to the river whilst still damp. By working on-site you'll achieve a fresh spontaneous painting. Set yourself a target, maybe only an hour, to complete the job.

Water-meadows fascinate me. It seems the landscape is floating, moored by invisible ties to the earth. At any time of the year they will inspire. It must have been early March or the dog-end of February that I came to Castle Acre not to paint the ruinous castle, nor the priory, nor any of the charming cottages. It was the River Nar that drew me and its hand-maidens the water-meadows lying between the gentle breasts of the shallow hills. The Nar was drifting along with ice on its back. The day was crisp, bright and clear. Even the air smelt clean. It braced.

By the river, Castle Acre.

I had set up on the footpath and using my pencil, was making my first rough sketches when I sensed out of the corner of my eye someone standing close by.

'Morning.'

'Morning,' I said, barely looking up.

'Cold.'

'It is a bit nippy.' I never mind people stopping to pass the time of day, but nor do I encourage it.

'What pencil are you using?'

'2 B'.

'And the paper?'

'Arches 3001b rough.' He wasn't going to go away.

He was thin and the word flew into my mind as he stood there, mincing. Kenneth Williams flashed into my head. I hoped I was not about to be importuned. I shifted nearer to the bank of the river and continued working. He shifted nearer. I could smell his after-shave.

By now I had completed the limited sketching the landscape demanded and was beginning to prepare my paints. I started to mix them.

'What colours are those you're mixing?'

I was preparing for the sky, Cobalt Blue and French Ultramarine softening to raw Sienna at the horizon. Do you see, I said pointing at my paints and reeling off their names. I suppose, I must admit, I was becoming slightly ruffled.

'I'm not bothering you am I?' He clutched his hands together and wriggled his shoulders in mock pique. Mr. Williams sidled into my mind again.

'Not at all,' I said. 'I run courses from time to time.'

He clapped his hands with glee. 'Good,' he said 'I'll go and get my camp chair. See you in a mo.'

Before I could stop him he was off along the footpath towards the village. He gave a little wave when I looked up. I longed for my sky to dry so that I could get into the car and finish off at home, but the cold early spring air had no warmth to help me. I waved my paper about frantically but he suddenly re-appeared with his folding seat. He came over, put it up, and sat next to me.

For an hour he taunted me with his questions. Why that colour? Why blue with umber? What was the sienna for? Wasn't that a bit too drastic? What about the water? Isn't that brush a mite too thick for the willow?

I was amazed that I contained myself, that I didn't hit him. I thought about abandoning the painting altogether and drive off with a skid in my wheels. But in truth he was harmless. As harmless as a gnat. And when I had finished my inquisitor disappeared as quickly and as silently as he had appeared.

Feeling as exasperated as I had, commentating on every mix and brushstroke, the resulting painting was in an unfathomable way disquieting. Certainly it was not my usual style. It was – how can I say? – loose, free, quick. If my usual style is close, introspective, accurate then this was open, almost impressionist.

But I know this, if ever I felt the need to paint another picture as free, as open as this then I would take that Kenneth Williams doppleganger with me.

'A perfect day and gentle . . .'

Glandford

John Constable sat on my shoulder that day at Glandford. He kept whispering in my ear. He understood that sky. The cottages, the trees, the footbridge, the church he knew. I am not saying that he influenced me in my painting. My teachers and my gods are other than he. And I paint who I am, or vice versa. But Constable lurked in the Englishness of the scene, although for me it was specifically Norfolk and especially the landscape of its northern region

It was a perfect day and gentle. One or two people had been to enjoy the River Glaven gliding quietly under the bridge towards the mill. The church had just rung out one of its hymns. Indeed, the peel of those melodious bells danced over the rippling surface of the water when a clamourous school bus turned off the road to Wiveton and along the lane towards me, stopping only feet from the water's edge. There is a ford, I remembered, but too deep for all but a large 4-wheel drive. The bus wouldn't make it, that was for sure. I watched and waited.

A minute passed. Suddenly a gaggle of dozens of school-children

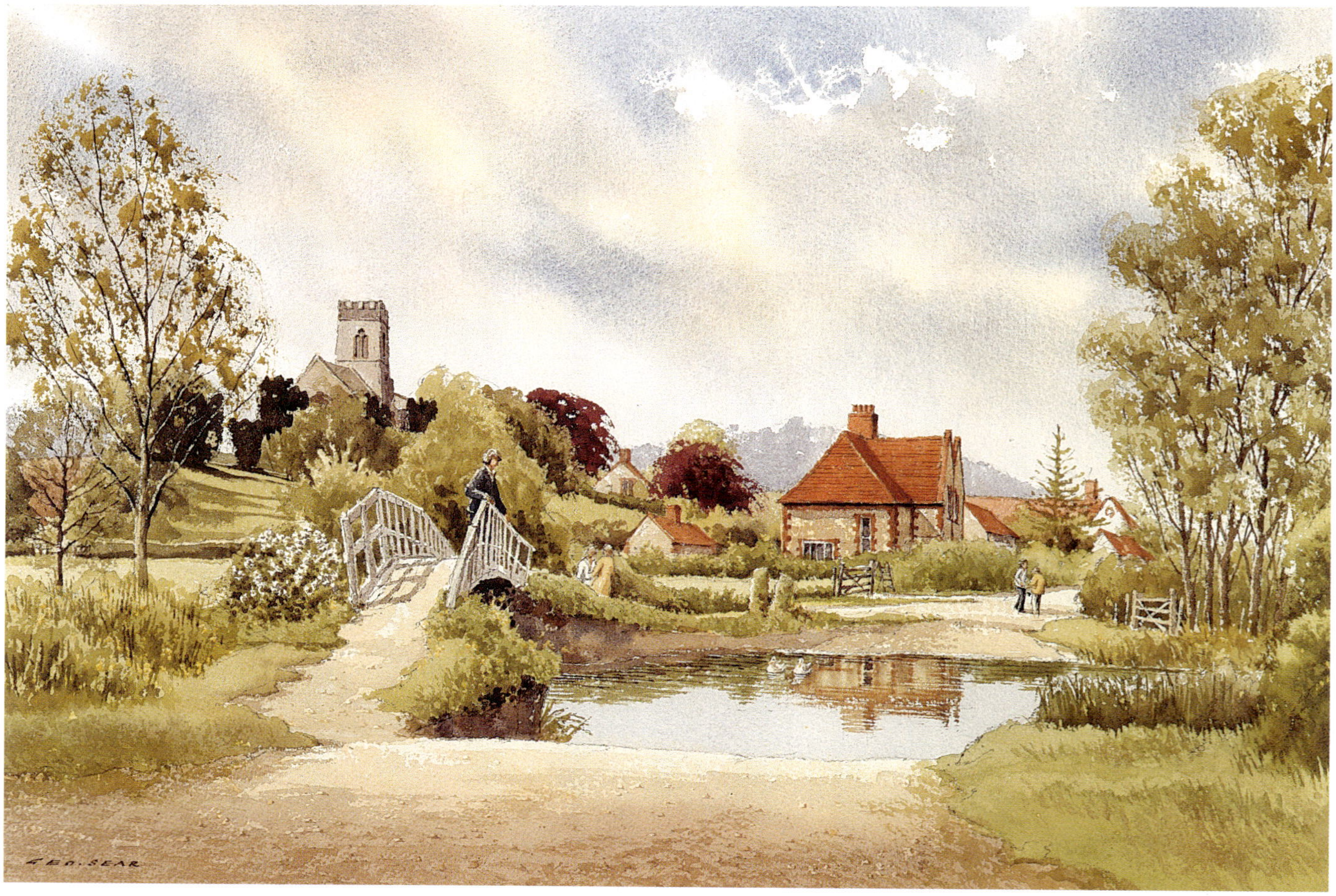

Glandford in the Spring.

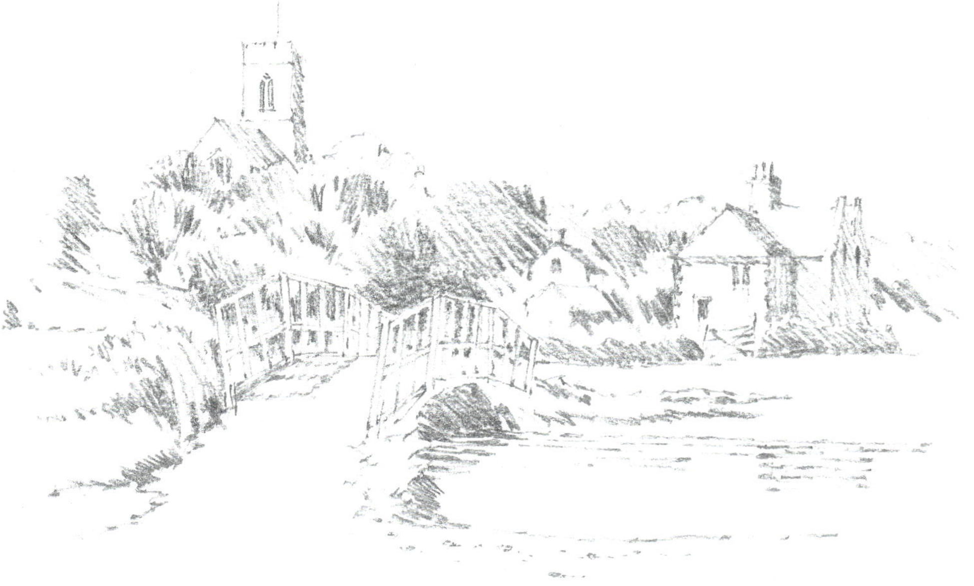

poured from the coach door. Shrieking and squealing they ran excitedly hither and thither everywhere. Two teachers ran around shouting, trying in vain to control them. They could have been geese on the loose.

It soon became apparent that they were out on some sort of field study or some such organised riot. Some of the children were carrying poles painted with black and white bands. Others had the kind of tape-measures that architects carry. There was a young boy and his companion, a little girl, with stop watches. Was this, I wondered, a competition between the sexes of some obscure kind?

Mayhem reigned with boys splashing about in the river up to their knees. Kids were throwing stones from the bridge, making them skim across the surface of the water. A boy was in tears and a girl screamed with laughter. Pandemonium. Anarchy. The teachers hoarse from shouting.

At last a little order prevailed. Poles were stuck into the banks of the river. Those with tape-measures, seriousness and concentration lining their little faces, measured between the poles. Then they all seemed to be waiting for something to happen. They were all looking over towards the parked coach.

One of the teachers, a pompous-looking young man taking himself with awed self-importance, came round from the back of the coach wearing high green waders and carrying, in a ceremonious almost ikonesque manner as though he bore the Holy Grail, a black and white chequered object. It was coffin-shaped sitting in a flat-bottomed miniature boat. Perhaps this was a primitive Inca-inspired burial ritual for a pet hamster? Or a sacrifice to the river-god Isis? Or was it to be a demonstration of the speed a river flows? The pleased-with-himself teacher solemnly lowered the coffin onto the water to loud cheers and applause from the children.

But the chequered ikon started to float away towards the mill. The teacher tried to retrieve it, but it moved along the water faster. The teacher became more and more desperate, chasing it along mid-stream in front of me. The children goaded him on at the tops of their voices, jumping up and down. The teacher stumbled and fell into the river. All pride abandoned he staggered to his feet, lost them again and went down on all fours. By now a dozen or so of the older boys had joined him chasing the coffin. But by now it was almost at the mill and in deep and dangerous water.

On the banks the poles had been dropped and the tape-measures sagged. The spectacle in the river had been abandoned. The teacher helped the soaked boys from the river. The dry teacher herded them all with their poles, their tape-measures their slurping shoes and their dunked pride back into the coach. It drove off.

I was left in silence. The little chequered coffin was sucked into the mill and disappeared. Then the church bells rang out another hymn. I looked round. Constable had gone.

Fact File

Arches 300lb. Rough paper was used, and lightly draw in the scene with a 2B pencil make every line count, don't over draw as this can become a habit, sub-consciously putting off the inevitable first brush strokes.

The paper was dampened with a large brush, down to the buildings and behind the church, leaving a few spots dry centrally at the top. A pale mix of Raw Sienna was then dropped into the damp areas, and a mix of French Ultramarine, Burnt Umber, and Alizarin Crimson, a slightly stronger mix to form the cloud shapes. Finally with a stronger mix of French Ultramarine, make a break in the clouds using the dry parts to form the cloud edges.

Build the painting from the distance forward, keeping the trees open as it is Spring, and noting both the foot-bridge and the gate to the field on the right are painted by putting in the background between the woodwork, unlike the gate in the centre which is painted dark onto the lighter ground.

'Dancing shadows in the polished cobbles...'

Elm Hill, Norwich

It was early summer. The fresh young leaves of the plane tree at the top of Elm Hill in Norwich made dancing shadows in the polished cobbles. Few people were about. Those cobbles in the small intimate square, the bench around the base of the tree, the colourful window-boxes and the shuttered windows, the wall lamps and the old iron hand-pump all conspired to create the atmosphere of an ancient little town in Brittany. I felt intoxicated by the beauty.

Within a few minutes I chose my position. I rarely take longer. First impressions are best. I started to sketch, happy in my work. Even the birds sung. Shortly after I had begun I noticed two figures, one short, the other tall, appearing in the distance at the bottom of the hill. They were approaching upwards.

The small one was female and she wore black garments from head to toe which flowed about her like an ominous cloud. The taller figure was a young man dressed in black leather. But it was his hair that disconcerted me. The sides of his head were shaved and along the top of his head ran an upstanding tuft of hair in the style of the Mohican Indians. It was bright canary yellow tipped with orange.

What was more disconcerting was that as they drew nearer and nearer it seemed they were heading directly for me. Indeed, they were. The young man came straight to where I was sitting, stopping only when his heavy black boots touched the legs of my seat. He looked down at me from what seemed, from my squatting position, a great height. He put his hand on my shoulder. I thought I was a gonna, or at best was in for a spot of bother.

'You're sitting on my spot,' he said.

I made to get up. He kept his hand on my shoulder.

'You're sitting exactly where I was before I had me dinner, mate.'

'I'm sorry, I wouldn't want to....' and I started to move for him.

'Nah, you stay where you are, mate.' He was almost being friendly. 'I'll sit right next to you and carry on with my painting.'

And he did, got out his seat and his easel and we had a pleasant afternoon chatting and painting together. He offered me a fag, which I politely refused, of course. Peering at his canvas occasionally I could see that in terms of technique and interpretation we were poles apart. He was an art student on the threshold of his career, experimenting with possibilities. His style was stark, angular, somewhat crudely primary in colour. The sort of thing people laugh at. But who am I to judge another's work?

Indeed, people did laugh at his work, openly, unkindly. We happened to be on the route of guided tours who stopped where we were in the picturesque little square. They gathered in groups behind us, the Birmingham accents saying loudly what rubbish the lad was painting, call himself an artist, wouldn't give it to the dog to play with. All the while, though he must have heard, my companion artist made no reaction to the cruel criticisms of his work. He carried on painting as if he were alone. I felt sorry for him and ashamed of them.

Then I remembered that I had also judged him by his appearance alone when he had come up to me earlier. For a moment I felt ashamed of myself.

When we had finished we shook hands and wished each other well. I think of him and wish him well.

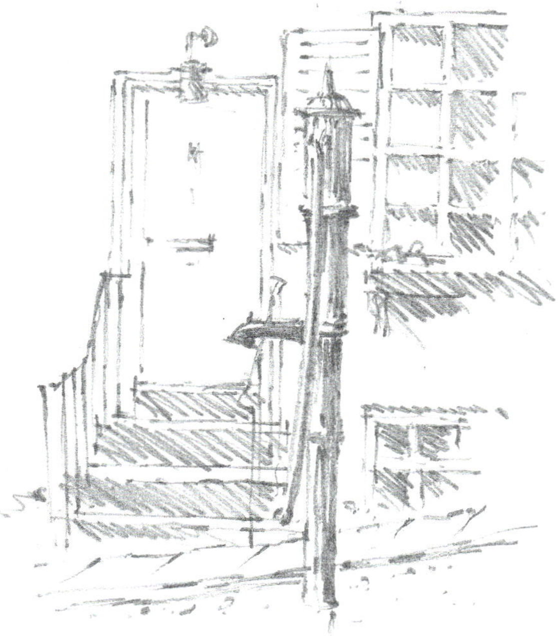

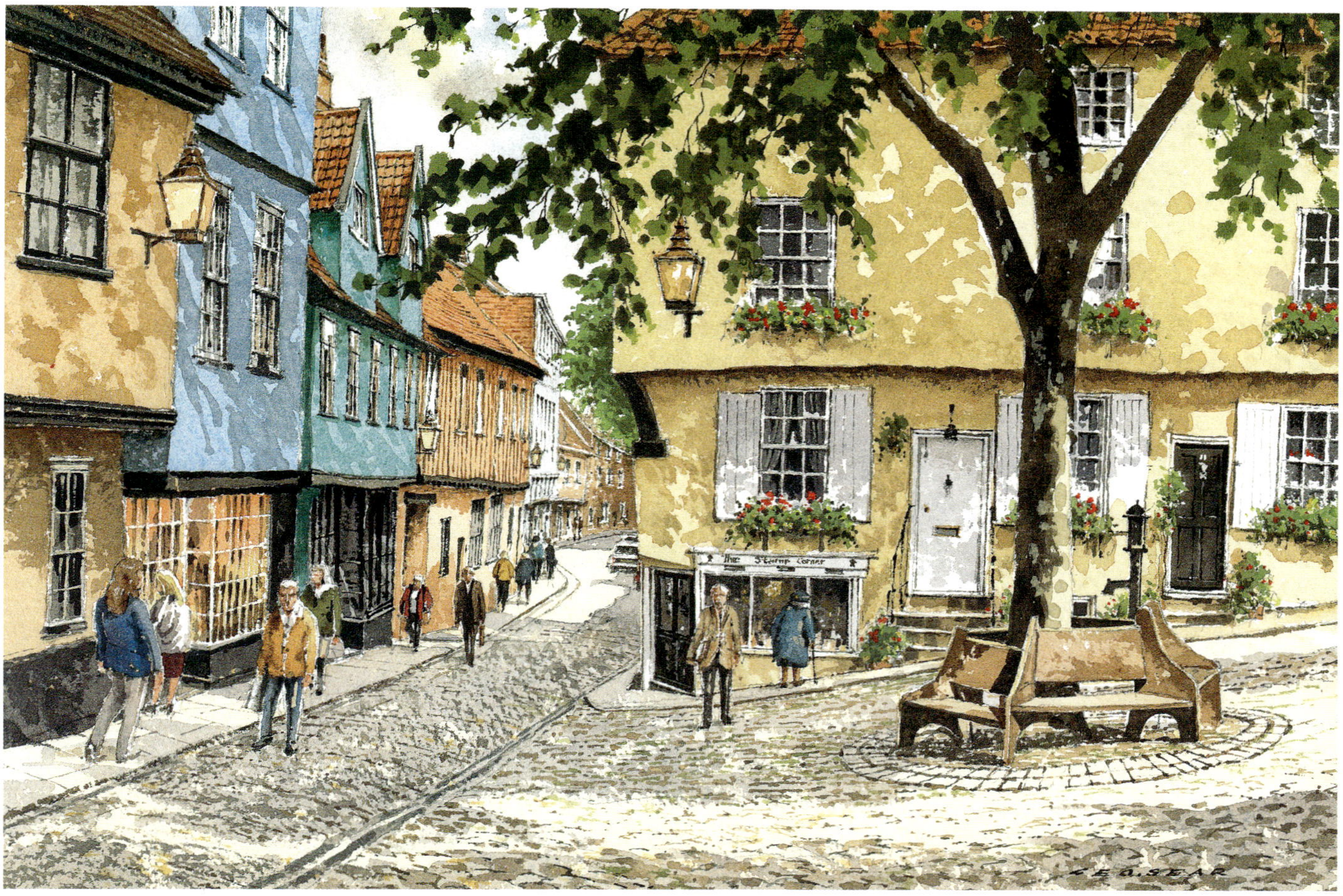

Elm Hill, Norwich.

Fact File *More care needed at the drawing stage.*

Looking down a street, one has to take a little more care at the drawing stage. The horizon line in this picture is just below halfway down the painting, so I did not want the vertical break to be central, I adjusted my view point leaving just enough of the cobbled hill to twist into the distance.

Multi-coloured buildings with broken shadows on the walls, passers-by hurrying about their business the scene gives a light and airy briskness. Observation is needed when drawing the seat that is round the tree, as it is built on sloping ground. The tree leaves were painted first before putting in the tiled roof behind, The cobbled effect was achieved with dry-brush application, dragging the brush over the rough texture of the paper.

'Early morning paddle'

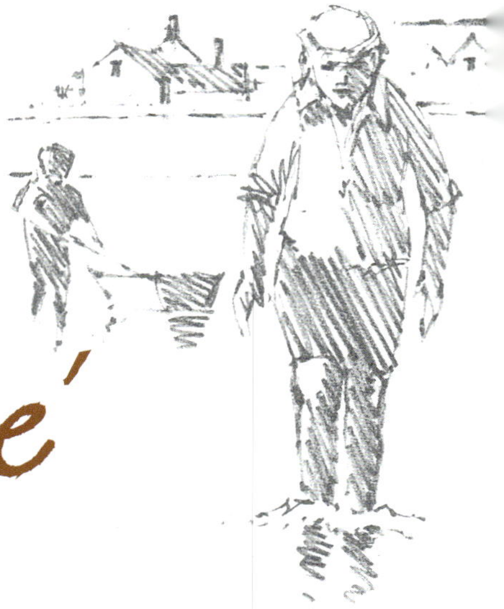

Wells-next-the-Sea

The morning had hardly started. The tide was retreating. It was going to be, I sensed the makings of it everywhere, one of those rare primrose-yellow days. That strange and unique Norfolkness of the marriage between light and water, between the moods of the clouds and the solemnity of the sea were uniting, even this early in the morning when visitors were cornflaking and the fishermen come home all intertwined to create a yellowness to the day. Cadmium and Raw Sienna would dominate my palette.

I set up my stool and board at the very rim of the receding tide on the concrete slipway. Before me along the quay that familiar building across the road still welcomed grain ships from the Low Countries. The morning was yet to be peopled. I felt strangely detached and the beginnings of my picture were unusually slow, like the morning itself.

Three men and a dog came down to the beach in front of me. It was a bumbling Golden Labrador who thought itself amusing. The men were in their late sixties probably. One of them, the tallest, had an air of authority about him. He had a vaguely military manner, a ram-rod back and a pencil-thin grey moustache.

It gradually occurred to me that they had come down this early onto the beach on some sort of mission. They seemed incongruous for they were not locals. They kept pointing across the channel, across the withdrawing water, towards a row-boat drawn up and tied to a pole sticking out of the marsh that, when the tide runs high, is often completely submerged. It became clear that the men wanted to cross over the channel and bring the row-boat to shore.

An hour went by, my painting grew well, the men were becoming more and more agitated, shouting and pointing and gesticulating. They were rolling up their trouser-legs as high as they would go and one after the other tried to wade across the channel. Every attempt failed in raucous laughter. There is a way across, but only locals know it. But the men kept taking turns to try even though the tide had not yet ebbed completely. Still they yelled. Still they laughed and the dog must have thought they were laughing at it for it kept running around in circles, its tail a propeller.

They were boys again, of course, and enjoying their regained childhood enormously. I couldn't help smile myself as I watched them. Eventually the 'Captain', being tallest, got across and shouted to his companions to come over, admonishing their timidity. The dog swam across as the other two waded painstakingly to the other side. The

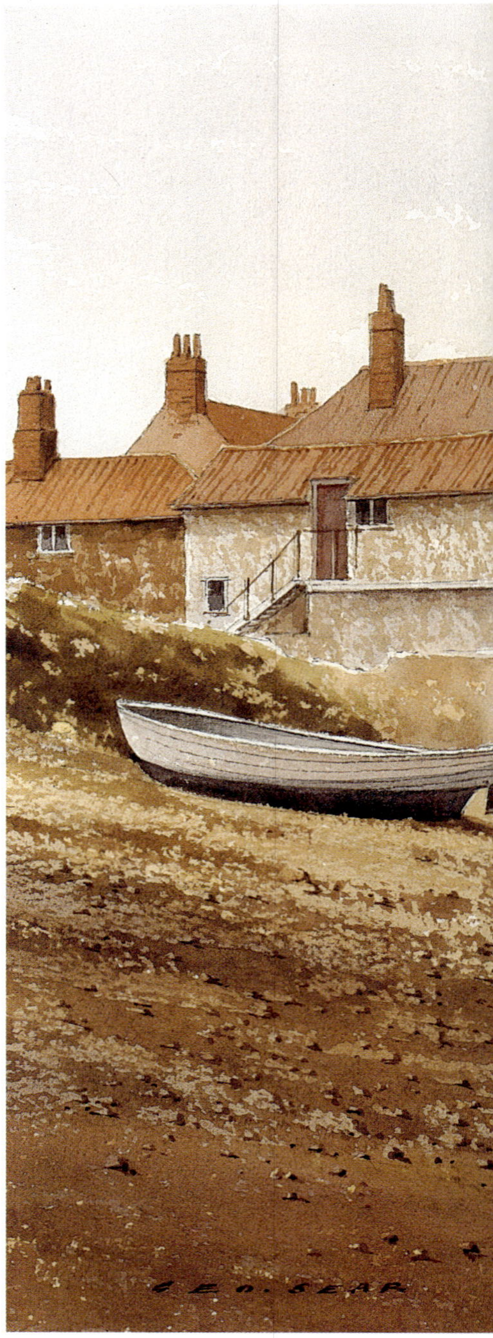

Early morning paddle, Wells-next-the-Sea.

boat was a dead weight and they struggled another hour to get it down into the shallow water. When they finally did, the dog jumped into the boat and was pulled across barking all the while.

I had finished all I could do to my painting and left the three men and their dog looking as if they were waiting for the tide to come back so they could have a row in their boat.

They had amused me with their boy-like antics so much that I put them in my picture.

Fact File

Stones and mud in the foreground.
Having considered the alternatives, you choose to sit by the waters edge, make sure you know the state of the tide. You do not want to make a hurried exit half-way through the sketching stage. Do not place figures into the painting too early, let the scene grow on you and you can then decide. The horizon line is just above the central figure's head, this making all the buildings on the quay on the left hand side slope down towards this, both left and right.One of your main concerns may be the way to tackle the mass of stones and mud in the foreground. I approach it like this.First a wash of Burnt Umber and Raw Sienna, not too strong at first, was painted on to the whole area, except the boats, down to the water's edge. When this was beginning to dry off, a slightly stiffer and stronger mix of the same was dry-brushed over the surface of the rough paper, with brush strokes from left to right in a downward manner, following the contours of the mud and stones, as this is drying but not dry, an even stiffer mix is applied to the front edge.
In the first and second washes it is not pressure that forms the stones, it is the lack of pressure that counts. When all is dry half close your eyes, and you may be able to distinguish some of the larger stones. Define these with a shadow on the right hand side.
Study the painting in this area to see what I mean.

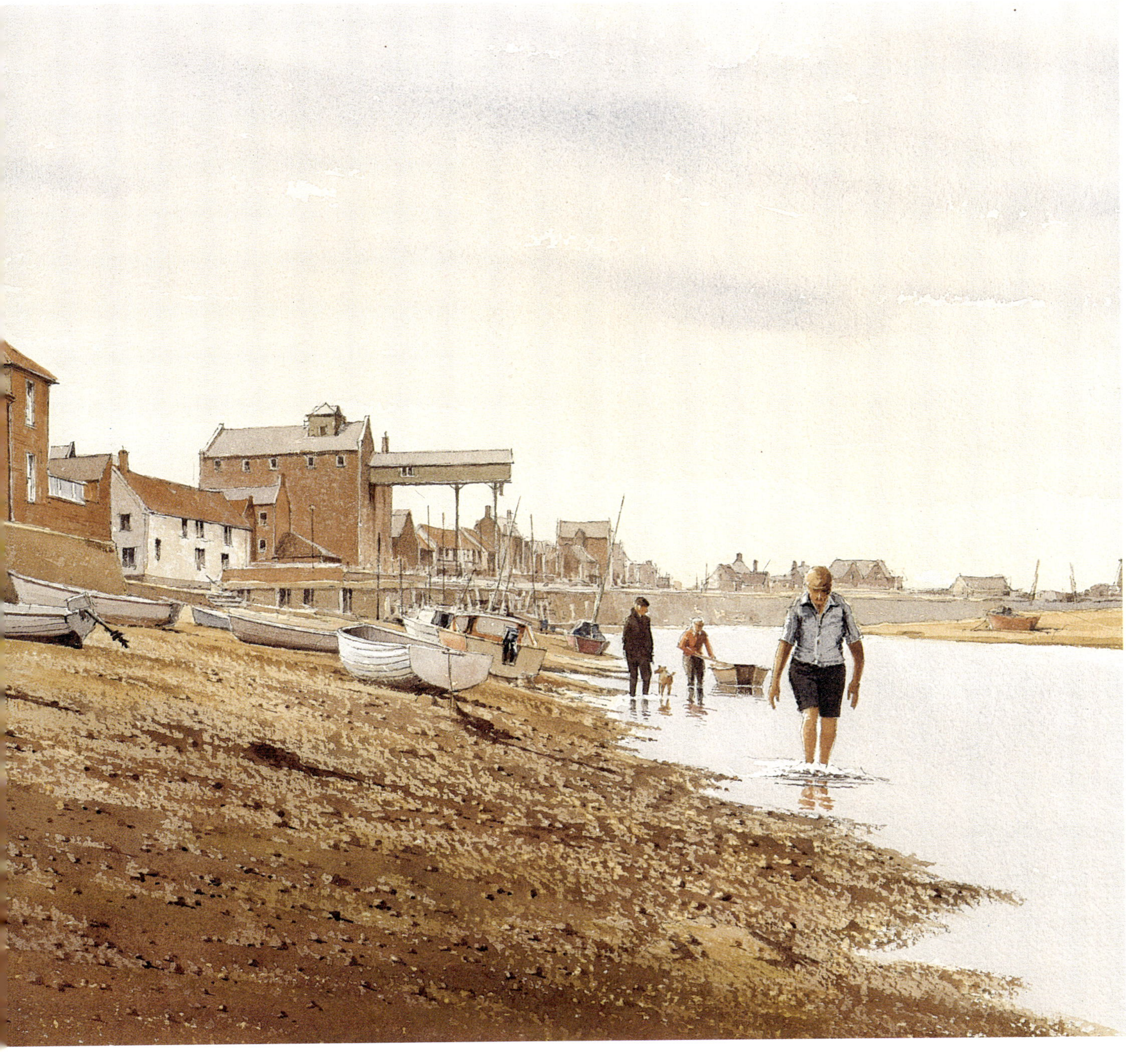

Landmark of a Fine City

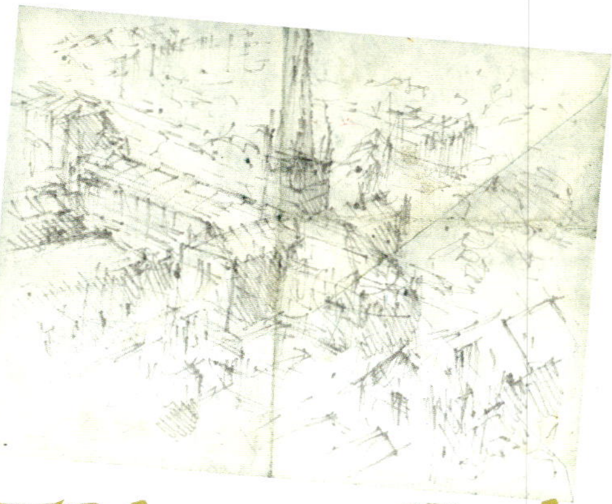

Norwich Cathedral

When they were handing out competitiveness I must have been somewhere near the back of the queue. You do your thing and I'll do mine has always been my maxim. The proviso is, of course, that each of us must strive to do the best we can. And that is what I did when Priscilla, Lady Bacon wrote to me.

She wrote to me in September 1995 on behalf of the Publication Committee of The Friends of Norwich Cathedral. The following year was to be the 900th Anniversary and they wanted a special painting of the Cathedral to reproduce as celebratory cards - they sell 90,000 cards every year. The thing was, though, she was inviting 'many Norfolk artists' to submit work. In other words the thing I am shy of, a competition in all but name.

However, the project stimulated me. I had no idea how many artists had been invited to submit their work, nor who any of them were. But what I did know was that I had to do something different. But what? It seemed impossible to find another perspective of the building. It had been painted from every possible view and angle by amateurs and geniuses over the centuries.

Suddenly, in a flash, I had the germ of an idea. The phrase 'a bird's eye view' came to me, lower than a helicopter, higher than a building. I drew this rough sketch of the perspective that was in my mind on the back of an envelope. I had something to work with.

One day I went into the Gift Shop in the Cathedral and asked if they sold models of the building. No, but there was over there behind a display cabinet a model that was not for sale. I asked if I could move the cabinet. The girl went away to ask permission but before she returned I had moved it and photographed the model from exactly the bird's eye view I had in mind.

With half the time gone from the deadline for the painting to be delivered I spent days photographing the architectural details of the Cathedral that would be visible in my imagined view. There would be nearby houses around the Cloisters and the School. Lady Bacon had written that snow scenes were particularly popular so I imagined a huge snowman in the middle of the Cloisters with clerics snow-balling each other. This, in the end, did not happen.

On the day the deadline came I delivered my painting. Strangely, I was shown to an office high up in the building - it may have been the top floor - and from the window the view of the Cathedral was almost exactly the one I had painted,

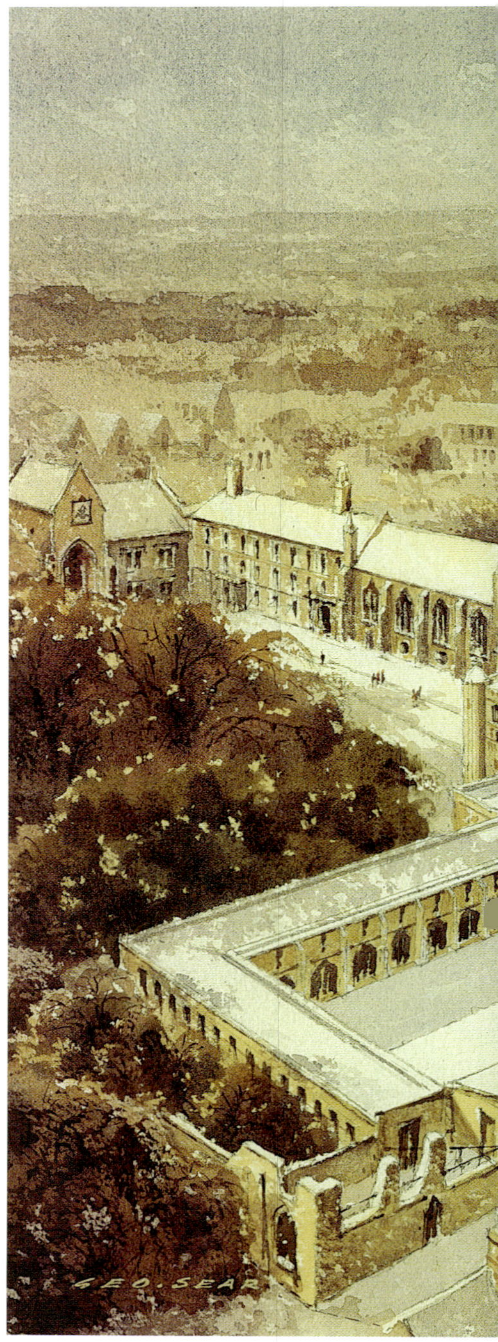

only my view was from a point 150 feet higher.

My painting was one of those accepted for reproduction as a card. However, I had put a great deal of hard work into the picture so I told them so, wondering if there might at least be a token payment. I explained that I already produced a large number of cards, printed by Richard Clover of Norwich. Indeed, I negotiated for the Cathedral card to be printed by my own printer. I was told that the normal courtesy payment to artists whose work was reproduced for Cathedral cards was 300 free cards. 'Oh,' I remember saying, 'really?' 'Yes,' they said, 'with envelopes as well.'

When the dust, or the snow, had settled Maureen reminded me that one of my customers who regularly buys my pictures had said that if I ever painted Norwich Cathedral she and her husband would like to be offered it first. I rang them and took the painting round. The price was rather more than they had expected, but decided to buy it.

Some time later the lady's husband sadly died. She said she felt strongly that the painting, although her property of course, truly belonged to the people of Norfolk and the Cathedral in particular. She made enquiries and then told me that she had bequeathed the painting to be held and shown in perpetuity in the Cathedral.

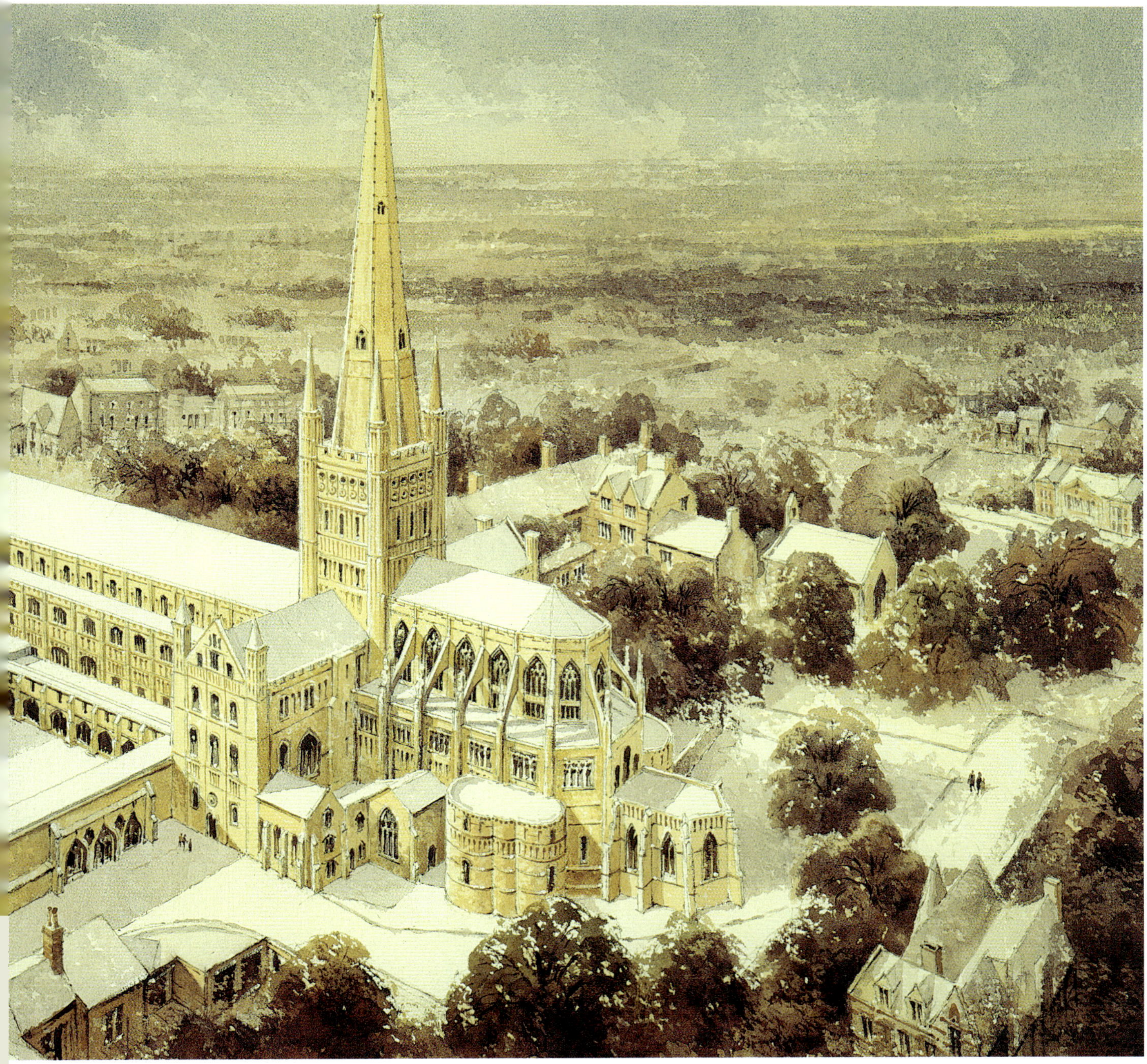

'A Splash of Red . . .'

The Letter Box

There is, isn't there, something very cosy, friendly and reassuringly familiar about the letter box? Whether free-standing as a pillar or as a box attached to a wall or even as a hole in the wall they are an integral part of the process of communication. Surely the new-fangled Fax and the E-mail will never replace them. I profoundly hope not.

A few years ago I gradually became aware that a growing number of my regular purchasers at my one-man exhibitions, particularly every August at Picturecraft gallery in Holt in Norfolk, were confiding in me that they had run out of space for them to buy and hang my larger pictures. They were beginning to ask me if I could paint something smaller for alcoves or arches or their halls - even for their lavatories.

Very much wanting to repay their loyalty and, perforce, by the nature of my work, responsive to market forces, I considered carefully my options.

Landscapes did not seem appropriate to a small format. I came up with letter boxes. And I came up with a winner for they have proved to be extremely popular, not only as paintings for the downstairs loo but in my ever-growing greetings card market.

As with most loveable objects I soon learnt that letter boxes had a fan club. I was contacted by the National Letter Box Study Group who kindly sent me the locations of fine and rare examples, not only of reds but greens and blacks. They also sent me the addresses of foundries in which they were cast. Therefore, in a small and modest way, I am becoming almost an authority on them. Certainly I take time in posting my letters.

Letter box fancying, as any other fancying such as of pigeons, make you look at their individual qualities with affection. You learn to spot a rare one, such as an Edward VII, from fifty yards. And although I am not what I call a 'nuts and bolts' man in that I do not often pick out the finest intricacies of detail, being more impressionistic, I am delighted that the fanciers of letter boxes find mine accurate enough to make them want to own either the originals or their reproductions as cards.

And, anyway, a splash of red gives the soul a frisson of pleasure.

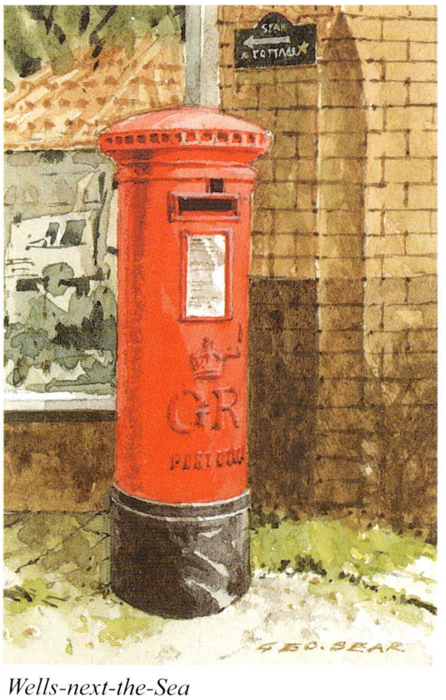

Wells-next-the-Sea

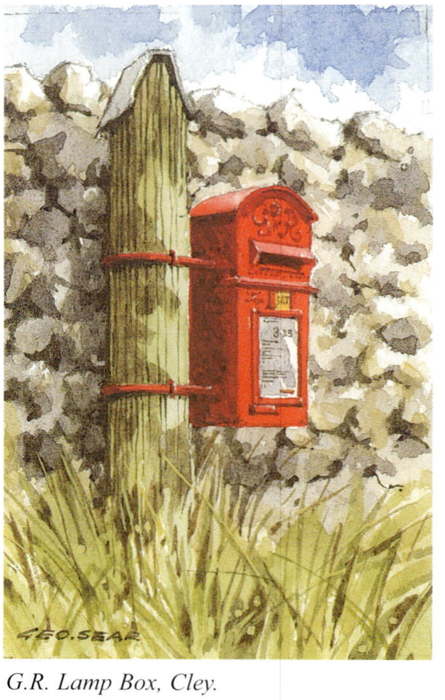

G.R. Lamp Box, Cley.

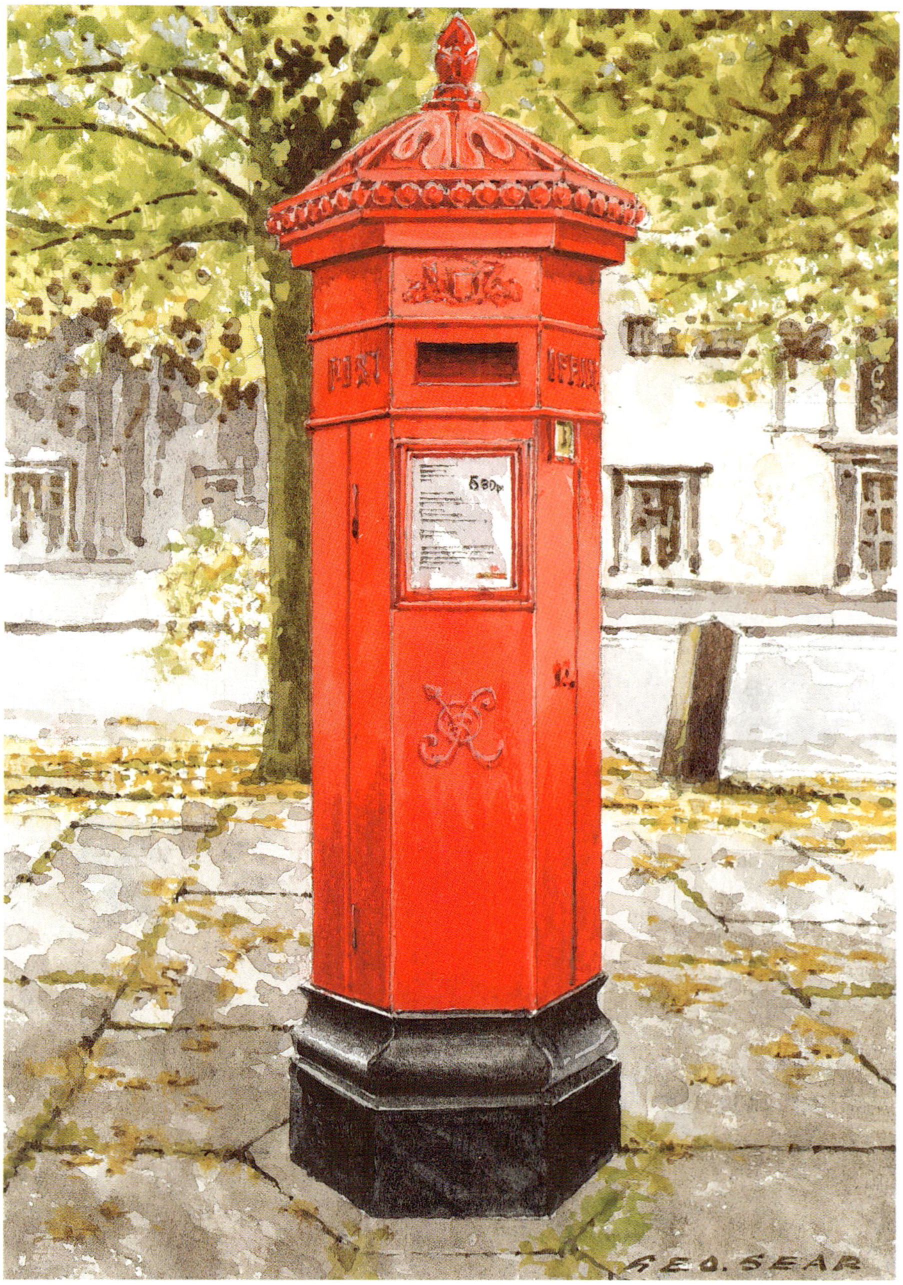

V.R. Pillar Box, Great Yarmouth

Fact File

The majority of my letterbox paintings are only 75 mm x 50 mm.

Mini watercolours are, in fact, treated in the same way as my larger works, only smaller brushes and more control are needed. I always paint the backgrounds first, and then when dry, paint the box on, using Winsor Red, mixed and toned with Alizarin Crimson, even a touch of French Ultramarine may be added to the mix.

Beware. The Winsor Red will weep into the adjacent background colour if that is still damp.

The Letter Box Study Group Tel: 01634 861714. secretary@lbsg.org

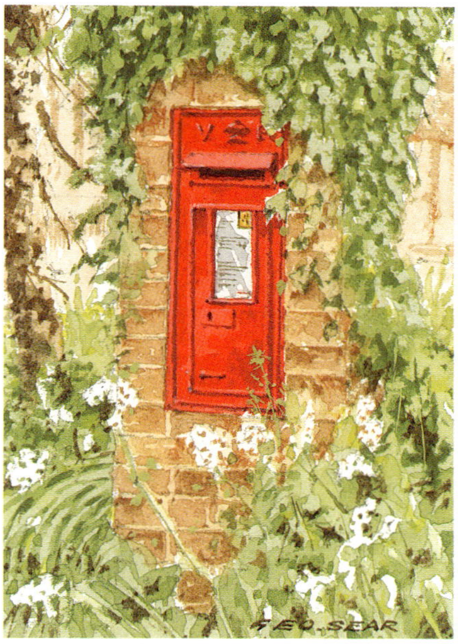

V.R. Wall Box, Gt. Ryburgh

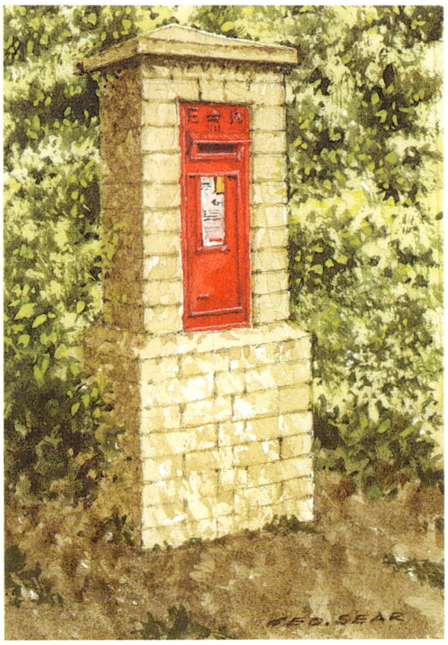

E.R. VII Wall Box, Thurne.

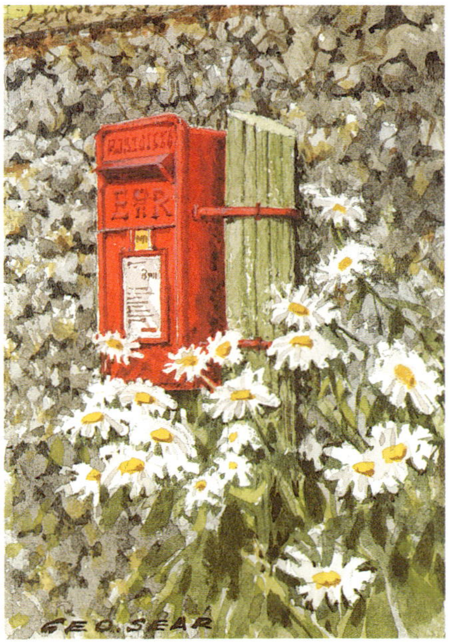

E.R. Lamp Box, Warham.

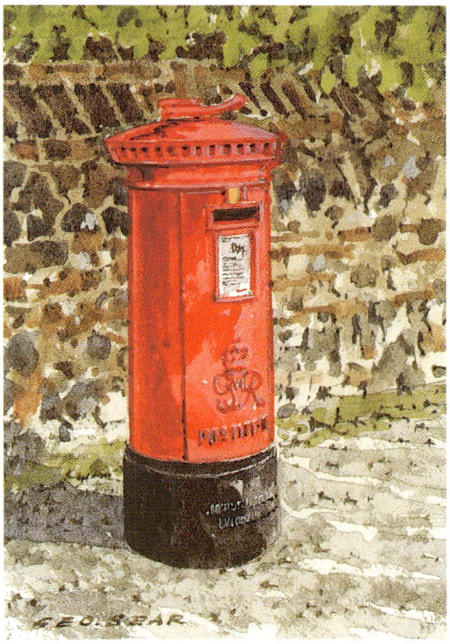

Cathedral grounds, Norwich.

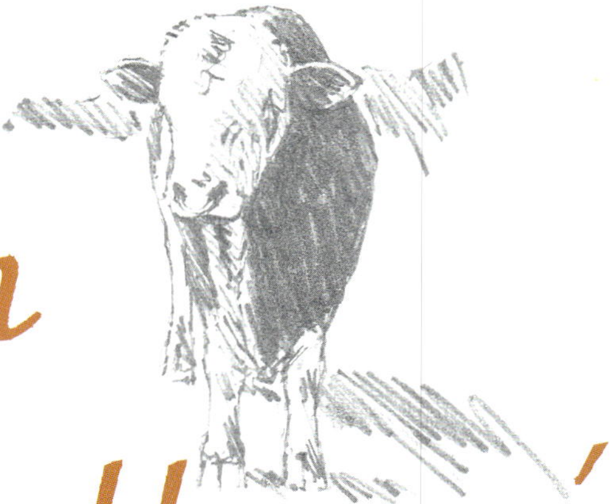

'A commission and a challenge'

Park Farm, Aylmerton

A commission is always welcome and a challenge. Not only is it charmingly personal, but there is an implicit vote of confidence in my work which soothes the spirit. For no matter how many paintings I may sell there must always lurk the fear that I might never sell another one.

John West, the farmer at Park Farm in Aylmerton near Cromer, had retired in favour of his son and built a new house in the grounds in which to do so. He wanted me to paint for him a portrait of the old family farmhouse and also his new house so that he could hang them on his wall. It was a rare expression of sentimentality in a farmer.

Painting the old farmhouse had been pleasant. Typically the old original house, much smaller than the house you see today, was nestling amongst the additions of the centuries. But it retains and wears proudly its honourable character. As I worked I could hear children playing not far away.

Painting the new house was not as easy. Put simply, compositionally it needed to be painted from a distance. From the bottom of the garden over a wall I could see a

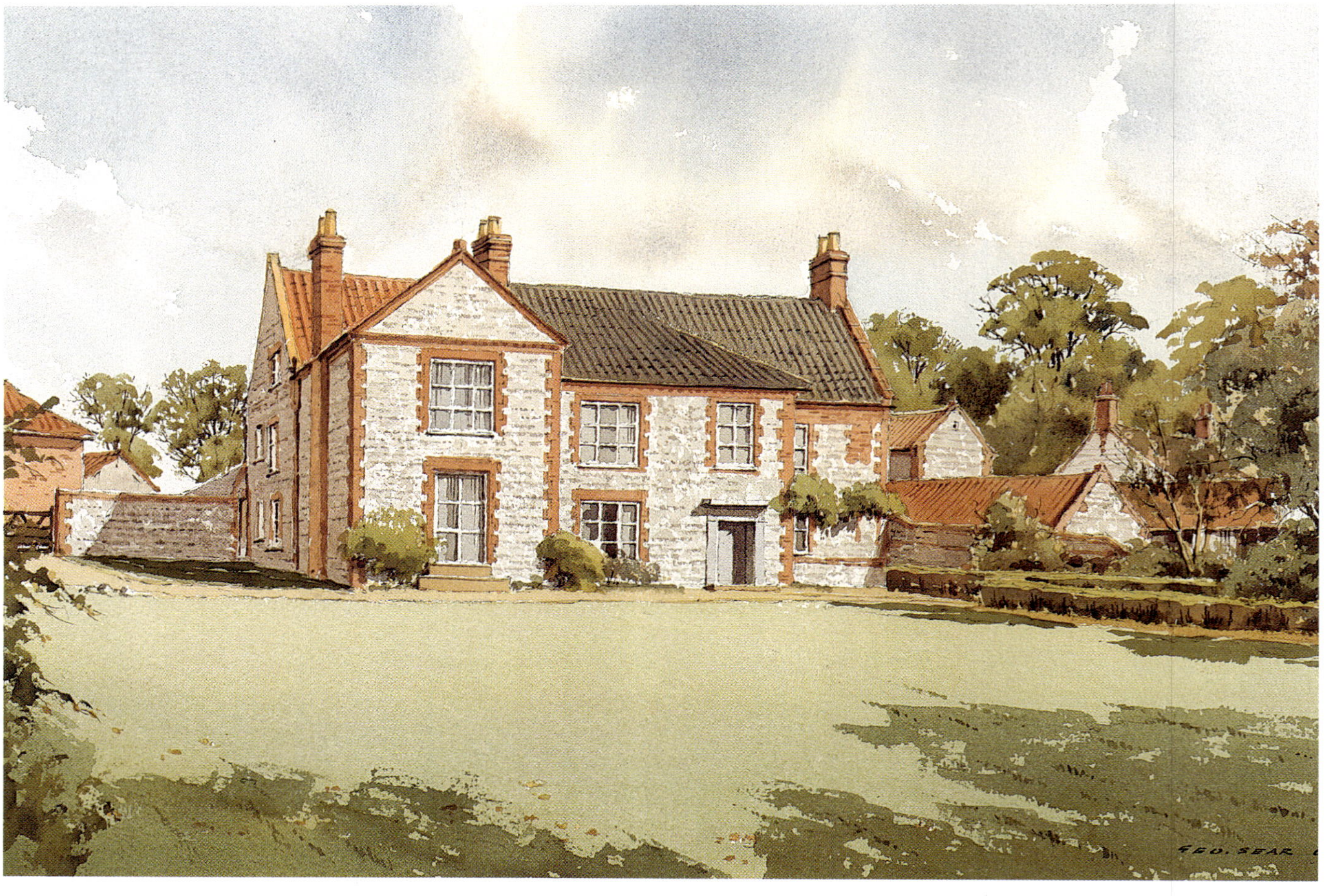

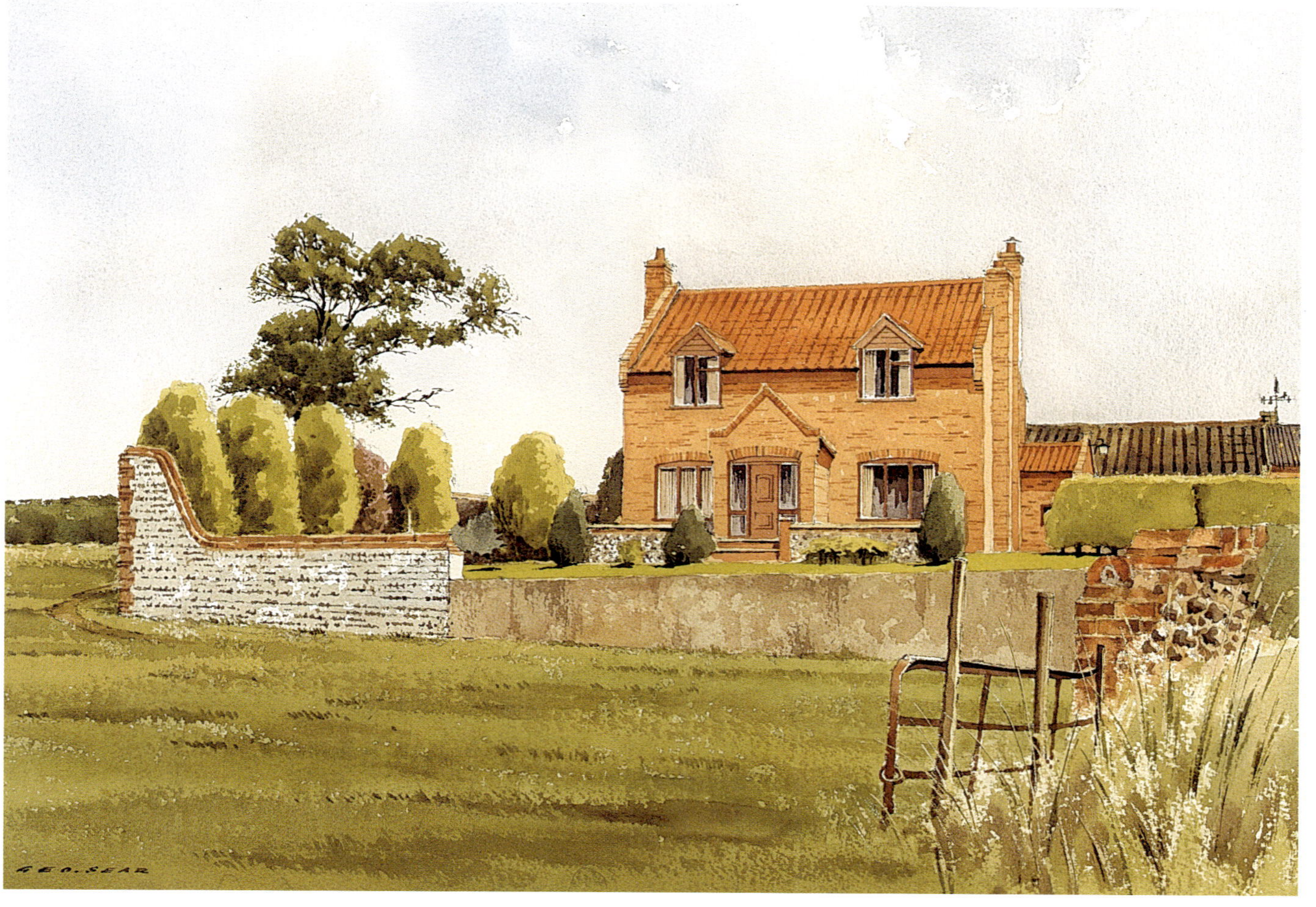

pond on the left in a field. It seemed a good position so John strimmed the area of long grass so that I could sit on my low stool without getting wet. In front of me was an electrified wire stretching across the field. I was assured that it had been switched off. I assumed it was a deterrent for cows or sheep.

'No,' said John, 'it's for Oxo, my French bull. But don't worry he's a pet really and as calm as a lamb . Wouldn't hurt a fly. Anyway, he never comes to this part of the field.'

I took his word for it and set myself up. My sketch came quite easily and I felt at peace. The sun was shining and the sounds of children playing and laughing came over the hedge of the old farmhouse. When the time came I opened my lunch-box and ate while continuing to paint. I wanted to finish as much as I could by 3.15pm as I planned to pick Maureen up in Holt and travel back down to Berkhamsted.

There was a hiccup in my painting, something not quite right. I became absorbed with watercolour washes, tonal balance and detail. Suddenly I had a sense that I was not alone. I looked up and there towering above me stood what seemed from my low position a gigantic bull. It was studying me with interested contempt.

With monumental self-control I told myself not to panic. DO NOT RUN. Instinctively I put the two tomatoes in my pocket out of view in case it was true what they say the colour red does to a bull. Absurdly, I wondered if it might not like art, although John had said it was French. With the pond behind me and a large hedge my retreat was cut off. My pride would not let me call to the children to help. I made a quick calculation of how long it takes a heavily-built artist to pack his gear, bob under the electric wire, leg it across 200 feet of uneven field and scale the wall to sanctuary. Ultimately it was the thought of Maureen waiting and worrying in Holt that made me run like greased lightning. At the wall I threw my gear over and, like a monkey up the rock of Gibraltar, skittered over the wall to safety.

Looking breathlessly back at the bull, it had turned to see what all the fuss was about. And behind me John was laughing his head off on his front steps.

He plied me with vegetables from his garden and, still chuckling, waved me on my way.

Fact File

When executing a commission, first ascertain if any 'Must not leave out' items such as a rose bush from Aunt Maud or an apparent spindly tree planted by Princess Diana, have to be included. I unfortunately found out too late, and had to make good my mistakes. Painting is all a learning curve.

I usually produce a pencil sketch to make sure the view pleases both myself, and the client.

The sun had got its hat on

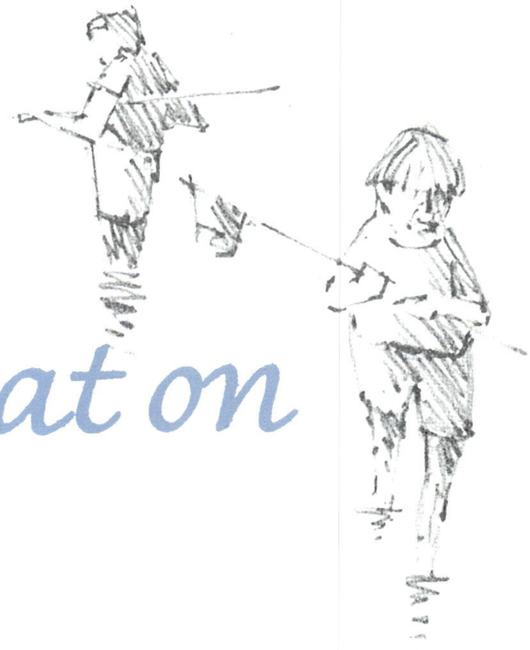

Blakeney

Blakeney is an experience more than a place; or, rather, a vast and ever-growing haven of memories. We have all experienced it differently and privately and, always, memorably. My recollections are no more special than yours. It is, above all, a family sort of place for mums and dads and kids to muck about together.

And they did as I sat just along from the car park looking across the narrow stretch of water at the tide's lowest ebb. In particular I watched a young family on the other side, having paddled across. It was a jolly hot morning and the sun had got its hat on. The two young boys had just been bought fishing nets on sticks. The eldest, about six, already had the knack of dredging the water for crabs and was lost in bent-over concentration. But the youngest boy, about four, solemn faced and introspective, would not use his net. He kept it held aloft carefully, safely. Mother tried to encourage him to use it like his brother. He wouldn't. He refused, stamping his little feet. It was as though he was frightened of getting it wet. Father tried to make him let go his tight hold. The child clung to it.

Memories of such a childhood dance in the heat of the sun like clouds of gnats.

Twenty years earlier I could have been drowned very near to that spot. I did not know then the dark hazards of the sea's edge in North Norfolk, the sly way the sea can corner you unawares.

We were staying at the Manor House Hotel and Maureen was still asleep when I crept out and into the grey morning and along past the duck pond and eastwards towards the marshes. I walked out a little way into them and started sketching seawards. Susie our dog was at my side.

Every few minutes I retreated backwards as the incoming tide crept forwards to finger my shoes. Sketch some more, ease away.

When I had finished my sketch, aware that by now Maureen would be waking and wanting a cup of tea, I turned to go back. Alarmed I realised the tide had cut off my retreat. There was sea coming steadily towards me and sea behind. I was standing on an area of marsh that was temporarily proud of the water.

Thinking quickly I realised that I must keep to the path and be guided by the posts to which boats were tied. Either side would be deep water. It was hard going, waist deep with my sketch book held high in one hand and Susie's collar in the other, for she was too young to swim.

Padding over the carpet in the Hotel reception I looked very sorry for myself - as did Susie. Back in the room, soaked to the skin, I was in time to watch Maureen turn over in bed and wake up.

Rubbing her eyes and sitting up she said, 'Tea ready yet dear?'

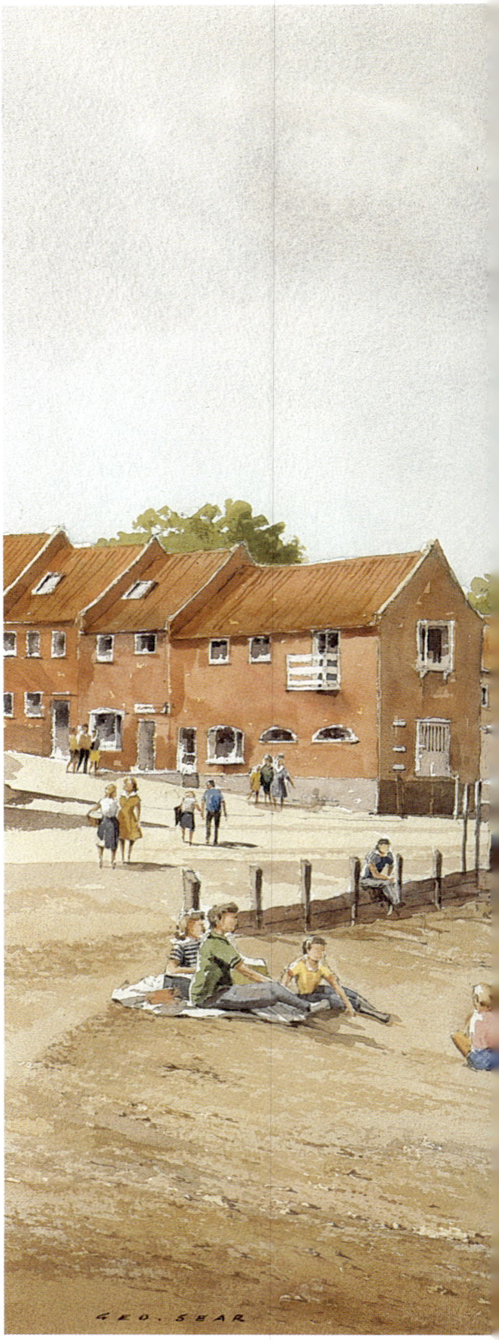

Plenty going on, Blakeney.

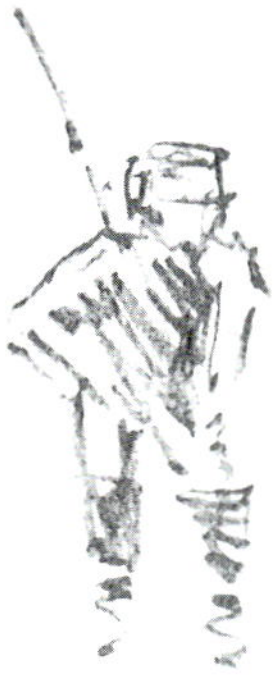

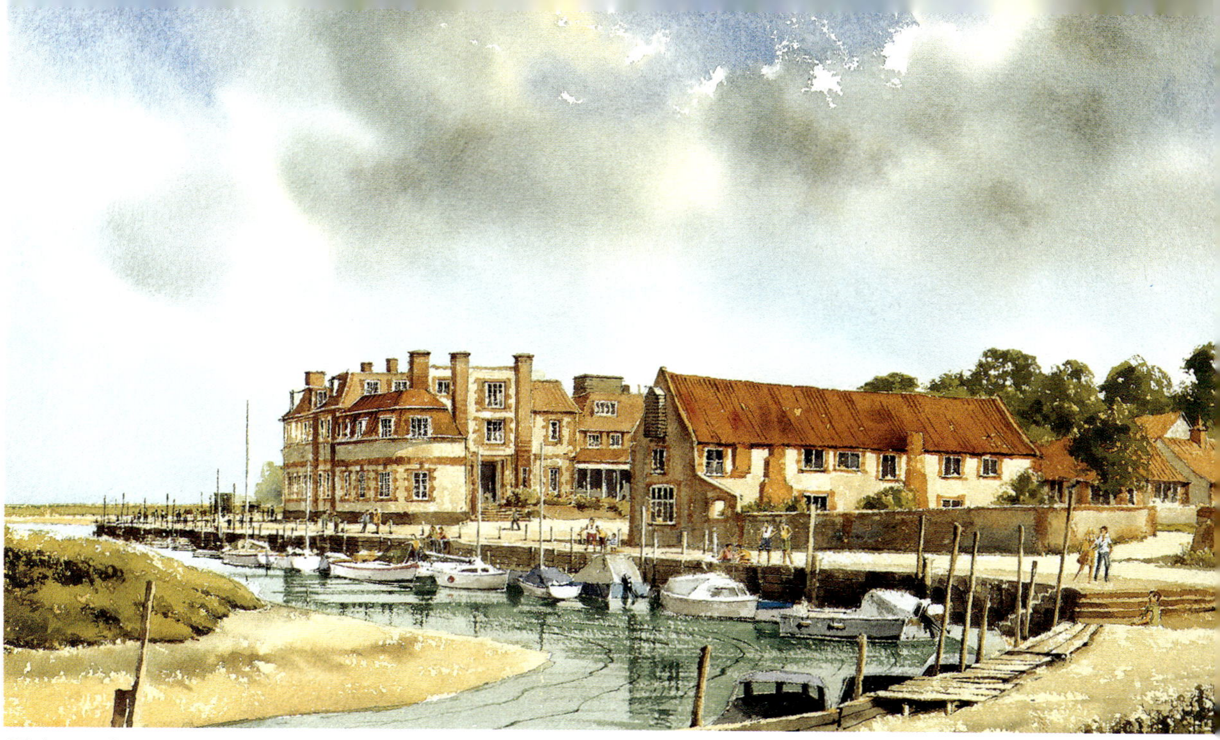

Blakeney Quay.

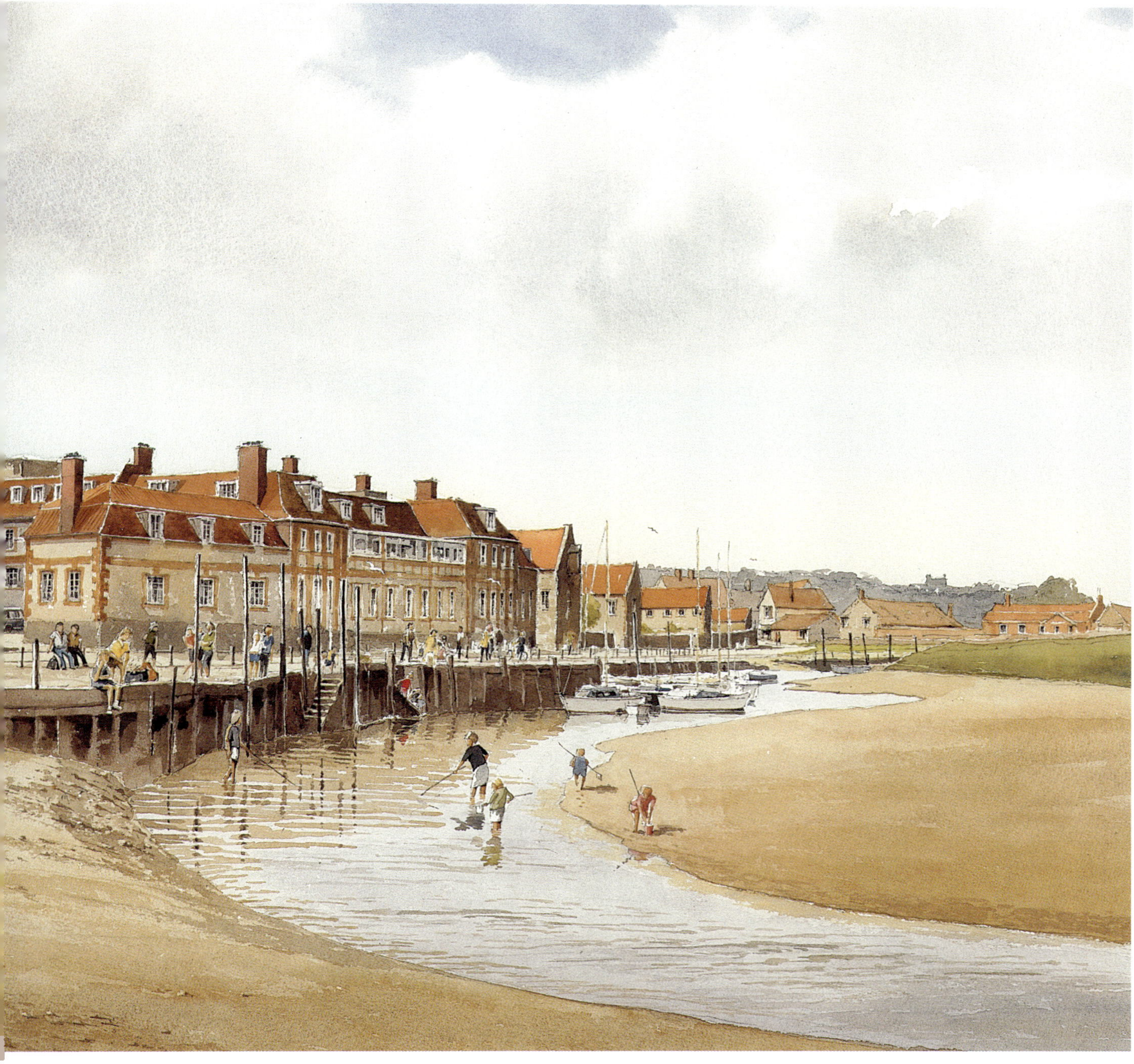

'When I paint Poppyland I paint the past'

Poppyland

How delicate, how frail, how vulnerable the field poppy, symbol of a nation's grief and remembrance. The blood in the field of fallen soldiers, of boys gone to war too young, too innocent to know why.

Poppyland has come to describe an area in North Norfolk around Cromer and Sidestrand, Overstrand and beyond inland. In fact everywhere in the county is Poppyland. Everywhere the earth yields masses of poppies when it is distributed by widening a country lane or building a by-pass. Their seeds are viable, endurable for years, like the memories of mothers.

When I paint Poppyland I paint the past. I paint memories of the past. Nothing in my poppy paintings resembles, or even refers to, the hand of man other than his praise of God by building churches to His honour. The hedgerow is the cathedral whose jewels are stained the red of poppies. The footpath along the cliff's edge is skirted with a fringe of poppies as guides. Immemorial the land, immemorial the poppy.

Poppyland got its name from the pen of Clement Scott, a journalist with the *Daily Telegraph*. Although he was a revered, indeed feared, dramatic critic he arrived in Cromer in August 1883 on an assignment.

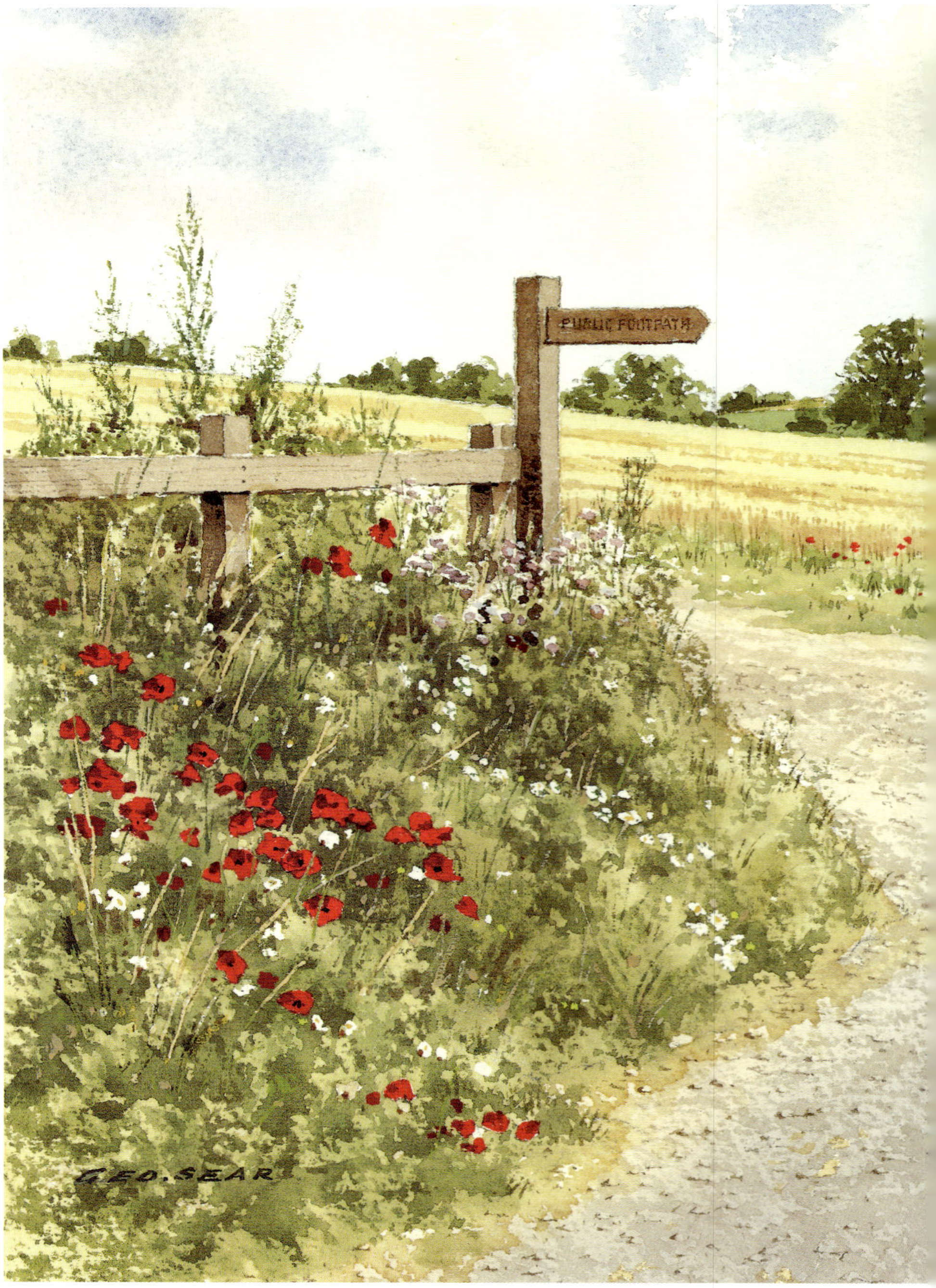

Pointing the way.

Taking a ramble up the crumbling cliffs into Sidestrand he was moved by the rustic charms of the poppy-encircled fields of hedgerows. He was also enchanted by the local miller Mr. Jermy, his old-fashioned mill house and especially by his daughter Louie.

Scott stayed many times at the Mill House, sometimes bringing with him his friends the poet Swinburne and George Sims. And he wrote a series of articles from 'Poppyland' which were an overnight success. Hotels and guest-houses were quickly built to accommodate the throng, arriving by railway and road.

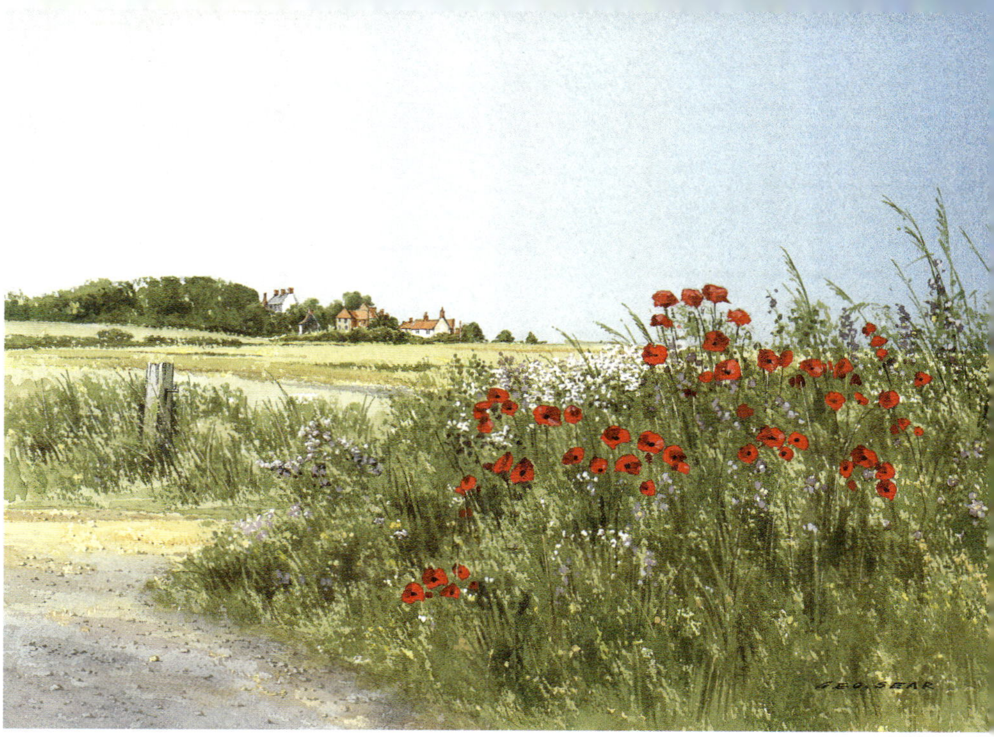

Wayside flowers.

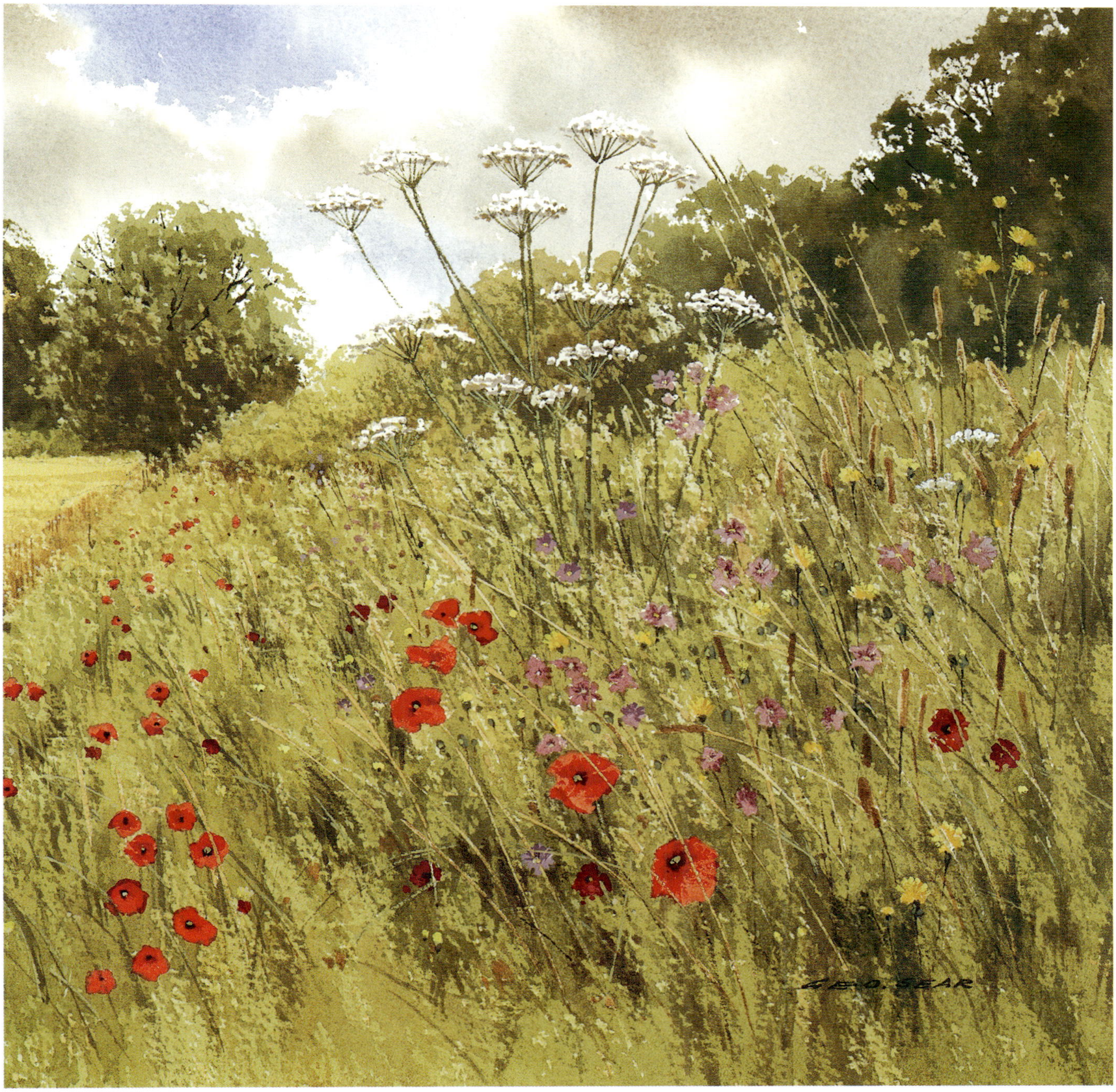

Field flowers.

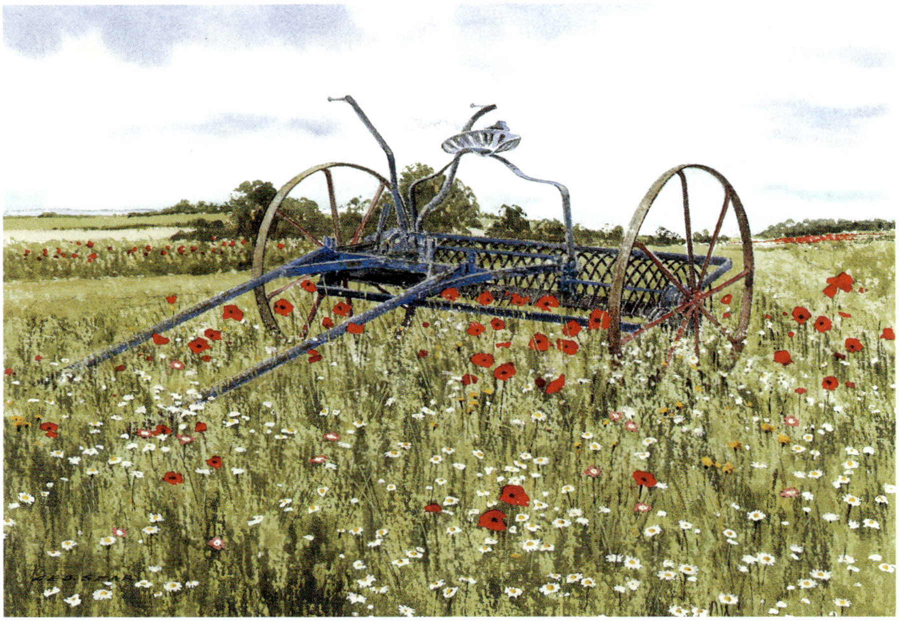

The Old Hay rake.

Yet by 1890, four years before his death, Clement Scott was to rue the days he popularised his beloved Poppyland. 'The Cromer that we visit now,' he wrote, 'is not the Cromer I wrote about but a few short years ago. It is not Poppyland, but Bungalowland.'

And yet, still, a few yards from the hurly-burly, over a stile, through a farmyard gate, the poppies greet in all their innocence and solemn beauty.

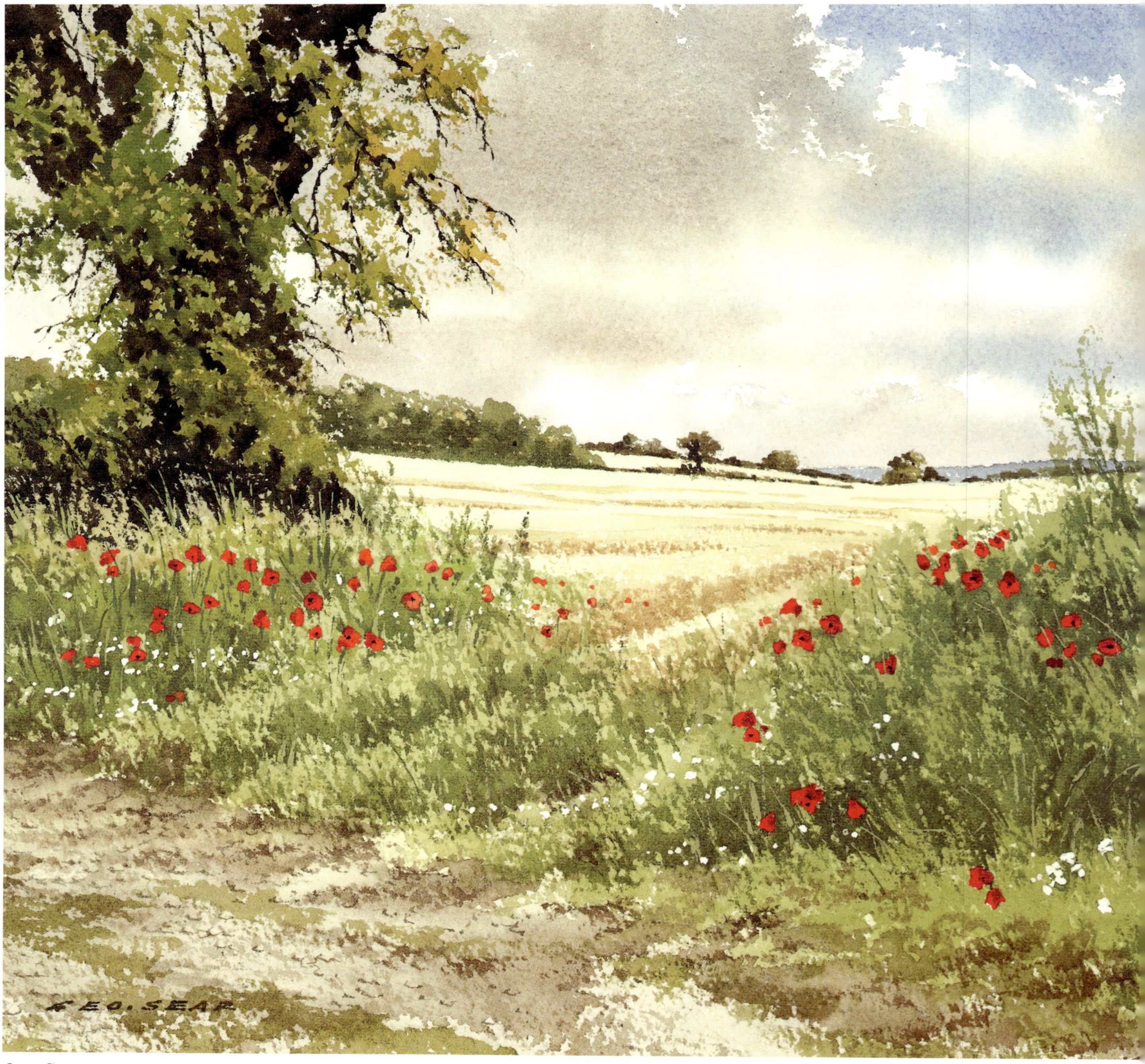

Late Summer.

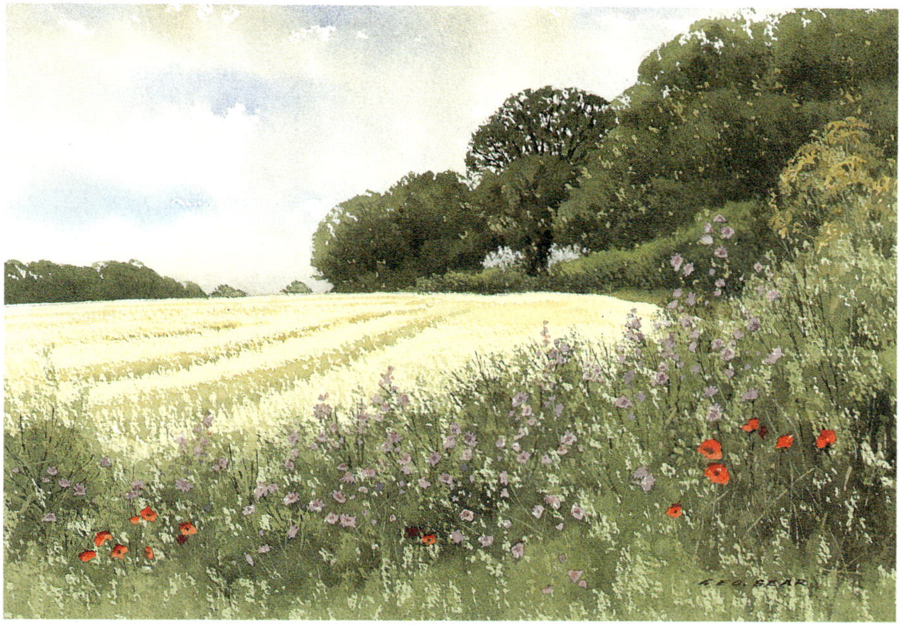

Mallow in Old Woman's Lane.

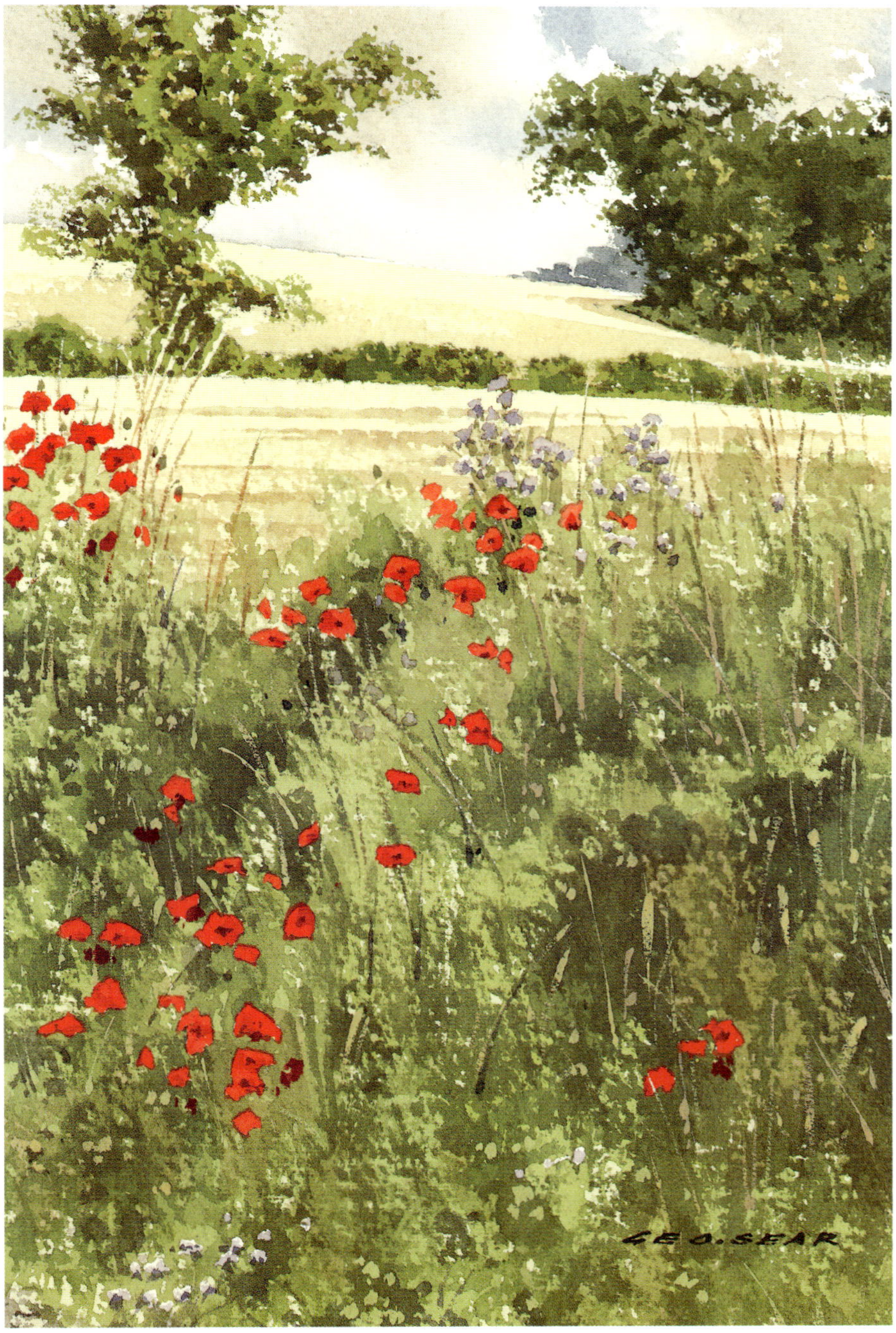

Ready for harvest.

Fact File

Get the 'feeling' of being on site.
All these paintings in the Poppyland group, were all painted on Rough paper, both Whatman 200lb and Arches 300lb. Most of my work over the last twenty years has been on 'Rough'. I was asked recently whether I chose Rough paper to suit my style, or did the paper influence my style? A difficult one to answer. I do know that preparing your paper properly, and getting to know its properties, using them to the limit, only comes with experience. My dry brush technique is improving all the time.
From a preliminary sketch I work out my composition and lightly pencil it onto the paper with a 2B pencil. After painting the distant view in the normal way, I mask out with masking fluid only the largest of the flowers, when it is dry, start with the lightest wash first all over the remainder. I mix all my 'Greens' with a range of Yellows/Siennas/ and Umbers, mixed with Winsor Blue. Always add the Winsor Blue to the others carefully as it is strong and powerful. Then add subsequent washes as the one before it is drying, each time with a stiffer mix, working from light to dark through the greens to brown colour range with the action of the brush following the direction of the grasses, in my dry brush application.
In the studio, surround yourself with notes, sketches and photographs to get the 'feeling' of being on site.
My poppies are painted with Winsor Red/Alizarin Crimson, onto the previously masked areas, and also on the green areas that makes them appear darker.

'A quick chilling wind engulfed me . . .'

Baconsthorpe Castle

To sit alone in a field trying to convey onto the paper in front of you the sense of the place that is a ruined castle, sleeping as it is in its memories, for hours and hours, makes you feel very alone. Not lonely exactly, but insular, isolated, an observer from the wings of the pageant of life. You are an outsider looking on without judgment, without joy. You cannot touch or be touched. And yet as your painting grows and becomes an image of your thoughts, your emotions, so too grows a sense of omnipotence, or having infinite power.

It was quite cold in that field at Baconsthorpe Castle near Holt, although the watery sun strew strangely sinister shadows across the broken flint walls. The open-eyed windows had tears in their corners. The gaunt tower capped with a cupola threw its long shadowed finger across the lawn, pointing almost accusingly towards me in my isolation.

In the making of any painting, but perhaps more especially a building in ruins, you are marooned on an island of intense concentration. Your eye constantly changes its focus from the subject then down close to the paper. The sounds around you, bird song, a distant aircraft, a dog barking farmyards away, they all become one and meld with your concentrated state. I would say that

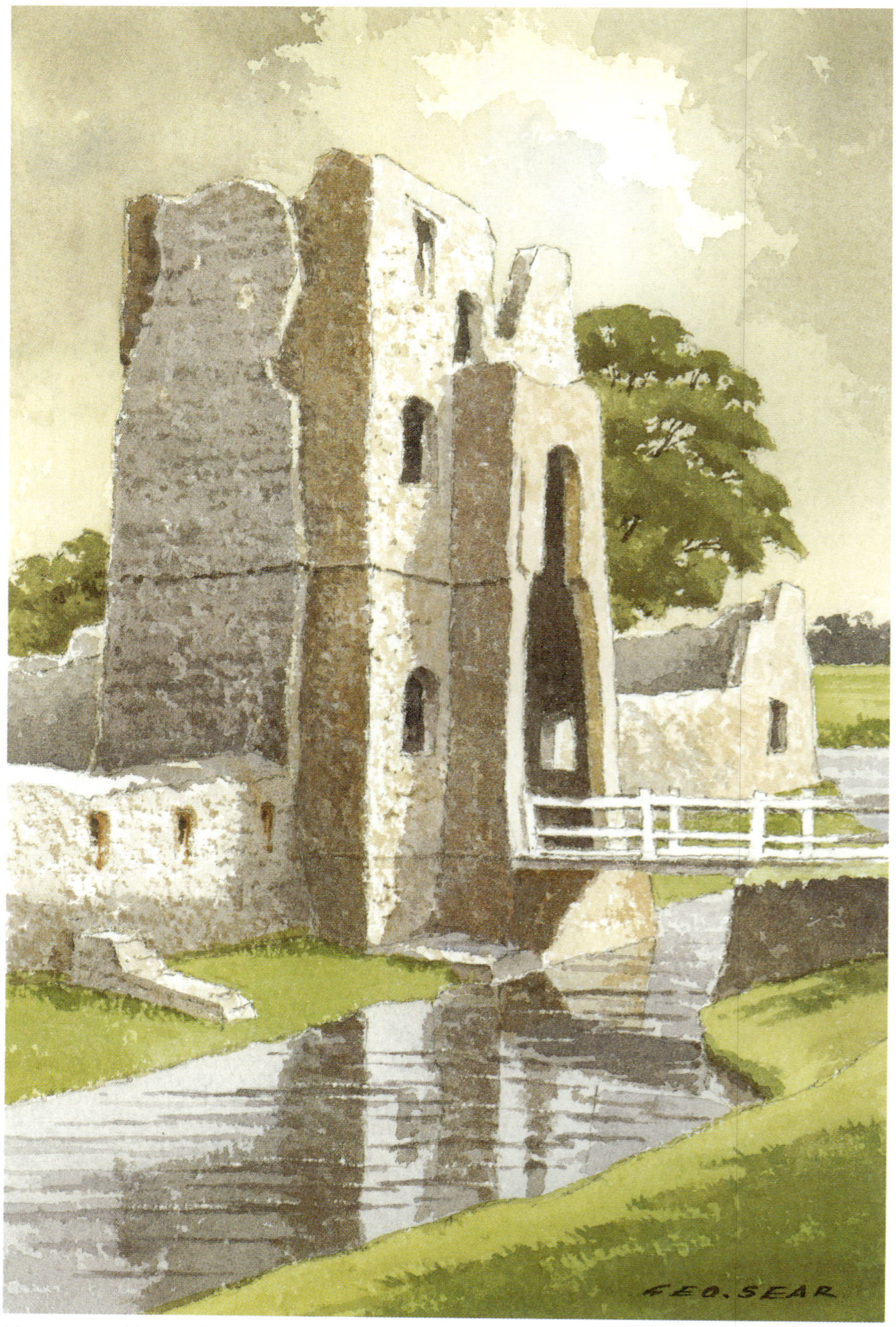

Entrance to Baconsthorpe Castle

your mind goes into a lull. Thus was mine as I translated those ancient stones into watercolours.

Suddenly and simultaneously the sun went behind a cloud and a quick chilling wind engulfed me. I shivered and was brought out of my lull. At that precise moment I looked up at the great entrance arch beyond the drawbridge and there moving out from the shadows was the ghostly figure of a woman.

I felt the flesh creep up my neck and the hairs moving. There was a tingling sensation all over my body. My eyes felt they were on stalks. In a word, I was terrified. But I could not move. I was frozen with fear. The woman was wearing Elizabethan clothes and on her head was a long, pointed wimple with a veil draped from it.

Her appearance and the disappearance of the sun and the sudden wind seemed strangely connected. The one made the other happen. And the cold breeze made the drapes of her dress and the gossamer veil of her head-dress dance and swirl. With her hands clasped together in front of her she moved slowly towards me, slowly, slowly. She was looking directly at me. She did not seem to be walking, simply moving, gliding. My brush was caught mid-way between palette and paper, dripping coloured water.

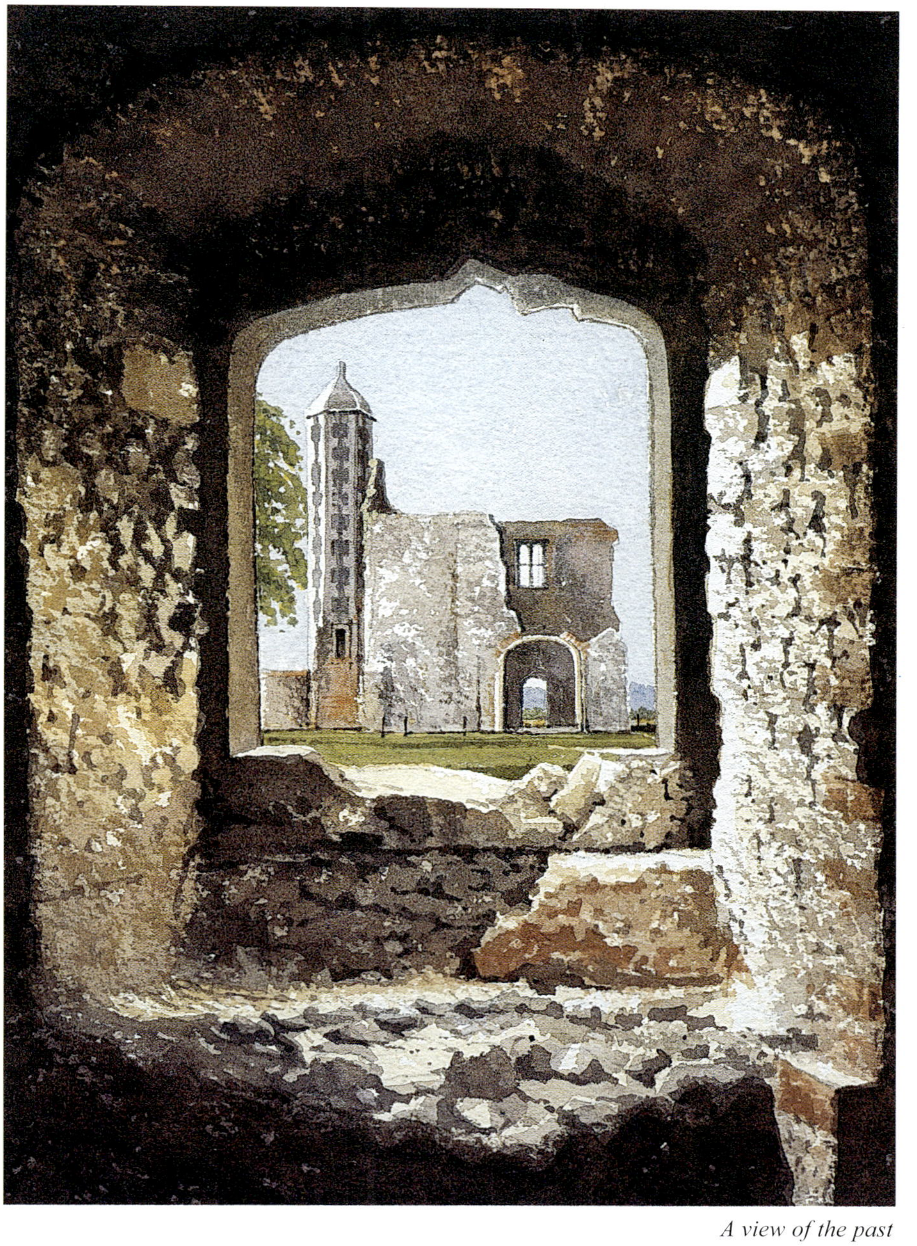

A view of the past

'CUT.'

The word sliced my brain in two. And then I was catapulted back into reality, into the present. To my right and hidden from view were a group of people with a video camera. I quickly realised they were making a film and the actress in Elizabethan costume had slipped into the entrance arch as I was concentrating on my painting.

They say that adrenalin made by shock can be good for you. Or give you a heart attack. I'm still here.

Fact File

Try to discover the unexpected.
The entrance to Baconsthorpe Castle demanded an upright painting with the drawbridge leading into the opening. I used a limited palette and simple approach, with emphasis on the lights and darks giving a dramatic feel. The other painting was a view out of the right hand lower window of the entrance looking towards the gatehouse. The shape of which, if turned 90° is echoed in the outer shadow of near window. It was this that attracted me first.

'She enchants still . . .'

Cromer

Cromer is a once elegant lady whose beauty and charms have faded with time. She does not wear her modern clothes well or comfortably. The huddle of her architecture dreams of its past. In her dear old heart her streets belong to horse-drawn carriages not domineering coaches and the crudity of lorries. She was not meant for amusement arcades and fish-and-chip shops. The haunt of a string quartet in the plush gloom of the dining room of the Hotel de Paris as she pushes her breasts out into the brace of the North Sea air. The echo of Royal heels still clip up the entrance steps, the foyer rustles still with taffeta and silk and a hush of awe. She did not deserve to be plundered by the crude and vulgar.

But she enchants still, especially on the shimmering August morning when I set myself up against the rails of the path that leads up to the lighthouse. From here the ravages of both time and commercialism fade from view and the town is its elegant past again. The beacon tower of the Parish Church gathers it around its skirts, the pier stretching long into the sea like a beached monster from the deep.

My drawing came easily, as though it had been waiting for my hand to set it free. The higgledy piggledy of the terraced hotels and guest-houses, the terracotta and slate roofs glinting dully in the glaring sun. The beach loving the caress of the sea, the sea in love with the shingle. Everything moved gently together.

A young mother and her daughter sat on the bench behind me in silence together, not wanting to interrupt me. The child was very good. I imagined they were on holiday, maybe a one-parent family.

My drawing was nearing its completion and the mother, her child and I started to chat. It was a passing of the time of day, merely. My drawing finished I sat with them on the bench. We noticed a crowd gathering below on the beach, gathering around a handful of people who faced the crowd. Punch and Judy?

'No. It's a Bible study group,' the child explained, 'who act out scenes from the Bible.We watched them doing The Resurrection yesterday morning, didn't we Mummy?'

I opened my lunchbox and started on my sandwiches. The mother and child left, waving time and again. Below the crowd around the Bible actors started to disperse towards the town. The actors went with them. They were off to lunch.

After a few minutes I noticed two elderly ladies making their way across the beach, each with a shopping bag. They made for the square area of the shingle that had been raised to form a temporary stage by the actors. When they reached it the two ladies decided that the landward side of the 'stage' was a good spot to sit, with their back supported by the side of the 'stage'. As I watched they took little parcels of food from their shopping bags and began to eat. They were experiencing Cromer at its best, the sound of the sea lapping, the sun in their faces, a gentle off-shore breeze in their grey hair.

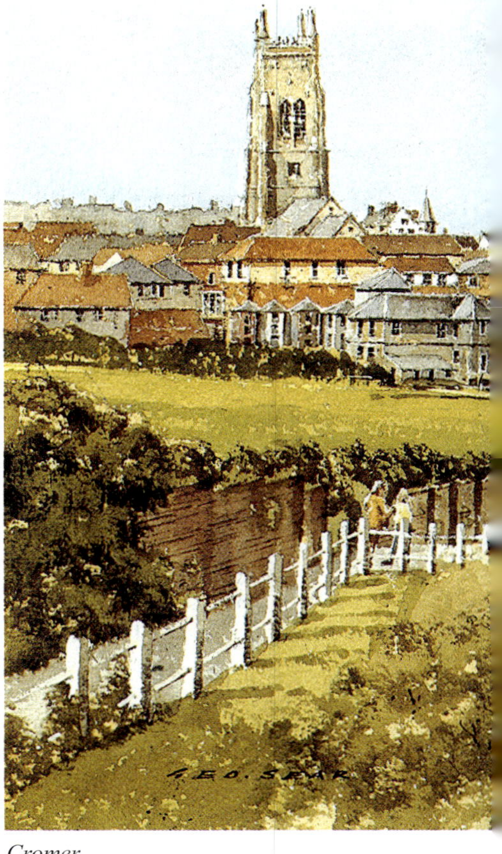

Cromer

As I watched their reverie I was aware that people were beginning to return to the place, to sit facing the stage. In ones and twos at first, then sevens, then nines, a crowd gathered, all sitting on the beach facing the stage expectantly. Soon an audience had assembled.

The two elderly ladies, still eating, gradually grew conscious, then more and more alarmed at why so many

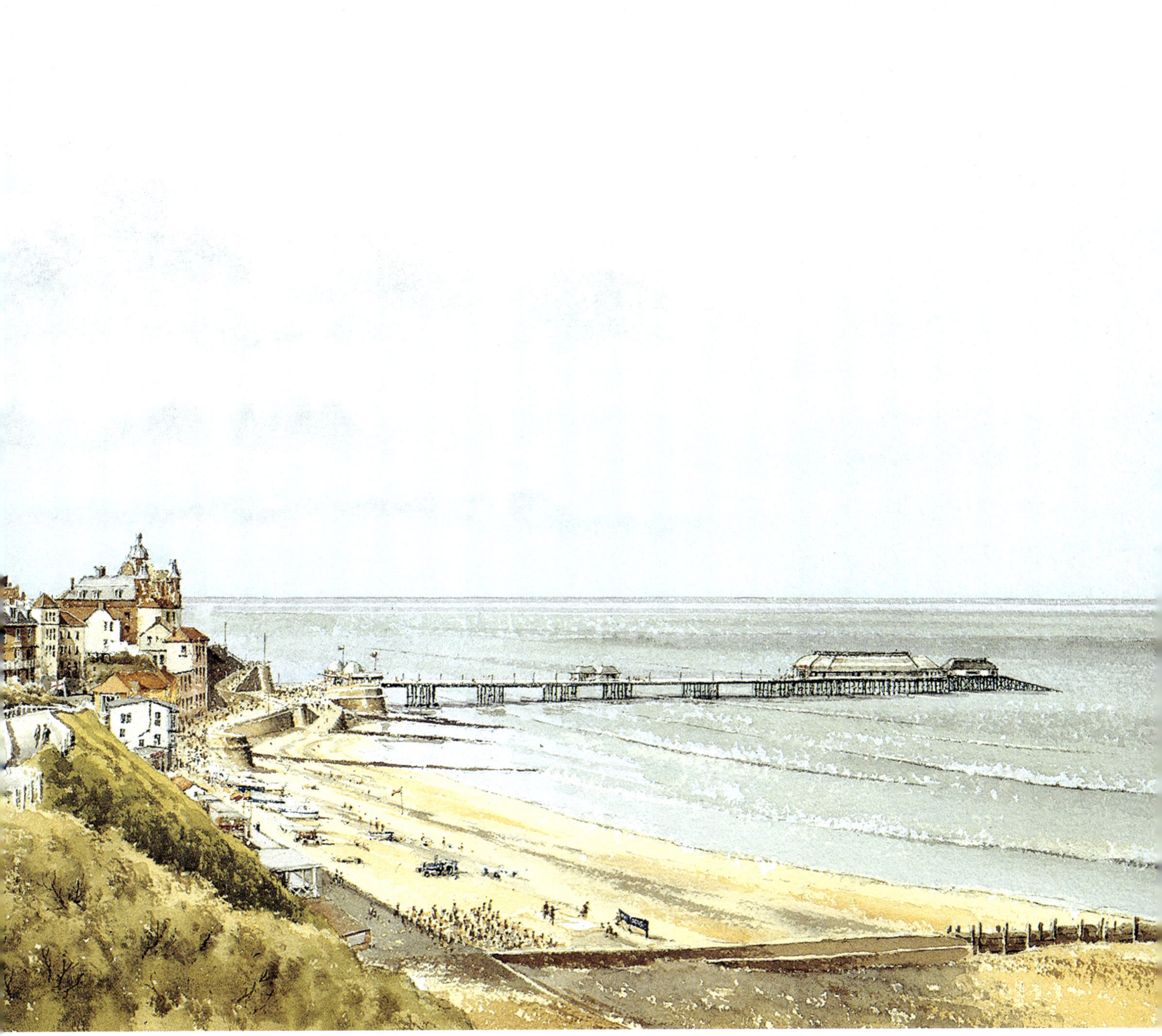

people had gathered to watch them eat their packed lunch. They looked at each other and then at the crowd. They began to hide their food, first in their laps then putting it away in their shopping bags.

Finally, embarrassed, humiliated, bewildered at being the centre of such attention they helped each other to their feet and they slunk off. They then half-ran towards the safe anonymity of the town. Confused, clutching each other, I watched them disappear up a side street.

And the sun glinted on the sea as the actors took up their Bibles for another performance.

Fact File

The atmosphere is in the detail.
Cromer, from this high vantage point needs concentration, and the fact that I was away from the summer crowds, I achieved this.
I started putting in the sky with pale Raw Sienna high up, and lightish clouds below with my usual mix of French Ultra, Burnt Umber, Alizarin Crimson. These on reflection could have been slightly stronger and more to the right, but I didn't want to distract from the summer crowds milling around the pier entrance and the gathering in the foreground. Make sure the proportions of the church tower are in keeping with the rest of the building. The figures at this distance need only the touch of a brush, but that still needs a considered approach. Together with boats and tractors on the beach, the safety flag on the sand, and that of the RNLI, all add up to create the right atmosphere.

'Practice brings confidence . . .'

Cley-next-the-Sea

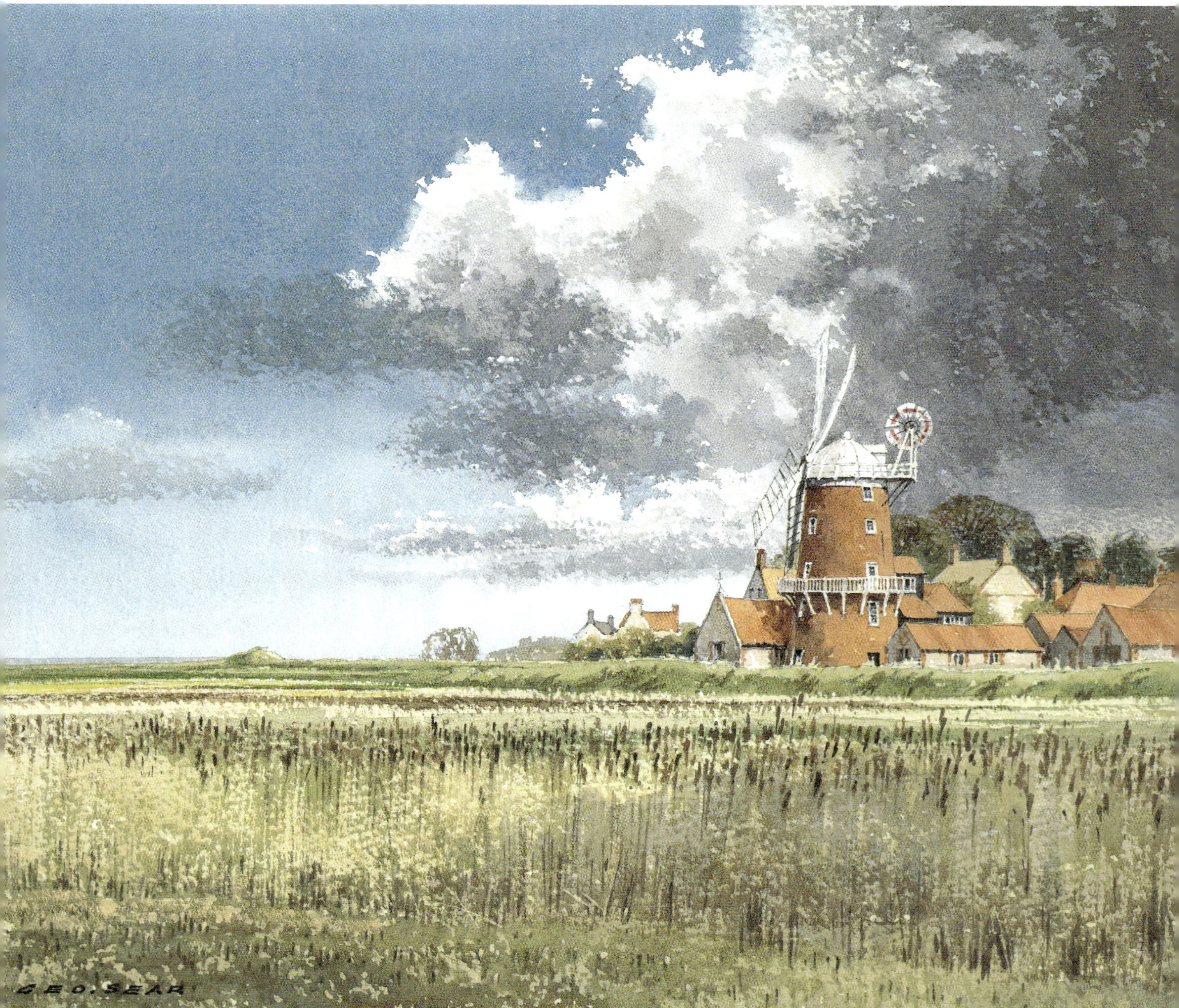

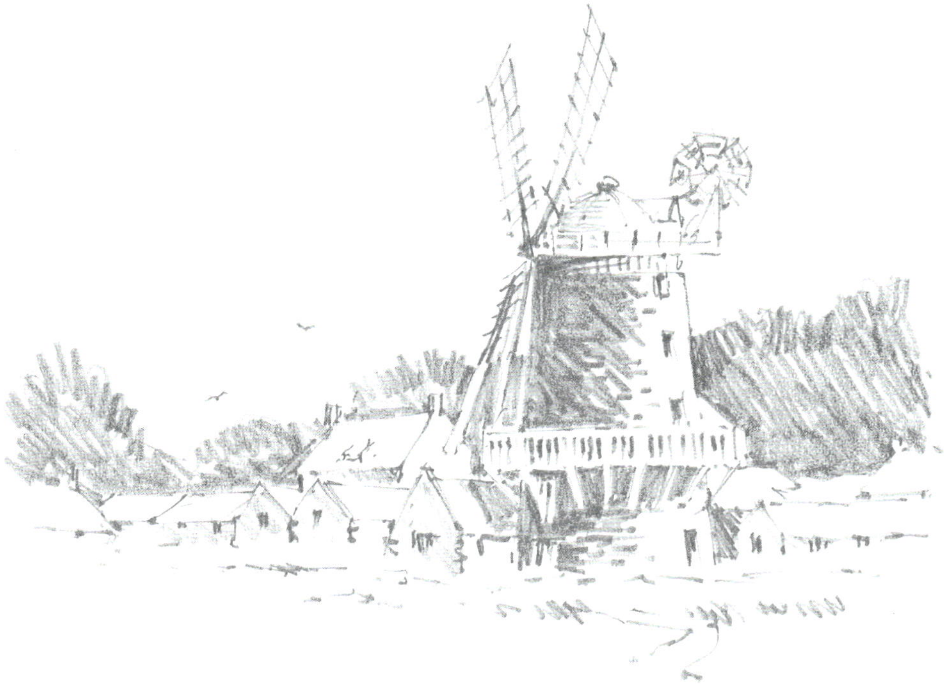

It must be one of the most painted features of Norfolk's landscape. It is virtually impossible for the artist to approach Cley Mill, pencil in hand or brush, with any sense of surprise. It's like telling an old old story, you search for a new twist to the tale, the unexpected, that evasive surprise. But to do so for its own sake, to surprise just to surprise is a fool's game.

Yet one day, down amongst the reed beds there, the mill above sailing in a cloudless sky the colour of lapis lazuli, the sun catching the bronzed tassles of reed flowers, I saw a different scene. I saw a storm being scudded across the landscape, inky, ominous, thunder wrapped in its depths, the clouds boiling and turning within themselves in anger. It was a single, isolated menace of a storm. Slanting curtains of heavy rain shifted across the marshes beyond sweeping relentlessly northwards towards me. The front edges of the storm were an innocent and fluffy white. The sails of the mill, forced stationary, seemed to demand to be set free and be allowed to spin wildly in the fitful gusts heralding the tempest.

It was a vision, of course, a dream, a surge of the mind on this still sunbursting afternoon with not a cloud in the sky. But the vision persisted. I took it home with me in my head after I had drawn the mill in its relative position to the edge of the sea, the reed-bedded end of the land.

The next morning I had half a painting on paper and the other, its sky, in my head. I had set myself a formidable task. Artistic licence, which the painter uses at will, is one thing. Invention quite another. At seven, before breakfast I started to paint storms in skies. At eleven I was still at it, discarded skies about me littering the surfaces of the studio. Lunchtime came but the sky had not. Why would it not come?

It would not come, I began to realise, because I had flown against nature. Not in creating a storm where a storm was not, that's licence. My fault was in painting in watercolour something that demanded oils. A subject will always tell the artist what medium it will give itself to, whether by the texture and depth of oil or by the soft airiness of watered colours. And I had known instinctively from the outset that this stormy scene in my head cried out for oils. It wept for them.

It was not until late in the evening that my storm became itself over the mill I had been waiting for it, not quite yet arrived except for its heralding wind. All that hard work, against nature, was a triumph of confidence in league with practice. For practice, time and time again, brings confidence. They go together, the one after the other.

Fact File

A brewing storm effect.

Once the preliminary drawing was completed, I masked the top of the mill and sails prior to painting the sky - this after many setbacks went like this.

A mix of French Ultramarine and Cobalt Blue was used in the left corner leaving dry brush work to form the white clouds. I moved down towards the horizon diluting the mix to make it lighter. Once this was dry, a mix of French Ultramarine/Alizian Crimson/Burnt Umber, to make greys of varying colour and strength, this I carried to the far edge. When this dried completely, I dry brushed with a strong mix of the same combination, trying not to stir up the pigment from the previous washes, to create a brewing storm effect, also with a few clouds on the left and onto the blue and reducing in size in the distance.

When I had arrived eventually at this point, the rest seemed plain sailing, making sure the shaft of sunlight clipped the village, and the reeds. A dry brush style was used with downward brush strokes, working from light to dark. Then I had a drink..

'The huddle around me cuddled closer . . .'

Morston Quay

It was young in the afternoon in October. A fierce wind was slashing through the marron-grass in a hiss of sand, slicing through the riggings making them sing and ring. The dark mud sucked as the sea slipped away. I had brought a group here on one of my four-day courses. The usual procedure is that after I had set them up they would, each of them, go to their own spaces, never near each other so they could glean their own individual atmosphere and sense of the place. Indeed, this was now beginning to happen, he and she going here and there, sheltering against the weather-boarded huts or in the lee of a marooned boat.

But the wind grew more fierce, lashing us with its fury. I called everyone together and suggested we all gather between the sides of two stranded boats for shelter. The wind seemed to sweep the sky bright and clean and clear. It was a spotless light. I began to paint, and encouraged my group to do so as well, a boat that had been put up on blocks to be scraped and maintained. It stood proudly off the sand around it. It was directly before us.

The huddle around me cuddled closer as we worked. They did as penguins do on the Antarctic ice-floes, those on the cold outside shifting inwards for warmth, those in the warmer middle sifting backwards and outwards to allow those who were cold into the warmer centre around me. I, at the still centre working with my brushes on my portrait of the boat on blocks in front of us, with the impression that I was a stove, something to warm themselves upon.

The afternoon grew older and ragged as the wind dragged grey clouds down from the north. The light was dousing and the shadows lengthening. Around me I could hear teeth begin to chatter and I sensed that concentration was drifting like the shining sand. The song of the curlews became melancholic and the boats darkened like coffins.

My thoughts turned to Maureen and the St. John Hall in Holt where she would soon put the kettle on to make tea for us with sandwiches and cakes. It was time to go. I suggested to everyone that it was time we all went and they all readily agreed. We hurried to our cars.

All except one. A dear friend who had come up from Berkhamsted to join the course. She was the doughty, no-nonsense lady secretary of my own art club in my own home town. She would not leave with us. We must go if we liked. But there were a few more details of the boat on blocks that she wanted to capture, to fix in paint onto her unfinished painting. You all go,she insisted, I'll meet you back at St. John Hall.

We went reluctantly, almost guiltily, for the place had become hostile. The nagging wind and the gathering gloom, the ominously turning tide and the dominating wilderness made us sense she was being made vulnerable by us leaving her alone. But, characteristically, she would have us go.

Later, warmed and laughing together in the cavernous St. John Hall in Holt, hot tea steaming, cheeks flushing, cakes and sandwiches piled on our plates, the grim desolateness of Morston Quay seemed a long way away. And as we were all chattering away in animated groups of this and that suddenly the double doors swung open and my friend whom we had left alone amongst the furious elements stood before us.

She was not wretched as you would suppose. She was not chilled to the bone. Although her hair was dishevelled and blown about she herself was quite calm. Yet there was a glint in her eye, the astonishing glint of humour. And she began to laugh.

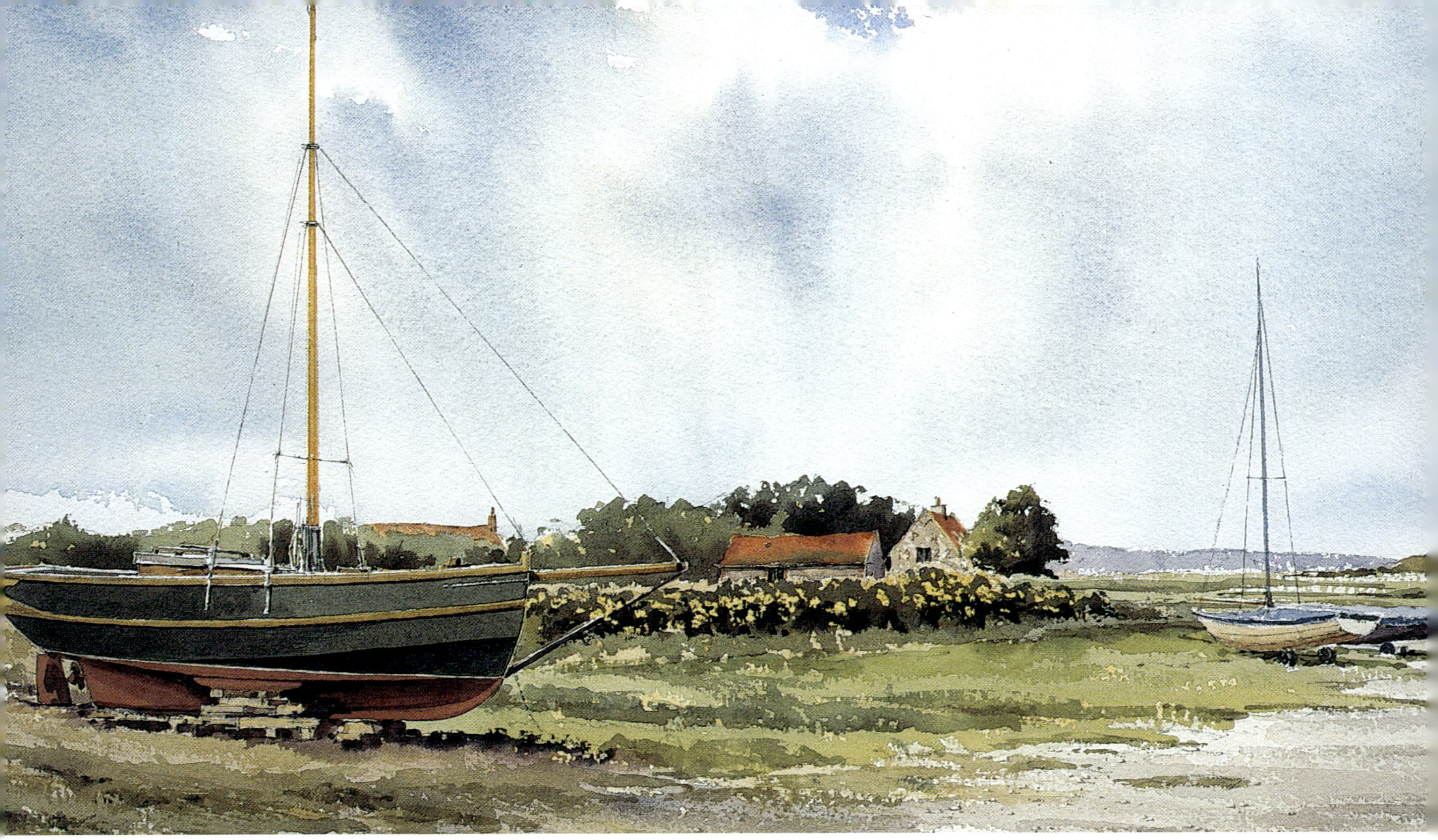

Boat on the blocks, Morston Quay.

We gathered round her, gave her tea, here, a cake, some sandwiches. She waved the concern for her down, a flapping motion with her arms, a cup and plate at their extremities. She then told us the story.

Minutes after we had all left her sheltering from the gale between the boats a car had madly sped up from the coast road, careered along the pot-holed quay and skidded to a halt in front of her. The driver jumped out and ran crazedly towards the boat on blocks we had been painting and she was painting still. He rushed around it, the jacket of his unbuttoned suit flapping wildly in the wind. He spread his arms and hands against its sides. He moved round it, caressing it, his expression was of intense relief and of disbelief. He seemed to be thanking God as he moved around feeling its sides, smoothing his hands almost sensually along its barnacled hull.

My friend, alarmed at his strange behaviour, called out to him and asked him what was wrong. Was he alright? She is the kind of lady who would do such things. He, in turn, was alarmed by her appearance skulking there between the boats. He stopped and stared at her. Then he approached her, laughing with his relief.

Shouting against the roar of the wind he explained that he had had a telephone call to his office in Swaffham to tell him that there was a gang of people painting his boat on Morston Quay. His life, his world was his boat and he could not bear to think of it being vandalised thus, of it being daubed with paint. He had jumped into his car immediately and sped off to the coast. As he drove, he shouted, all the while he was fearing what on earth awful colour the sods had painted his pride and joy - day-glo pink? Orange? Puce?

Fact File

This is a study of a boat on the blocks, ready for early spring repairs, and a new lick of paint.
Draw in carefully the outline of the craft, together with the marsh cottages and distant boats to help the balance. The sky, after being dampened, pale Raw Sennia, was applied followed by French Ultramarine/Burnt Umber washes on this cold spring day. Notice the distant trees at Stiffkey are pale blue with a touch of light red. After painting the cottage roofs, run a brush of green along the guttering and let it creep up to indicate moss. All the greens were a mix of yellows and browns with Winsor Blue, and the bushes dry brushed, leaving spaces for the yellow flowers. A few stones are indicated on the shore. The rigging can be painted in the studio from photographs taken at the time..

The Narnia Syndrome

Binham

It must have always been so that the artist is the child of chance, the plaything of circumstance. Because they deliberately and wilfully walk out amongst the world searching for visual pleasures for the soul, fate plays with them. Indeed, I have found that she teases. She dallies.

I had spent a large proportion of the day painting The Street in Binham. And it was going well. The little flint cottages with their ever-vigilant eyes of windows and the pantiled hats of their roofs. The low brick walls that encase the fragments of front gardens. The dense copper beech half way down, a dark purple bonfire. The parked cars and the telegraph pole I would probably magic away.

All the while, however, almost like an irritant, a wasp at a picnic, from the corner of my eye to my left, something kept whispering at me, pulling the coat-tails of my attention. Paint as I might, mix as carefully as I did my colours to capture the flints this other thing to my left nudged.

It was a gate, an almost derelict blue-painted gate in a wall. No big deal. But it tantalised. When I had finished my painting I went over and stood in front of it. I sketched it and took photographs of it. But why?

It is, I suppose, the Narnia syndrome, the longing to know what is on the other side. There is an obstruction, something barring your way, a gate or a door, and we yearn for the other side. Will there be the magical, undiscovered world we have always been searching for since we were children?

I return to this shabby old gate at Binham as one returns to a well-loved, dog-eared book. It gets older as do I. In the Hollyhock days the heat of the sun blisters its blue face. Snow sits along its narrow top for a moment in winter. In all the years I have known and loved it, it has never been opened. The post its hinges cling to leans away from the wall at crazier angles at each visit.

I do know what is on the other side. I couldn't resist one day and stood on my seat to look over. But I will not tell you. I must respect your dreams.

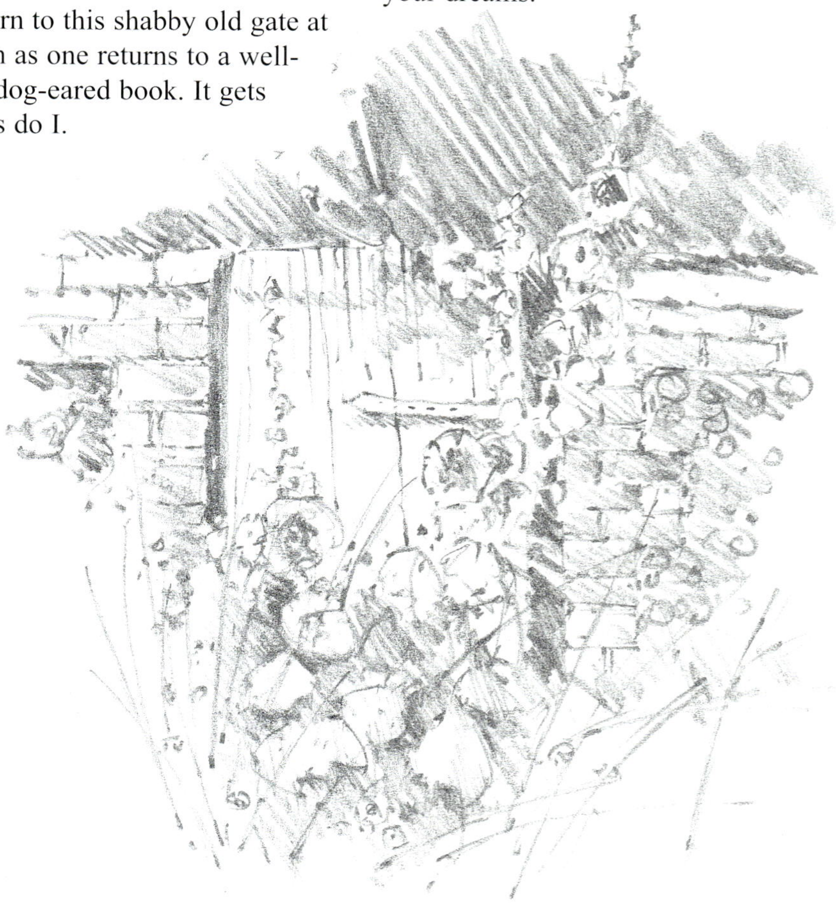

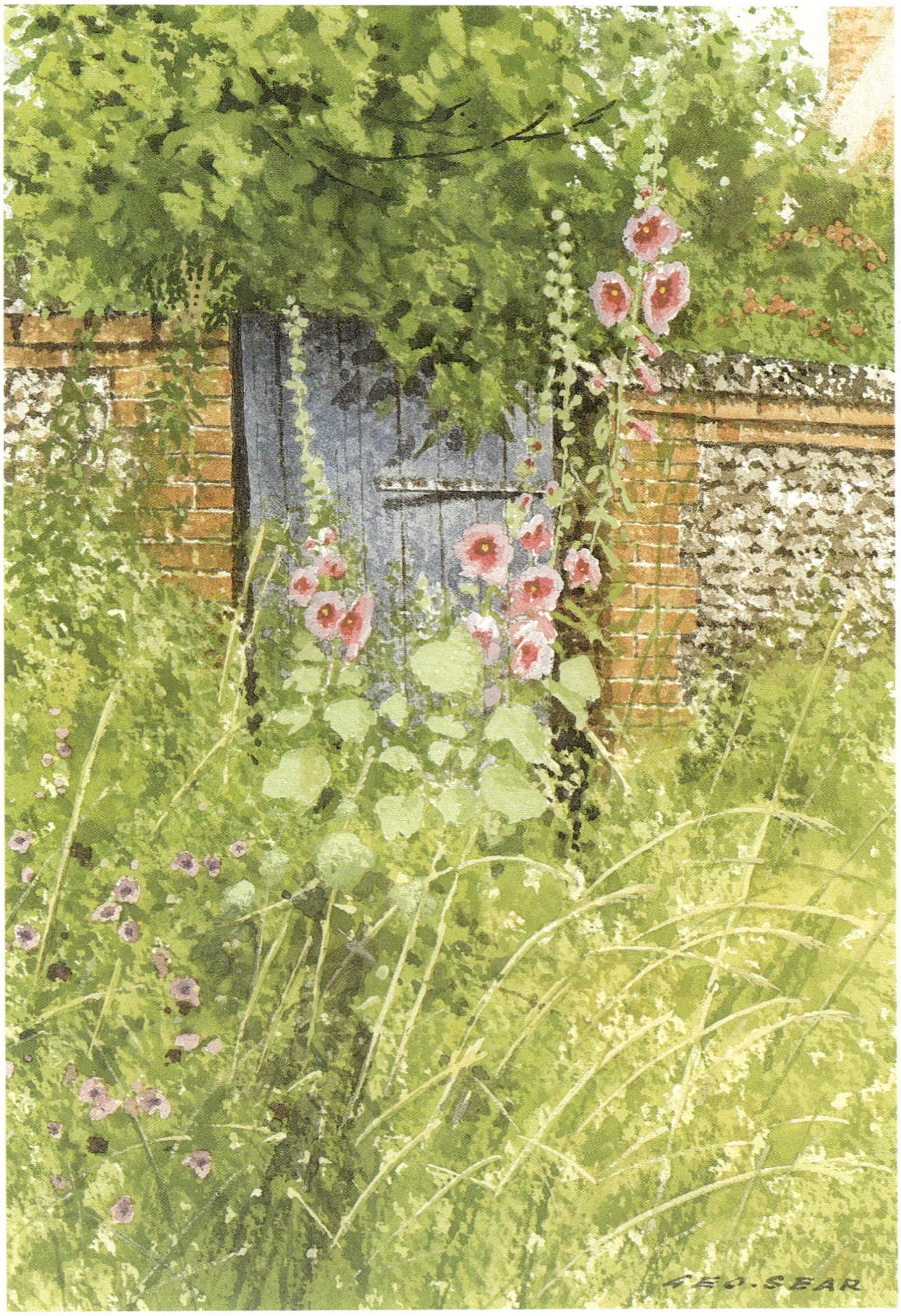

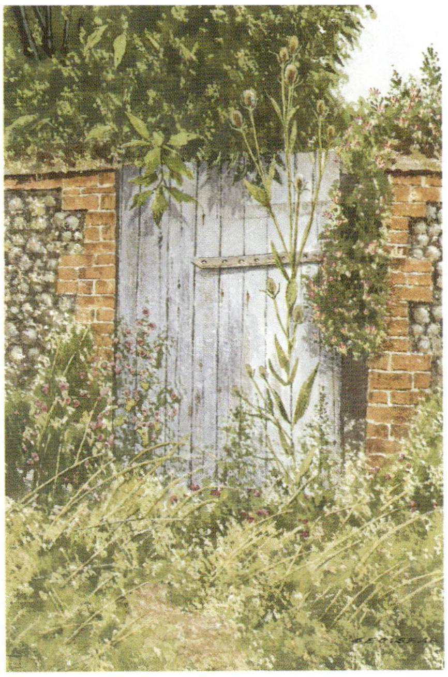

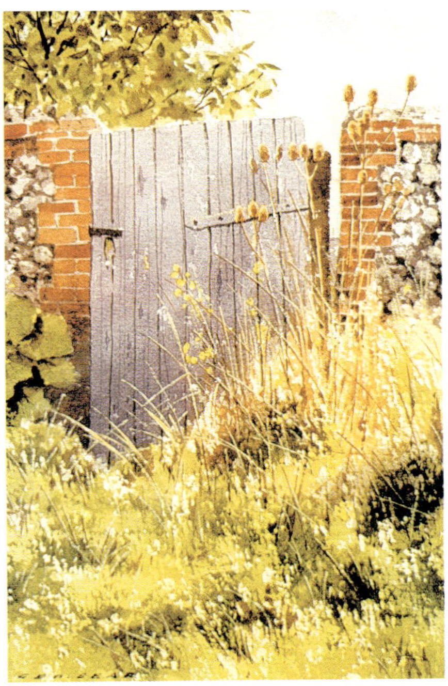

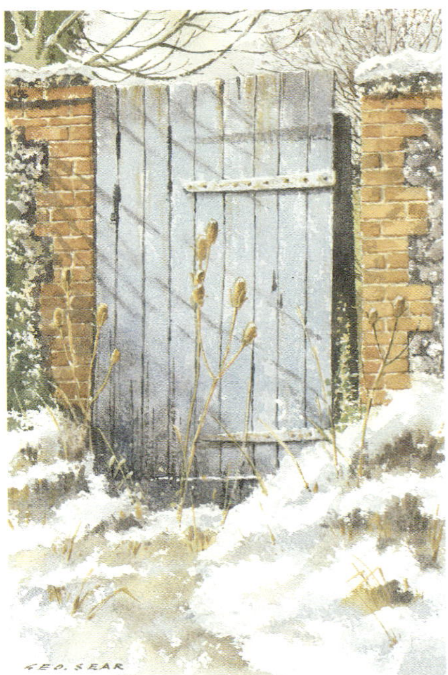

Fact File

Keeping the character of the scene is all important. The way the gate leans, the way the hinge curves away from the wood. The red of the brick-work, and the colours in the cobbles with the jumble of flowers and weeds throughout the seasons, all add to the mystery.

As usual, the larger of the flowers were masked and some of the larger hollyhock leaves. After the lighter washes dried, I masked some of the thin grasses, then continued with the greens. When the masking was rubbed off, the grasses appeared...

'Inspiration quickened my hand . . .'

Stiffkey Marshes

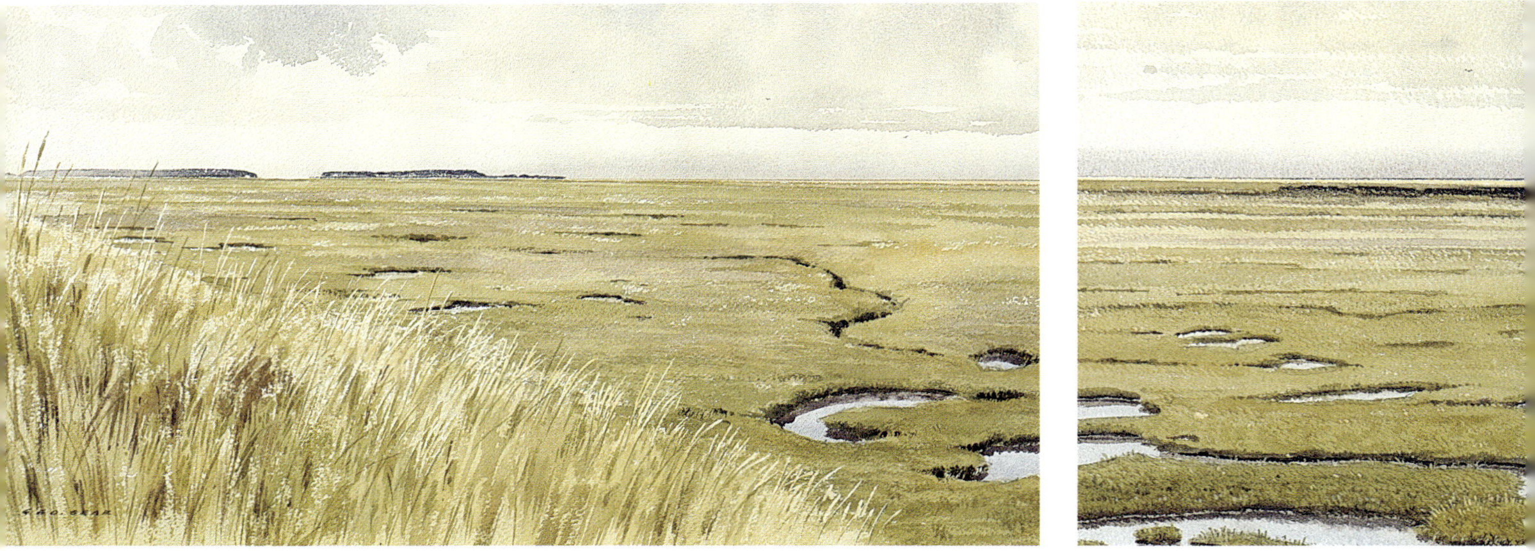

If the artist were clever with words he would probably have become a writer. One of the headaches that painting a picture creates is to name it, to give it a title. People expect what they buy and hang on their walls to have a name. The cliche is the last resort. And the first. So when, that summer's Wednesday, Maureen and I were walking Greta and Susie our dogs along the tufted edges of Stiffkey Marshes a wonderful and very special thing happened. Gazing at the glassy, still rivulets of water amongst the swathes of sea lavender and marron grass she said if I painted due north with the light catching the water I could call it 'Marsh Mosaic'. I was gob-smacked. What a title. It was worth painting for the title alone.

As it happened I had my kit with me. Maureen said she would walk the dogs round to Wells if I settled there on the spot to paint. It was magic. Even as she and they became spots in the distance I was engrossed in my work. A marsh is a marsh is a marsh. But on that day on this marsh it was different. It was inspiring. I had never seen so many shades of sage green at the same time. And the jewelled water, fragments of liquid sky lacing and snaking through the mudded banks. The mist out to sea giving the horizon a luminous mauve, an elongated opal slithering the distance between sea and sky, a slip of heaven. The clouds mere souffled incidents.

Inspiration quickened my hand. It was done, all that I could do there. I picked Maureen and the dogs up at Wells as arranged and we went home, I on a high.

We all domestic differently. You might have your dinner at noon. They might have a cooked tea at five. We eat at seven. Afterwards I put the painting of Stiffkey Marshes in the fireplace. Not, of course, to burn it but the better to see it from the settee, to assess the day's work, to observe it from the distance of others. I had washed the sky and put in more details of the marshes and honed the reflections on the water. And again, for the second time that day, a magic happened. The painting spoke to

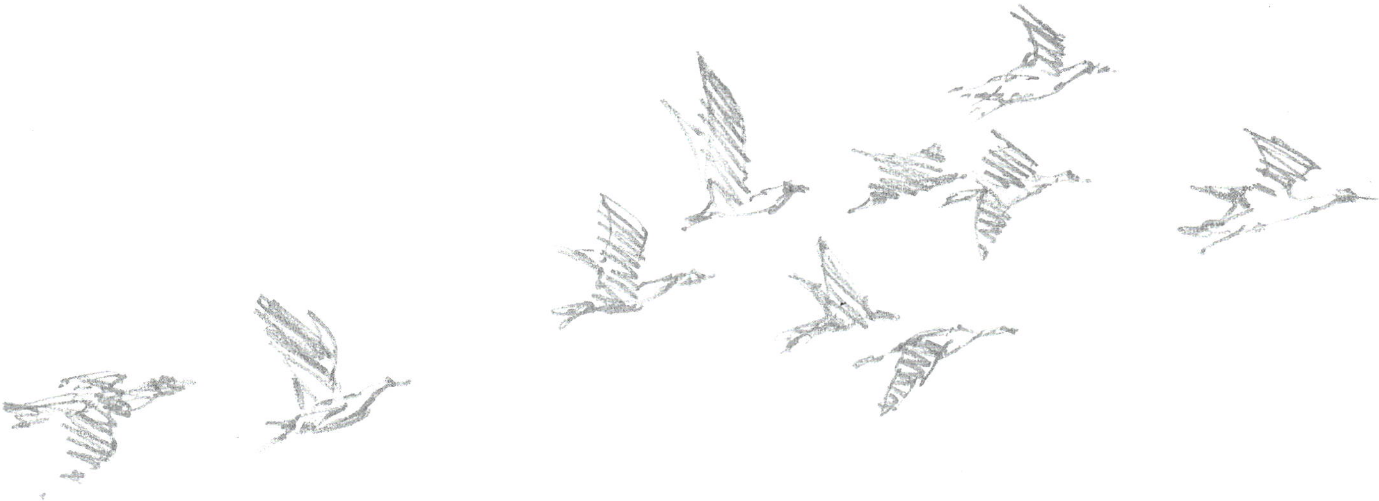

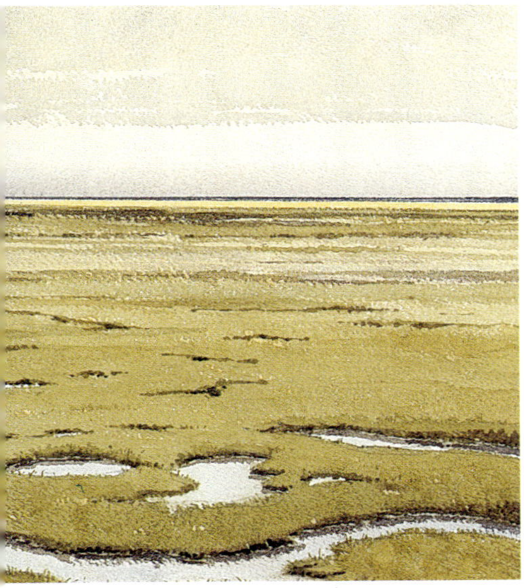

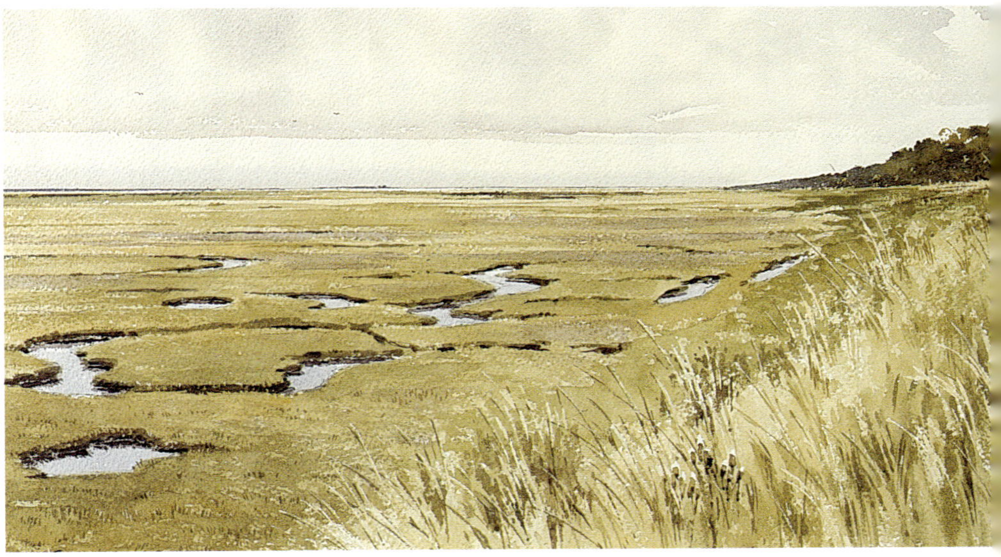

me. It said - more. More? What more?

Of course it needed more. It longed to reveal more of its marsh-scape, that to its left horizon and that to its right. It wanted to be, it demanded that it was a panorama. But, as it was, it was nevertheless complete in itself. So what was it saying? The evening ended with the question hanging. We went to bed. I slept on it.

The dawn brought the answer. 'Marsh Mosaic' needed to be a tryptych. It had to be three paintings to make it complete, to present the mystery of that enigmatic marshland. I could hardly wait to get back to Stiffkey. But it poured with rain all day. I was livid with frustration.

The next day, Friday, and then the Saturday, were fine although different in quality. But then no two days are the same. I went back to the spot on Stiffkey Marshes where I had worked two days earlier and did drawings of towards the left horizon that culminated amongst the pines opposite Wells Bar and to the right towards Blakeney Point. I could not take the light into account because that which prevailed on Wednesday must be my measure.

When I had painted the Friday Wells aspect and the Saturday Blakeney's my tryptych was complete. And they had to be sold as one work, the three together. And they had to be hung together and live together hereafter.

Fact File

I cannot look at the marshes without recalling Jason Partners phrase, told to him by his art master and subsequently, told to me. Aim to get six miles distance in depth of a $^1/_4$' (6mm), thus avoiding the marshes appearing to rise. Sayings like these are priceless, enabling you to remember before you paint instead of afterwards when the damage is probably irreparable. Others in the same idiom, 'Leave enough holes in the trees to let the birds fly through' and 'An area of blue in the sky, enough to patch a pair of sailor's trousers'.

Keep the marsh pools crisp and clear with a small reflection from the bank, and a thin highlight where the water laps against the edge. The tall grasses at both sides are light in colour with darker dry brushwork. Add a few thistle heads here and there.

Great Yarmouth

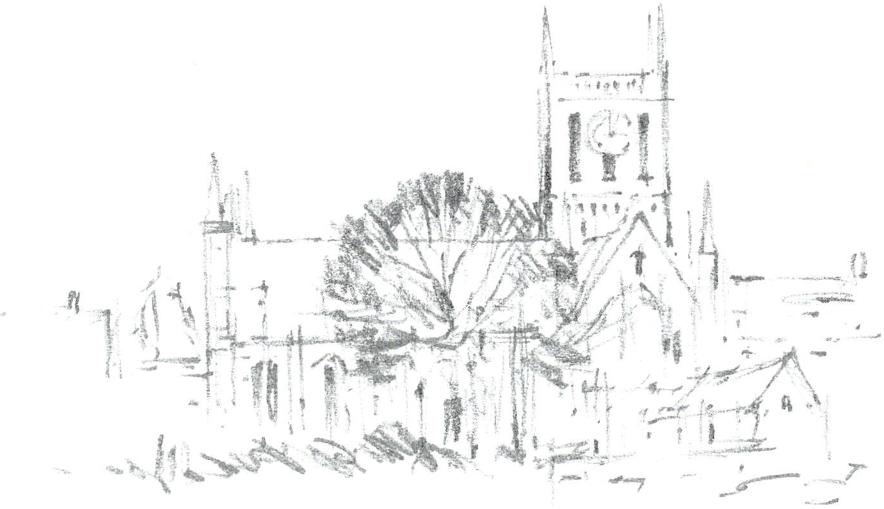

The commission was for a Christmas card of the Market Square in Great Yarmouth. There had to be snow. Of course, I said. And families shopping together. No problem, I said. Oh, and the church, you must paint the church. Fine.

When I got there the problems started. It was one of those mind-numbing, raw, intensely cold November days that only Norfolk knows how to deliver. Maureen wouldn't leave the car it was so freezing. Muffled to the hilt I set myself up in the Square.

Trouble was there were no market stalls, it wasn't their day. Nor was it snowing - yet. The church was too far away and I had to pull it forward in my sketch. And there were no happy families doing their Christmas shopping together - it was too darn cold. The few that there were, were running to get out of the blast of iced wind. And to cap it all I was confronted with more street furniture - bus shelters, railings, telephone kiosks, ugly street lights, road signs, traffic islands - than Piccadilly Circus.

In desperation I went into a newsagents and bought an aerial photograph of the square on Market Day to give me the positions of the stalls. The rest, as they say, was left to my imagination. I had to do away with the visual vandalism of street furniture. I had to imagine the snow that was surely half way down the North Sea and on its way. And I peopled it with the happy families of never-never land. You have to make people believe in what they see on the front of their Christmas cards.

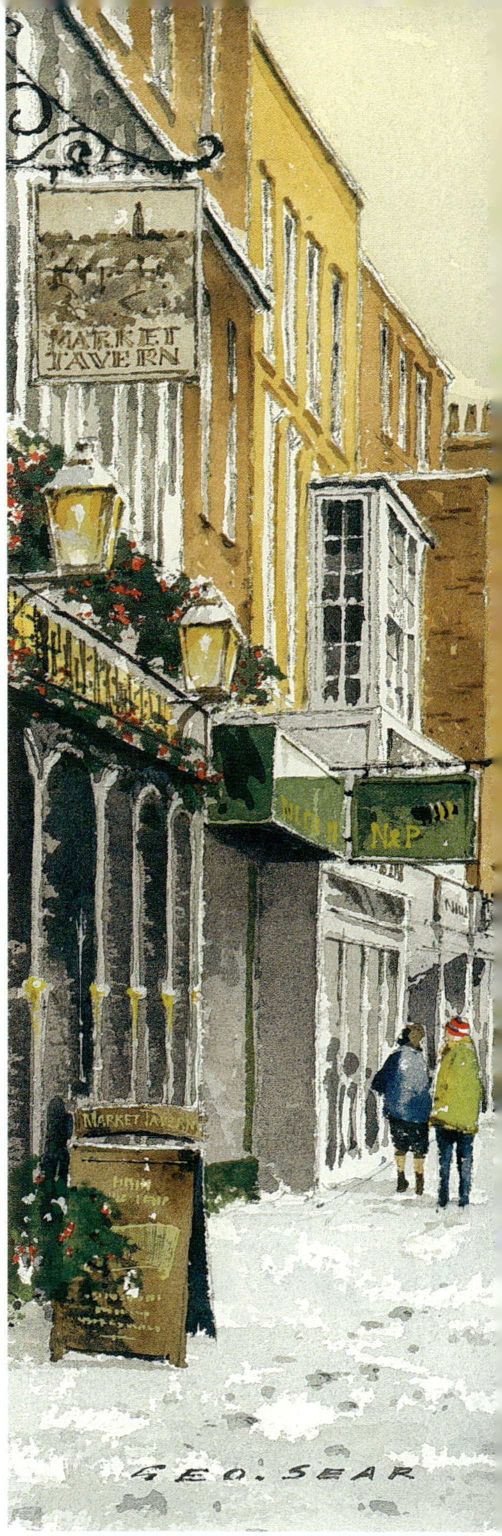

'The rest was left to my imagination . . .'

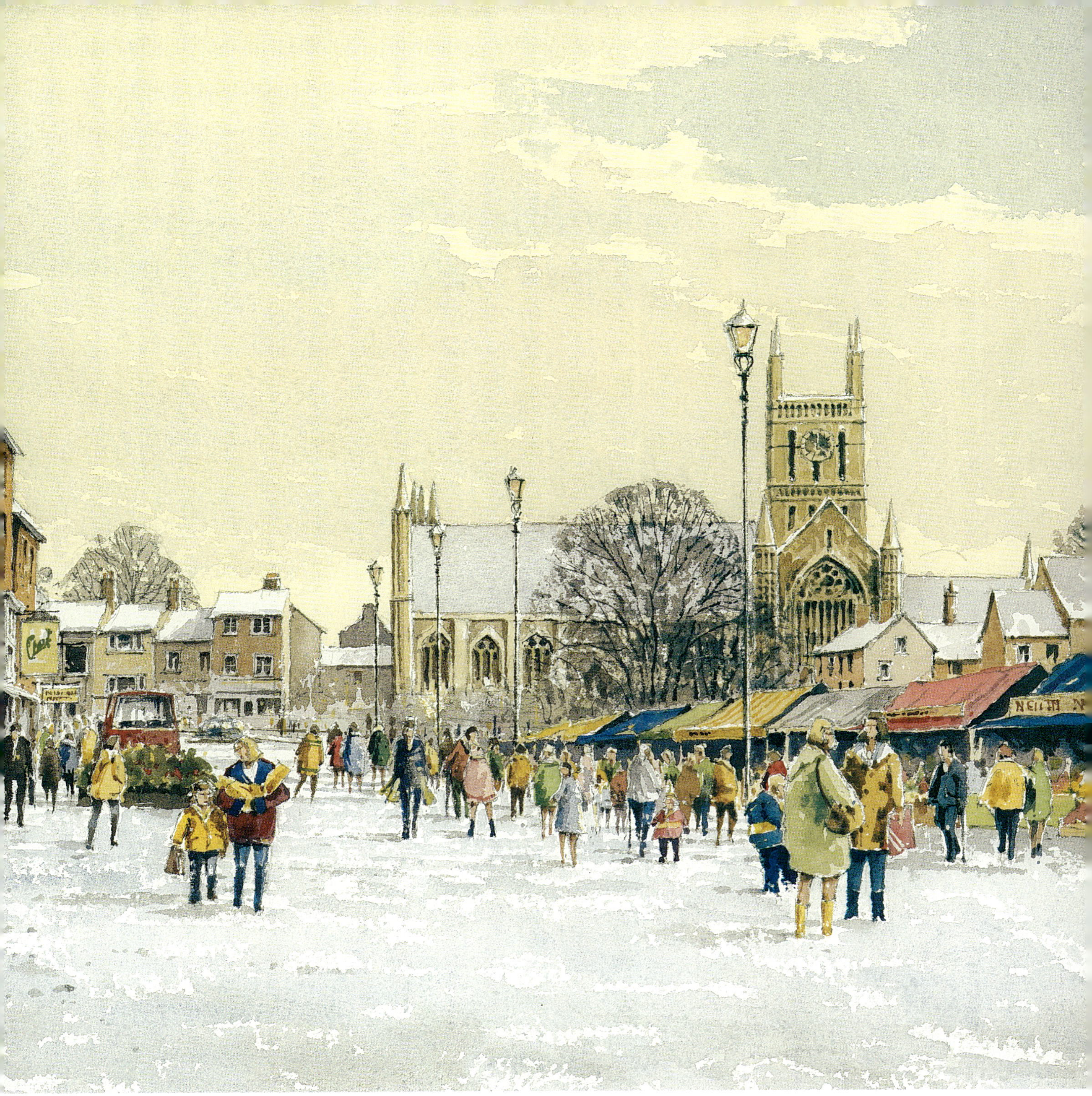

Winter Market, Great Yarmouth.

I was finished, almost, grateful and ready to get back to the car and Maureen.

'What you up to mate?' A voice over my shoulder.

'Painting a Christmas card,' I said. 'Pity there's no snow.'

'Hang about,' he said. 'It'll snow before the day's out. Bloody cold innit. I'm off.'

'Me too.'

I completed the job in the warm comfort of my studio.

Fact File

Give the foreground a chance to sparkle.
When I had completed the drawing stage, I didn't draw in individual figures at this point, just indications where they would finally be.
The sky had a complete under painting with Raw Sienna and a touch of Burnt Umber, not too strong. When this is completely dry, put another sky over the whole, it gives a unifying effect which gives the snow in the foreground a chance to sparkle.
Practice your figures on separate sheets, this will give you more assurance when they are inserted into the painting. Imagine what the people might be saying to each other, it helps with the general ambience.
I used Whatman 200lbs Rough paper as this brand has a white finish, thus making for cleaning snow, as that is the paper showing through.

'He stopped to encourage ...'

Salthouse

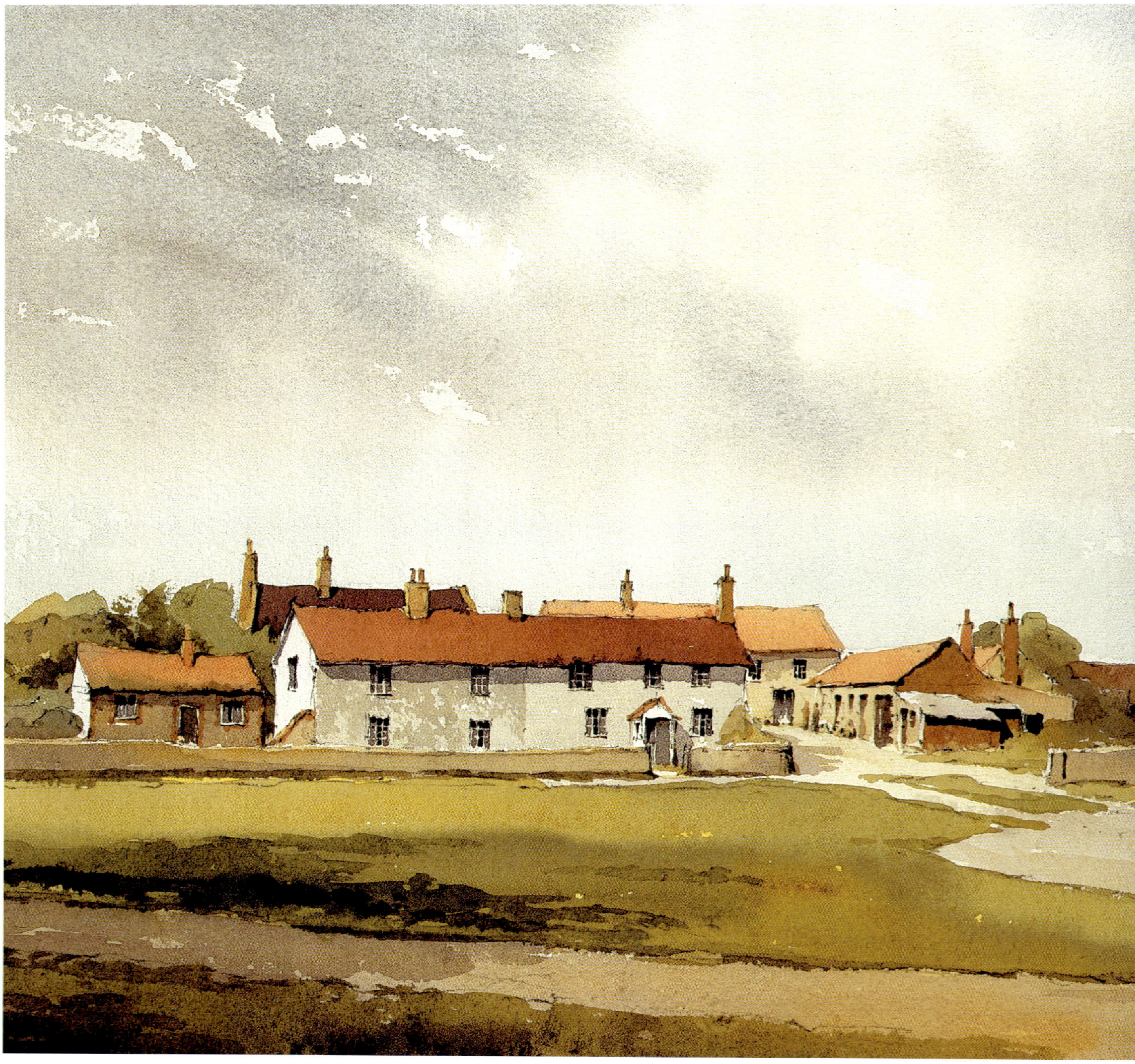

Sooner or later during one of my courses in the St. John Hall, Holt the class will insist that we spend time down at Salthouse. It is a favourite place because it is made for watercolours. It is almost a mirage on certain hazy days. But in wet weather the semi-tones of its colours are bright and clear.

So it happened, on this course and on this day, although it was pouring with heavy rain driven inland by a fierce north-easterly. They would paint from the comfort of their cars through the windscreen-wiper and they would have the heating full blast. Occasionally I would leap from work in my car and go visiting the members of the class in turn. I was delighted that there we saw many embryo pictures of merit. This was indeed water-colours with a challenge.

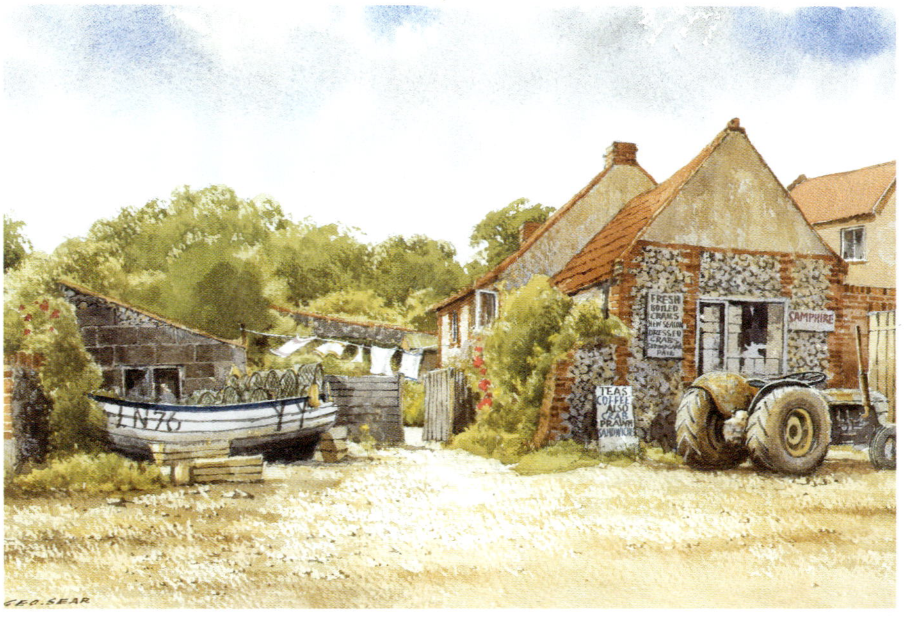

Wash day, Salthouse.

Maybe my enthusiasm for their work carried me away, but unfortunately as the dashing through the cats and dogs of rain from car to car wore on I got wetter and wetter until, in the end, my students became reluctant to admit me into their mobile studios because I was steaming up their windows as I dried off.

I took my leave of them and went home to change into dry clothes and met them all back at St. John Hall after lunch when we sat together finishing off our studies of Salthouse, pleased indeed with our results despite the difficulties.

On another very different experience of Salthouse the weather was much kinder. Half way through the morning it was clear to us all that the everyone's work was going well and that I was delighted. I was discussing a point with one of the class when I noticed the rest of them had all stopped painting and had gathered in a huddle near the bait shop.

They all beckoned us over, waving us to them, shouting.

'George, the Master has arrived.'

'The Master has come, he's here with us.' (Now, folks, I know this all sounds like a Lew Grade, low-budget biblical epic for Yorkshire Television, but I swear it's true.)

As I moved into the middle of the huddle I found to my pleasure that James Fletcher Watson and his wife had appeared as upon a cloud descended from Heaven. In fact they had been passing through on his way to make a promotional video in the area but had stopped to encourage the group. Being Salthouse he would probably have guessed that the class was mine. We are friends and I often tell him of my students progress in that little sea-swept village. It is a measure of his greatness that he stopped to encourage.

The Dunn Cow, Salthouse.

Fact File

Keep it simple.

The Dun Cow, Salthouse.

This view is one of the classic North Norfolk scenes, painted from different angles it never fails to please.
From this viewpoint, there is little to worry about regarding perspective, but make sure that the colour and tonal values of the pantile roofs fit nicely together, and counter-change between light and dark. Keeping detail to the minimum, show the sea defence wall on the right receding into the distance. This is accentuated by having the sign, wall and corner cottage in silhouette.

'It was one of those clear bright sea-days …'

Burnham Overy Staithe

The River Burn giggles to the surface in a field near Sculthorpe and meanders across the village green and even beneath houses in South Creake then follows the road up to North Creake, down through Creake Abbey, past Nelson's birthplace at Burnham Thorpe then it slips sinuously, peacefully into the sea at Overy Staithe. It doesn't live long on its snake-run to its home. It is here that I often find myself returning because it tantalises me. The solid mass of the buildings, the quiet elegance in the curves of the boats and the omnipresent sea and mud, the one ceaselessly remoulding the other like a dithering potter.

I was about to paint from a raised area of marsh facing east with the boat house on my right. Here and there were upturned dinghies hauled up out of reach and of any incoming tide. And two or three yachts grouped nicely high and dry to the left. A few boaty people were busying themselves tying rope and painting, repairing, retouching as boat people do between tides.

It was one of those clear, bright sea-days when half of Norfolk can feel that it is off-shore and being towed by the land. I was feeling good and the job in hand was coming along nicely. With the sun from the back of the boat house I had to make sure that I did not paint the shadow side too heavily, thus blurring the interesting details. So absorbed had I become with capturing every line, every curl

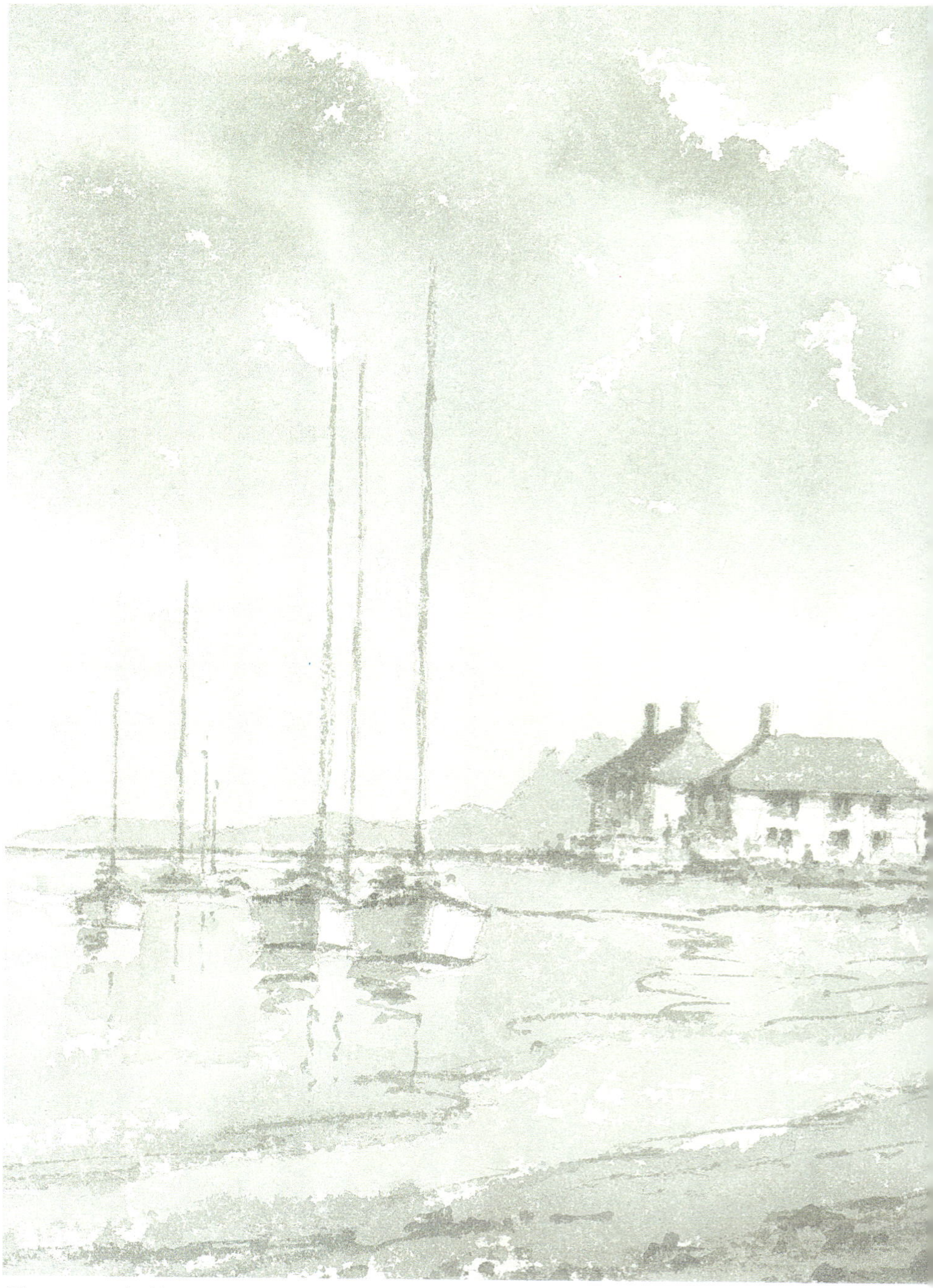

The missing half.

of rope that I failed to notice the incoming tide - as I ALWAYS DO. The group of yachts I had painted resting were now riding the tide high.

I hurried to clean my palette and pack my bag. Too late, of course, for water now encircled what had become my island. I was wearing fairly expensive new shoes and light trousers and had a painting I thought very good and worth saving. I did not want to wade back to the land.

Ah, rescue was at hand. A young lad who had earlier been watching me paint was even then launching a row-boat towards me. From his expression as he neared, rowing with one paddle like an Indian, he wanted to convey that he did this all the time, why were old people so stupid, but maybe he'd get something out of the situation.

'Could you get me ashore, do you think, lad?'

'It'll cost you.'

'How much? It's not far.'

'A quid.'

'A pound? You're joking.'

'75 pence then. It is here and back.'

We settled on 50 pence, which was a small price to pay for a dry watercolour and undamaged expensive shoes.

Two or three weeks later I was emerging from a period of turmoil one way and another, and I wanted to paint a medium-sized painting. I took from my studio plan-chest a sheet of watercolour paper and cut it in half vertically. Holding them up to the light to check the watermark to my horror I could see a group of boats were on the reverse. I had cut my lovely Overy Staithe painting clean in two.

Damage done no point in crying. Instead I had both halves framed. These were sold at an exhibition in Hitchin, Hertfordshire. Both purchasers begged the other to let them have both pictures. But they never would.

And so they live, my two pictures that once were one, in separate homes, under different house rules, as so many young families do today.

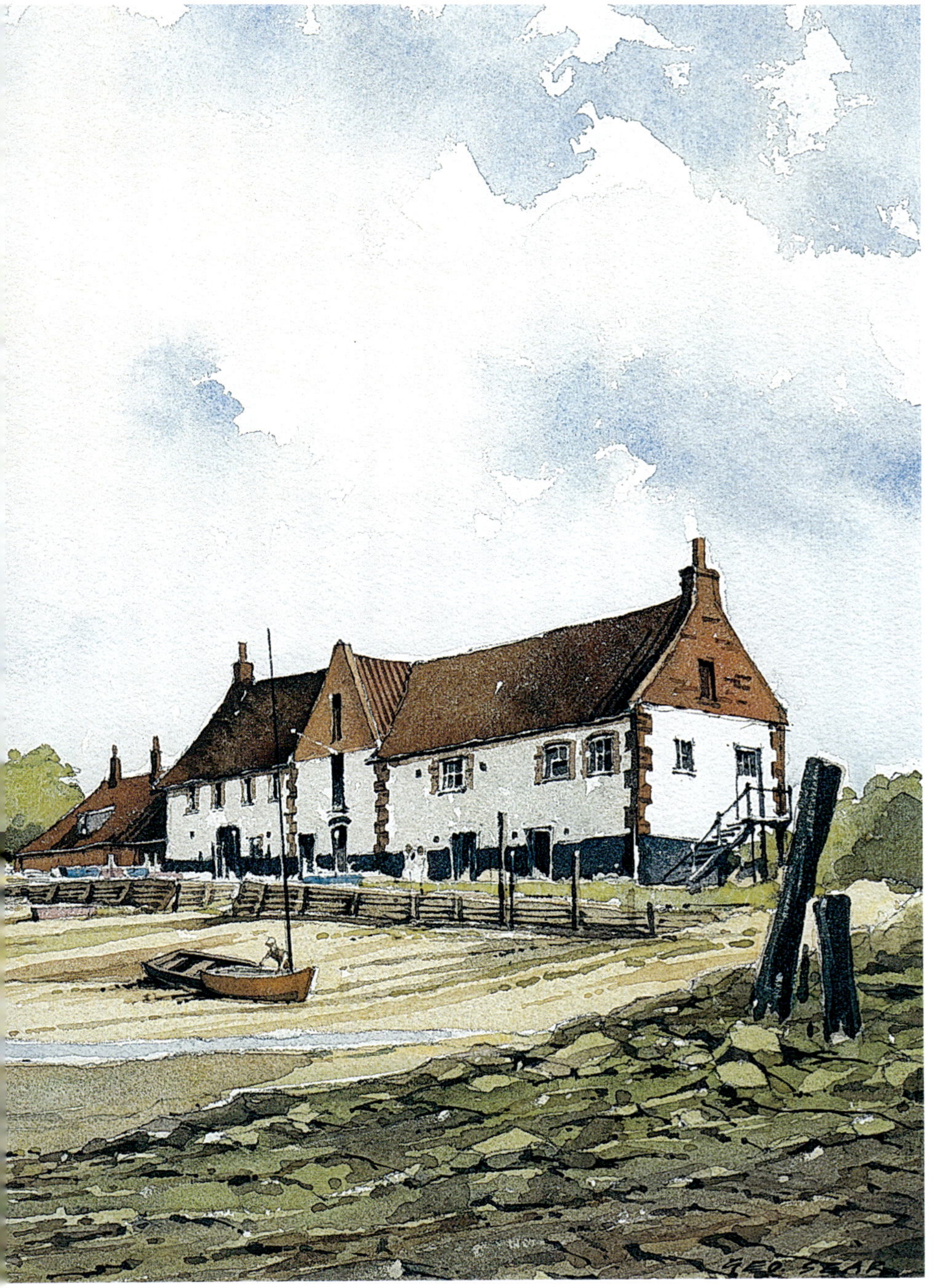

The half I found.

Fact File

Care in the Studio.

The painting of the Maritime shop/boathouse was produced a few years ago. I felt it must be included if only to emphasise the care needed of finished art work in the studio.
An attractive Norfolk Boathouse sitting on the quay, with an Anglian sky above.
I do not know of any other painting I have completed that this type of accident, would have resulted in anything but a complete disaster.
I only managed to trace one half.

'A painting is a segment of time . . .'

Holt

To arrive in Holt at the end of the journey, you must have climbed one of the several hills and, from all but one direction, penetrated woodland. Moreover, every path to the town crosses water.

From the north, from Cley-next-the-Sea, there is a crossing over a small stream in the dell of woods which, after prolonged heavy rain, becomes a ford. Thereafter the road winds uphill through more woods to the municipal graveyard and past a charming estate of cottage-style houses built in the 1930's and redolent of the Arts and Crafts Movement.

Eastwards the road ducks into the verdant tunnel of High Kelling and its substantial grounds surrounding houses of substance. Smaller lanes wind towards the town from the seaside village of Kelling itself and Weybourne passing Holt Hall and rolling farmland.

The main road from the south and Norwich rises steeply after crossing a stream at Edgefield up through the broad-leaved woods of Holt Country Park and its shoulder-high ferned mystery.

From Fakenham and King's Lynn the major road from the west meanders through the sleepy village of Letheringsett where it crosses the stripling river Glaven. Past the old flour mill the road runs up the hill to Holt town centre and Blind Sam, the decorative Victorian gas lamp moved from the Market Square to make way for the War Memorial, 'blind' because when it was lit by hand and pole it was always being blown out.

And from its south-westerly direction runs the road from Guist through Thornage and the hazards of the askew little bridge over yet another stream up the hill into town.

Upon such a distinctive and protected hill sits this fine Georgian market town, now, alas, marketless. Yet few visitors realise that it is Georgian because it bears no trace of its earlier history. There are no Elizabethan beams, no muddle of Medievalism. It is as though the town was suddenly thought of, or Brigadoon-like rose from a mist, at the turn of the 18th Century and the pageant of its history sandwiched between the then and now of three centuries. This absence of an historic past was due entirely to a catastrophic inferno that totally destroyed the town on May Day in 1708. Only a few scorched timbers and glassy-surfaced bricks exposed in one or two parts of old buildings in the centre of the town bear witness to the event.

The fire started when a spark from a stall in the market square, which was then at least three times larger than now, set light to the

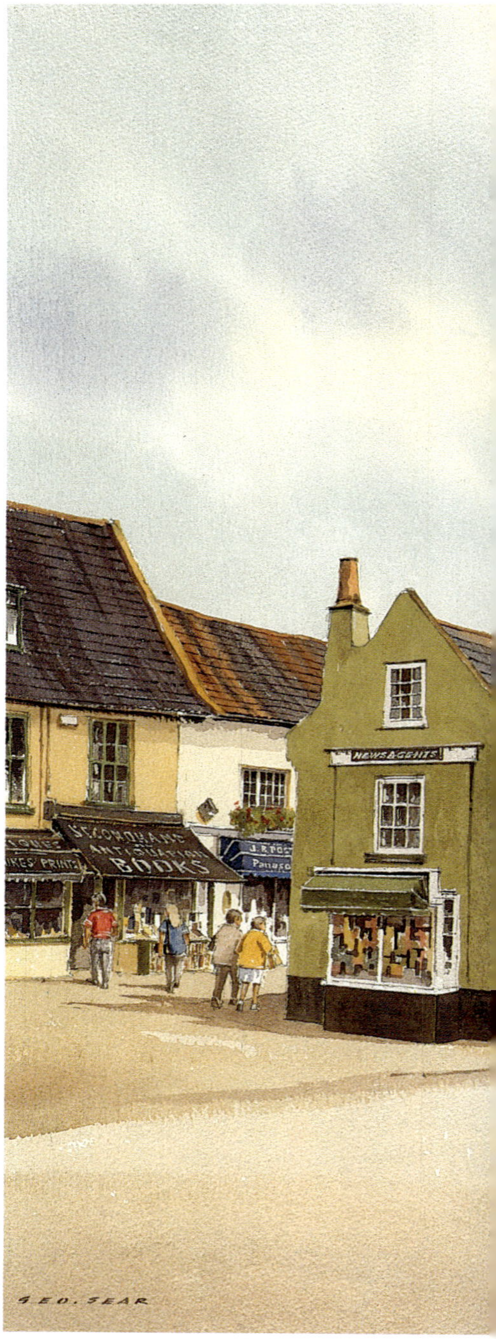

Market Square.

Fact File

Painting in towns and cities I know can be daunting, but working exclusively from photographs has its problems. A sketch book with a few washes of colour and notation, can help to create the atmosphere back in the studio.

On-site sketching enables you to register a lot more information that lurks in the shadow areas of a photograph. Start with small studies such as shops, flower shops and the like. Do not try for the big view, build up to this.

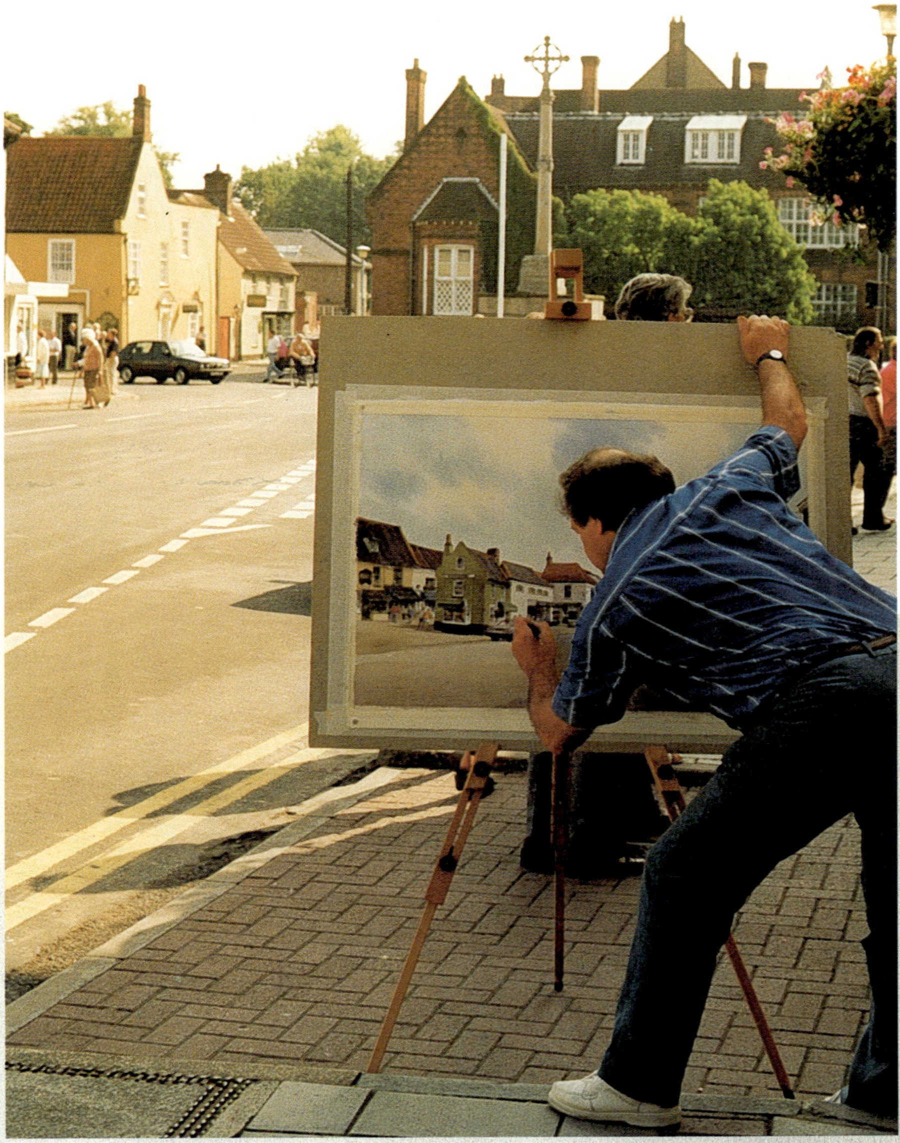

◄ *Completing the finishing touches.*

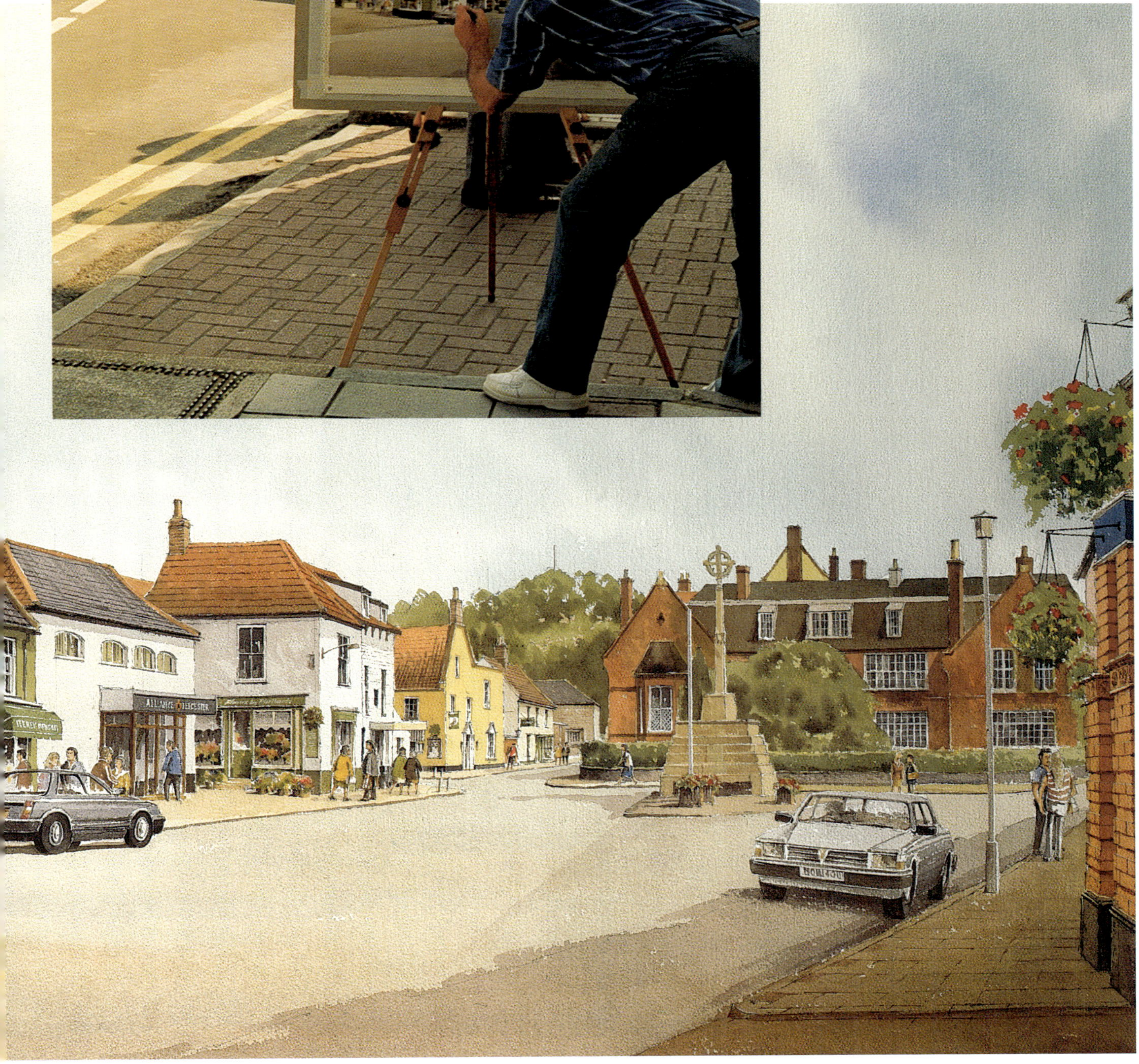

thatch of the church roof. The church was virtually destroyed and the fire raged through the town from east to west. In three hours all that was left were smouldering ruins.

By 1820 there were 212 houses in the town, mostly occupied by traders, craftsmen and farm-workers and their families. Clean water came by horse from Spout Hill and cost a farthing a bucket.

My love for Holt is a passion. The best of its heart shadows my own. Over the years I have painted her in all her moods and seasons. I have made tiny watercolours 3" x 2", small trophies of her charm. Full Imperial sheets 23" x 30". Larger even. The town is intimate up an alley or in a private loke or courtyard. She is elegantly and proudly proportioned along the rides of her main streets. Even her new estates have style about them, huddling to her skirts as they do.

My bottom, spreading widely over my low seat, is a familiar if not pretty sight amongst Holtians and visitors. Jokes abound; 'I wish they'd clear the rubbish from the streets.' 'I'd know that backside anywhere.'

A painting is a segment of time held on paper or canvas for as long as that painting exists. The painter holds in his hand a unique and precious fraction in the life of what is before him. Yet it is more than a mere objective representation that records the scene more or less faithfully; the painting speaks, it interprets the scene set before us. And it also reveals the painter, laying his soul, his personality bare for all to see.

Holt is always changing, ever evolving, though never, it must be

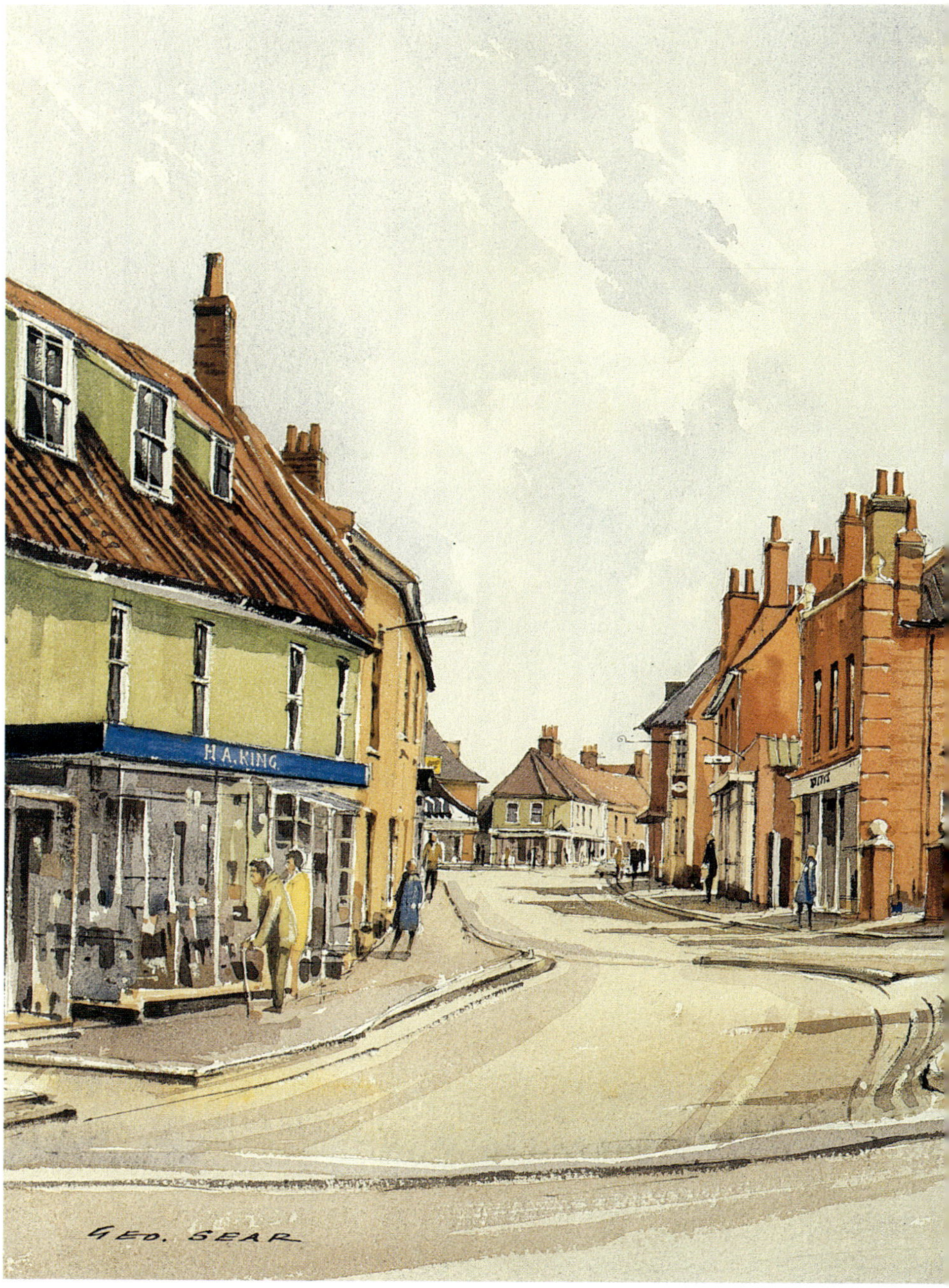

The High Street.

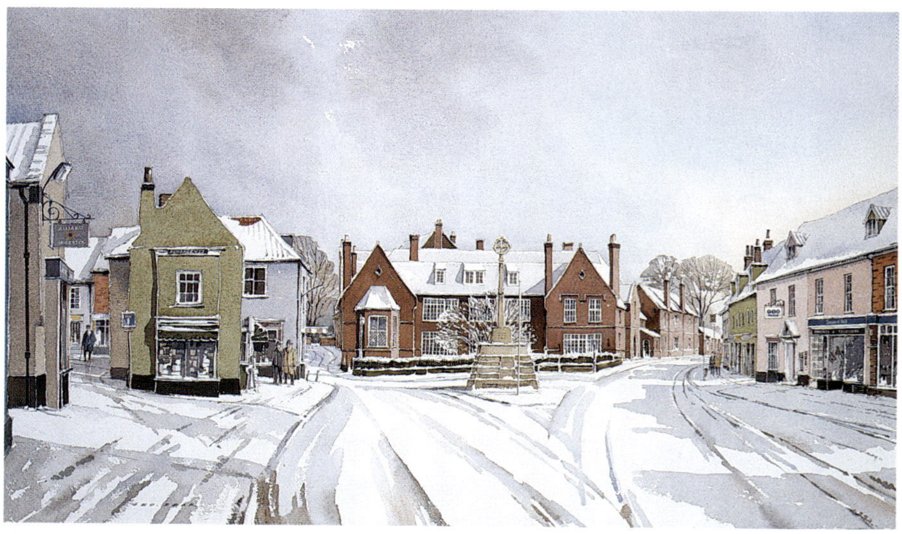

Snow arrives in Holt.

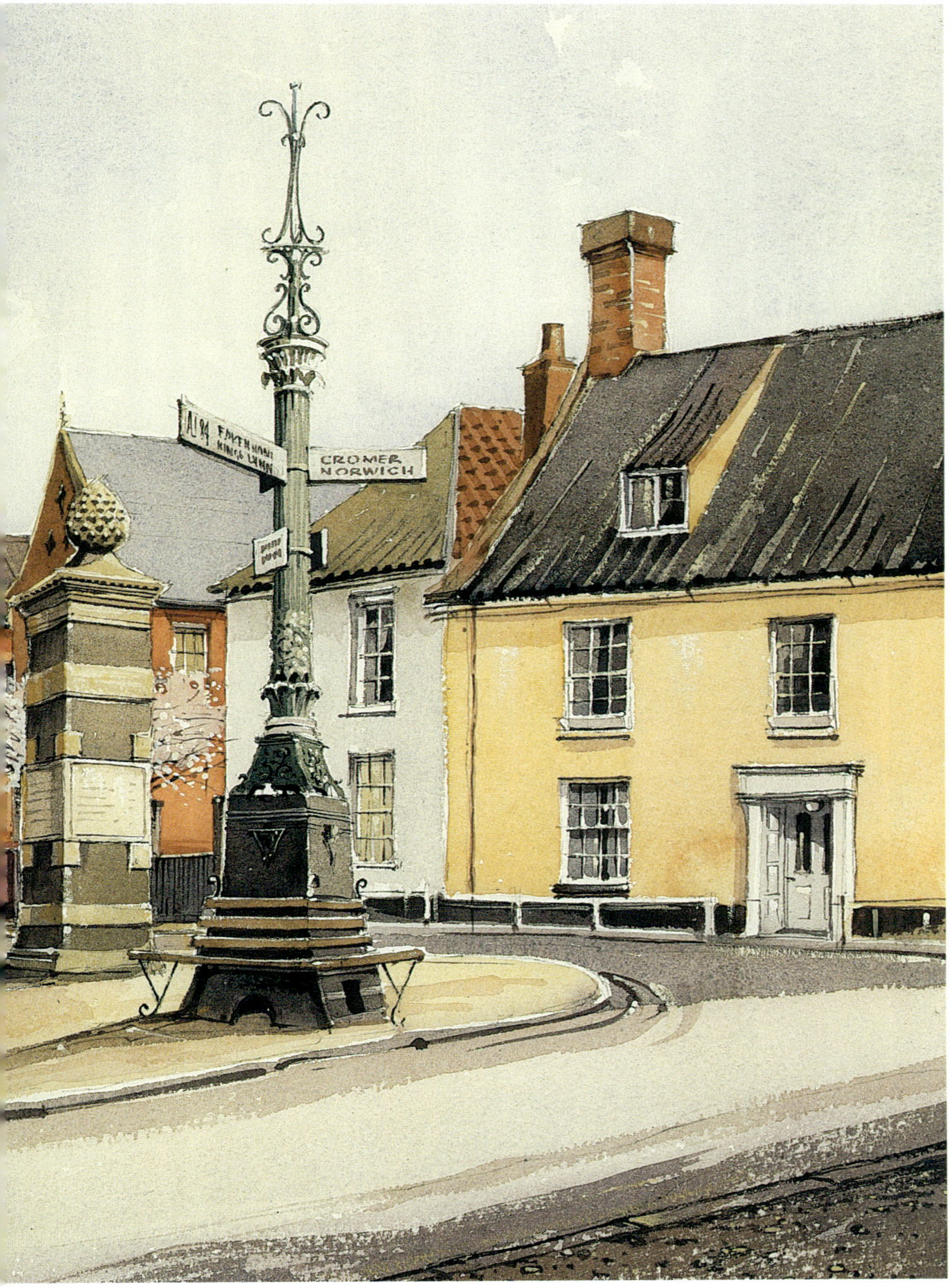

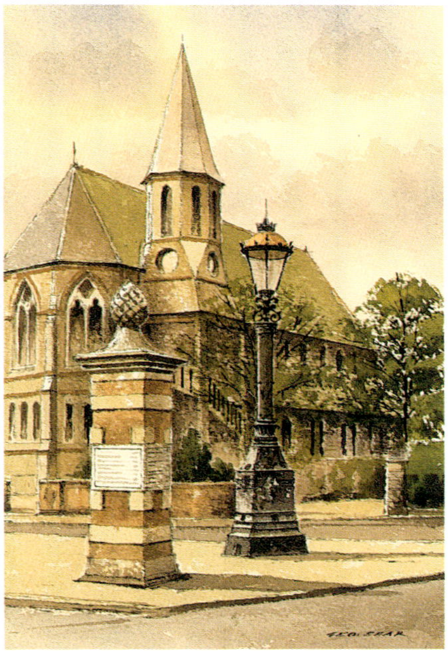

Blind Sam.

hoped, for the worse. That old green door I painted some time ago is sadly no longer there. Time moves on.

As if to prove the point that the painting imprisons for ever a fragment of time, this large watercolour of the centre of Holt was made by transferring small studies made on site - on the pavement outside Larners - onto my larger painting awaiting in my studio. It took between three to four weeks to complete. And when, finally, it was exhibited at my one-man show at Picturecraft Gallery some time later I noticed, indeed I could not help but notice, a local resident looking at it very long and tiresomely hard. I waited till he came over to me.

'I can tell you exactly when you painted that picture,' he said.

'Really?'

'To within three months.'

'How can you be so specific?'

He looked at me funny-like. 'From the installation of the church flagpole to the move by the Alliance and Leicester Building Society to a site opposite was within those three months. You can only have done that painting then.'

He was right, of course.

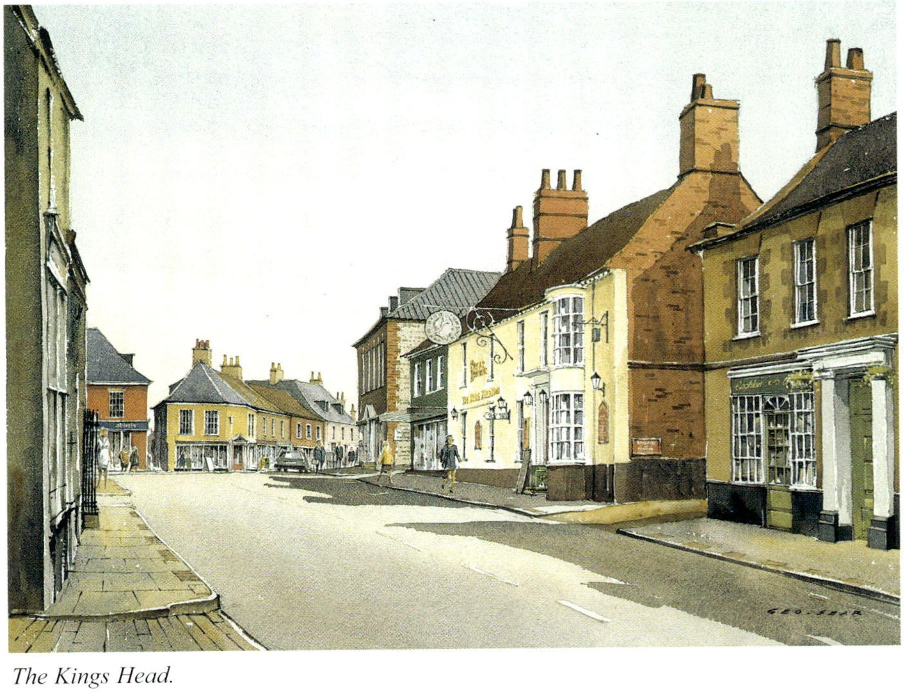

The Kings Head.

'So we go to the marshes . . .'

The Marshes

Marshes do strange things to people, perhaps because a marsh is the last place you would expect to see a person. What jars about our presence amongst the marron grass, the barriers of reeds and lakes of sea lavender is that we do not belong. We do not blend or harmonise with the wildlife and the birds whose home it is. Since time immemorial we have come here to kill for food and therefore have become not only predators but the feared. Oyster-catchers skirt round us. Avocets keep well ahead of our laborious step. Like the venomous snake in the under-growth our presence is heralded by

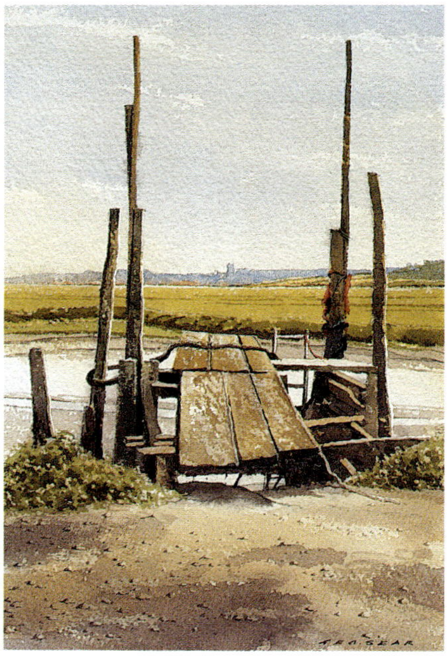

Centre stage

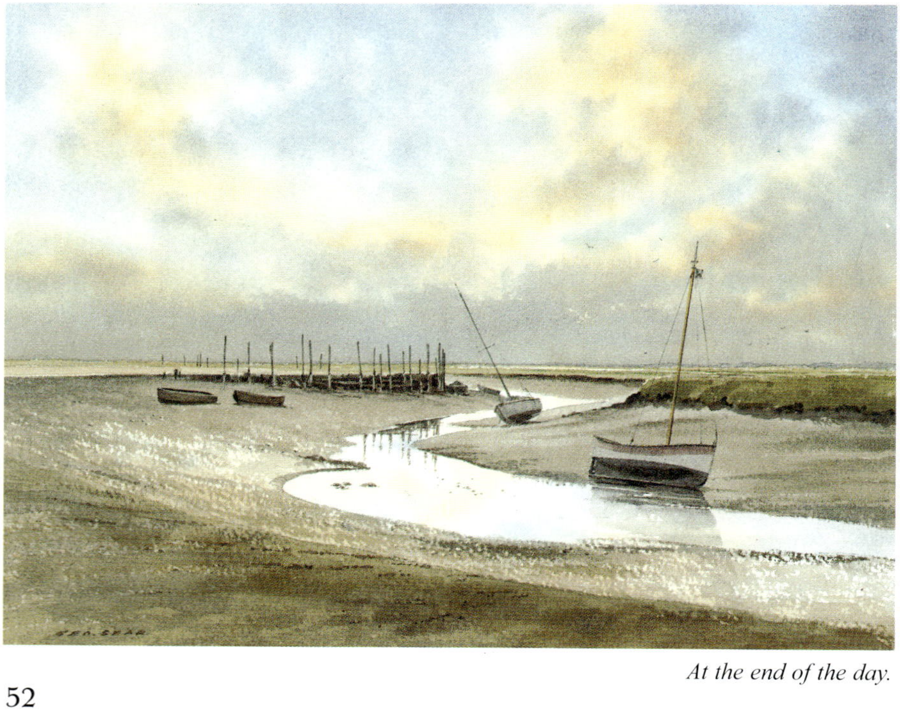

At the end of the day.

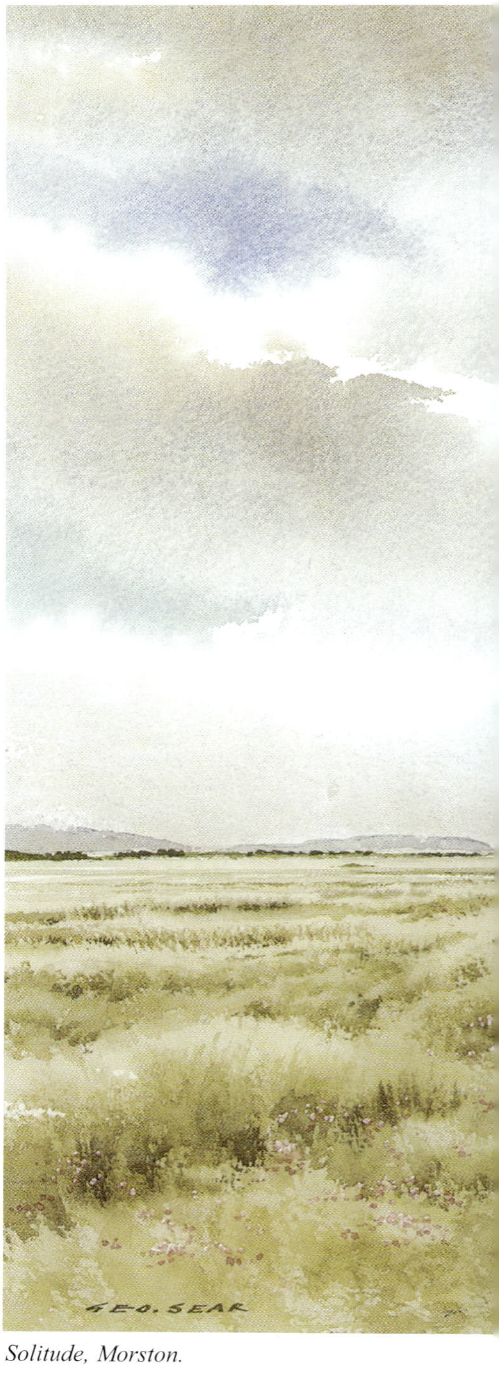

Solitude, Morston.

the anxious communities we pass through.

So we go to the marshes and, armed with knowledge of the potentially lethal caprices, walk amongst them. It might be a bracing wind with an iced rain in its breath. It may be still and hot and stifling. It was a bronzy autumnal flooding surge, with skin-coloured flotsam scumming its edges, that chased you away inland and it stayed behind like a baying guard dog prowling around making another sea out of the marshes, which it completely swamped. We go to the marshes, drawn to their mysteries, because no two days are the same. (Although I have known an eerie week of sameness when the marsh was uncannily still, pregnant with foreboding, a strange week in May when the weather got trapped in a rut of high pressure. The sea-mist stayed all day. This fret changed its colour from opal all morning into amethyst in the afternoon to a blood-speckled black pearl at sunset.)

What marshes say to us when we venture amongst them, wary of their indifferent dangers, is that they are and ever will be without us. We do not even enter into the scheme nature set for them. We are alien and all we can do is watch.

And that is the key to their fascination. It is in the being there amongst them with the only purpose of watching that makes the lure of the marshes irresistible.

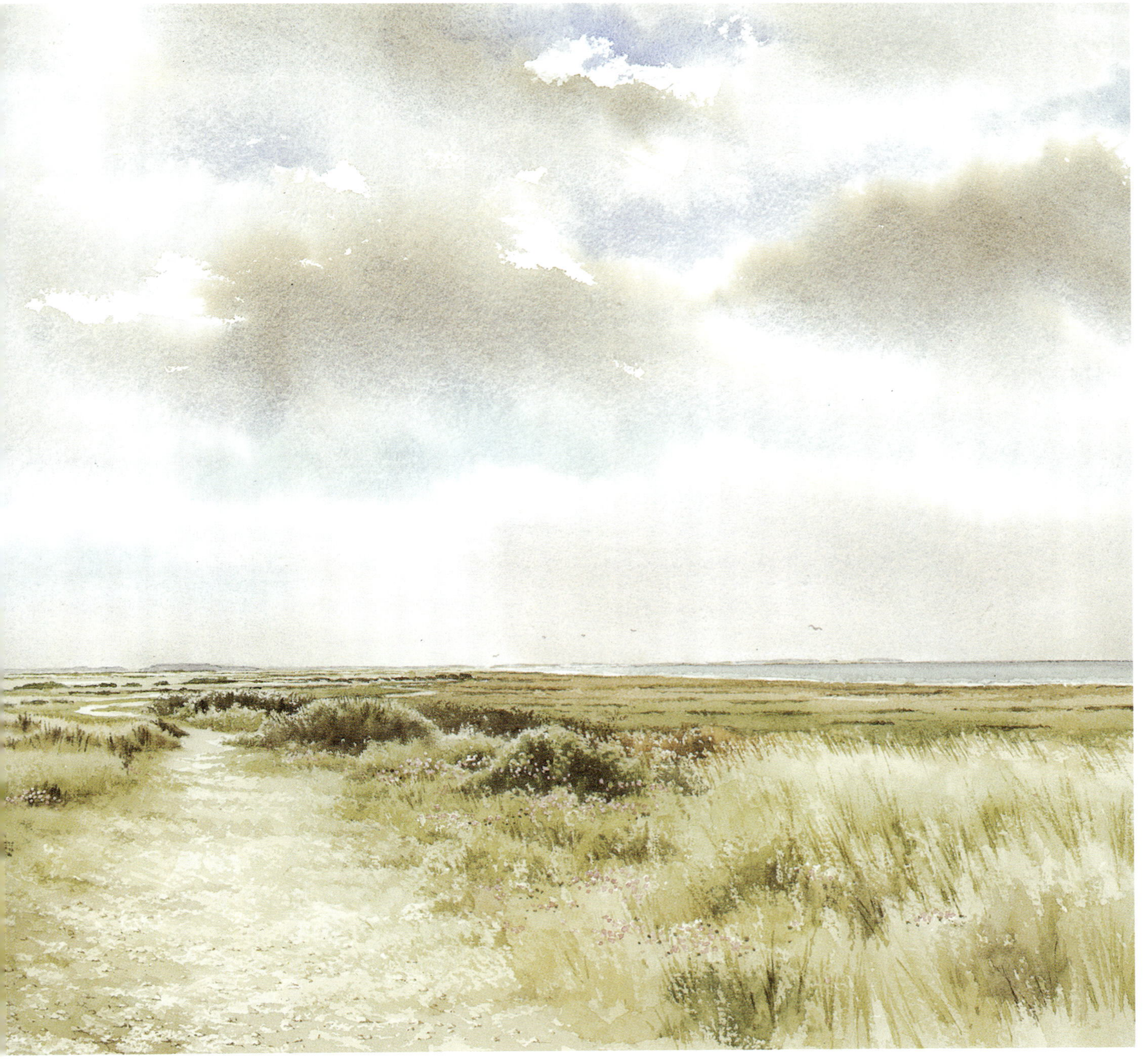

I know an elderly couple, although he is now dead, who returned again and again for that experience out on the marshes and knew its value. For years she had suffered chronic clinical depression. The demons that troubled her were unquiet. But they crept away to hide when her husband drove her to a particular spot overlooking Stiffkey Marshes.

She liked it best when he got her comfortably seated with a rug over her knees and he returned to the marsh leaving her with her own thoughts. Looking out over God's wilderness she marvelled at the sense of order to everything. The endlessly curving channels, the haunt of bird-song, the crouching line of sea in the lavendered distance were comforting to her. There was, she could understand as she sat there, a purpose for everything, all had a reason. Her turbulent mind ceased to be fingernailed by the unknowable things that taunted her. Yet when her husband came and helped her back to the car for the drive home, to the goading gloom, she knew that it was here in the marshes that truth and peace belonged and could be grasped.

After her husband's death she bought one of my paintings of Stiffkey marshes. She had come to the Preview night of one of my one-man shows at Picturecraft in Holt. She came over to me and

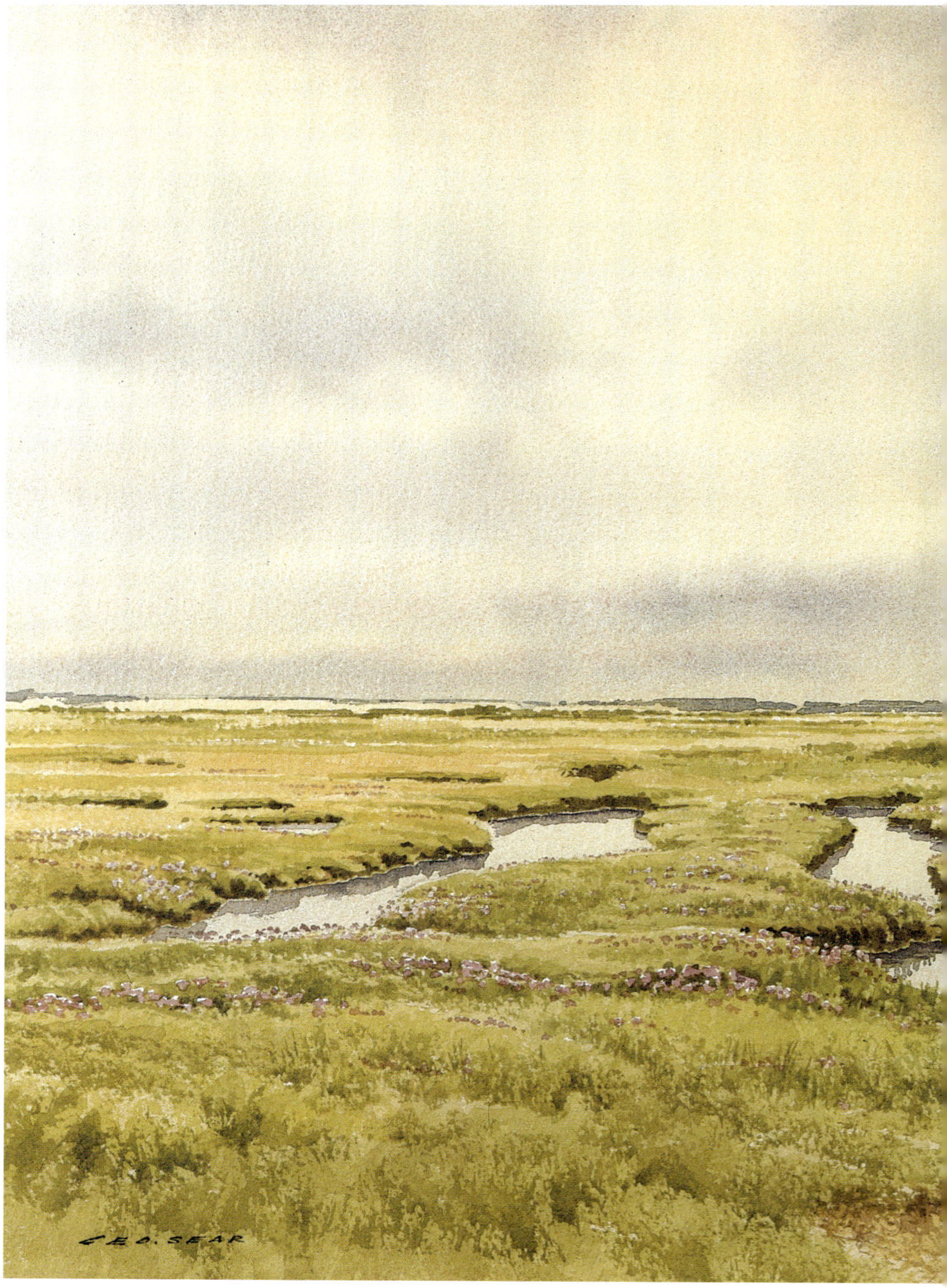

Mystery of the marsh.

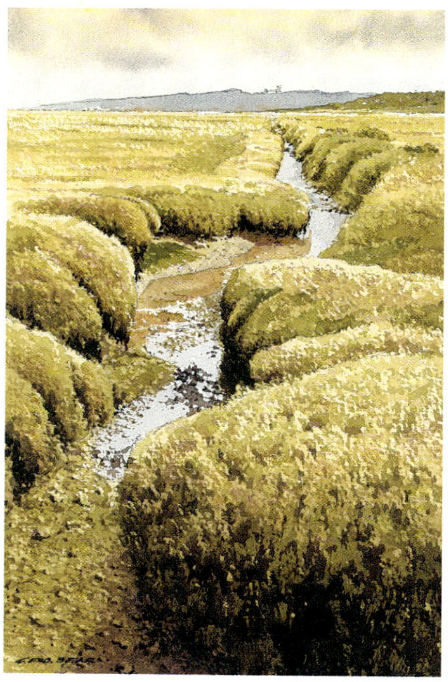

Muddy Creek.

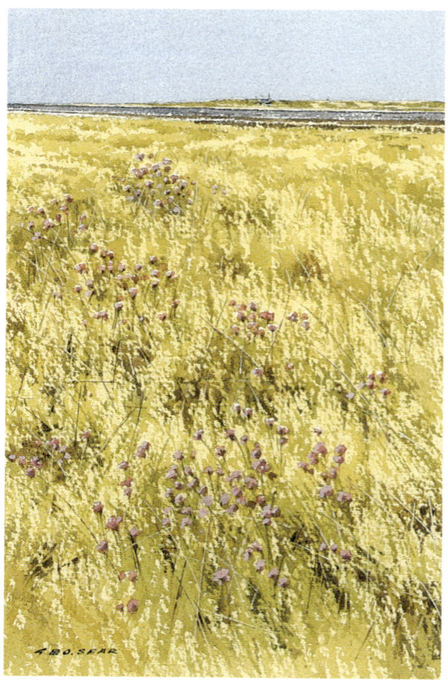

Thrift at Morston.

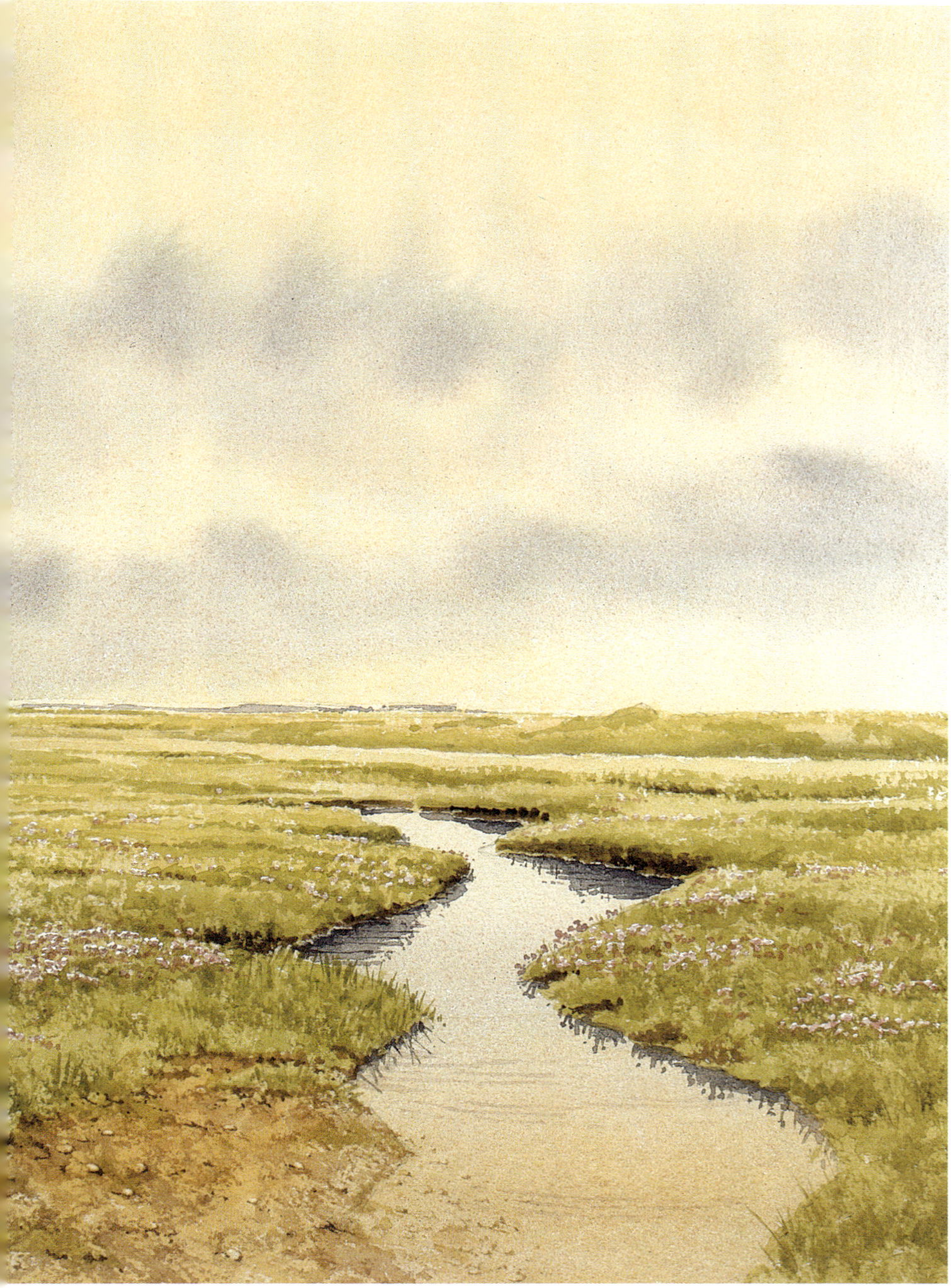

shyly thanked me. She told me that I must have painted it from the exact spot where she used to sit when her husband had taken her for 'therapy'.

'Now, with your painting above the mantlepiece,' she said, so pleased, so grateful, 'I can sit at home on the settee and get all the "therapy" I need.'

The marshes have that effect. The lady's demons have left her. They are at peace now as they always are. In the marshes.

Fact File

I have spoken about the marshes on previous pages. 'What to paint' is often the problem. One is surrounded by space, the sky, the distance, and the marshes seem to go on for ever.
Make yourself a viewer by cutting a rectangle 3' x 2' out of a small piece of card, say 5' x 4'. Use this to help you select an area you wish to paint, by holding it up and observing the subject through the hole. This tends to eliminate the distracting areas, and focus the eye on what is important, the large skies, distance, and the peace of the marshes.
Large brush strokes for the sky, and dry-brush and a little detail in the foreground. My painting 'Mystery of the Marsh' with marsh pools, was underpainted with Raw Sienna and Rose Madder, an occasional colour in my range, for a warm rosy evening glow.

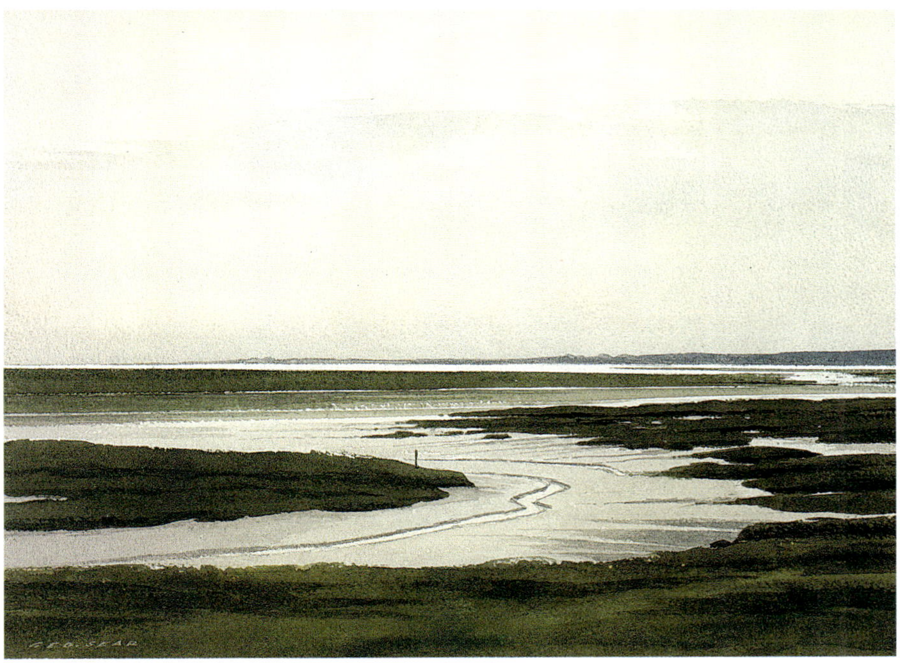

Silver Light.

'Serendipidy'

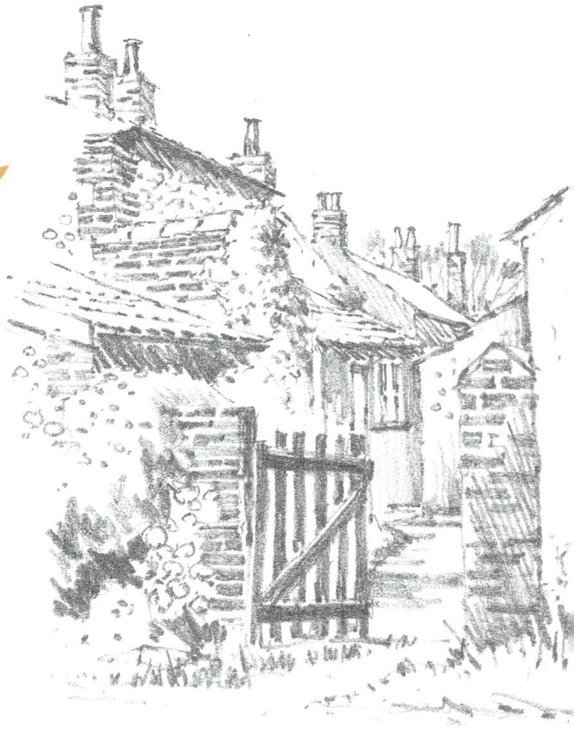

Binham

Setting off with some friends early one morning to paint at Binham I had a strange sense of the day ahead waiting to reveal itself. There was no feeling of foreboding or menace, simply that as the day unlocked and revealed its contents I would involve myself and experience to the full all it would offer. It is an odd thing to say but I felt as though the day had its finger on me, that it had singled me out. They speak of being in a state of grace. I have often wondered what that meant. This particular morning I believe I knew - and I still do not understand.

We got to the village and we all went our separate ways as the inspiration led. One set up outside the pub. Another opposite the butcher's shop. Two went up a grassy alleyway between two pantiled and cobbled cottages. Work progressed. An hour passed. I was deeply engrossed although not miles away.

A pat on my shoulder from behind made me jump.

'Some of your painters are upsetting the villagers.'

'Oh?'

'I'm Neighbourhood Watch and they just rang me to say that they are being menaced, threatened do you hear, over their garden wall. It isn't very nice.'

I realised immediately that seeing strangers holding up measuring sticks and waving them about could look menacing from the viewpoint of the privacy of your own garden. I apologised to the lady, explained that no harm was intended and demonstrated to her what an artist does with a measuring stick.

She understood instantly, indeed thought the misunderstanding was very funny. And she invited me in to her cottage for a cup of coffee. Sitting with her in her sitting room I was astonished to be surrounded by a group of large oil paintings on the theme of The Dance. They were magnificent, absolutely captivating, filled with colour and the essence of movement. She was pleased, in a very modest way, to share them with me.

She was not the only artist I knew who was working behind the watchful eyes of windows in the cottages of this village. I knew two others, each diligently creating their own masterpieces amongst the gentle domesticity with the cat asleep on the windowsill and the dog snoring gently in the wicker womb of its basket.

I returned alone the next day because I wanted to paint the Priory from a low viewpoint that would emphasise the romantic durability of the structure. I had to wait until late afternoon for the

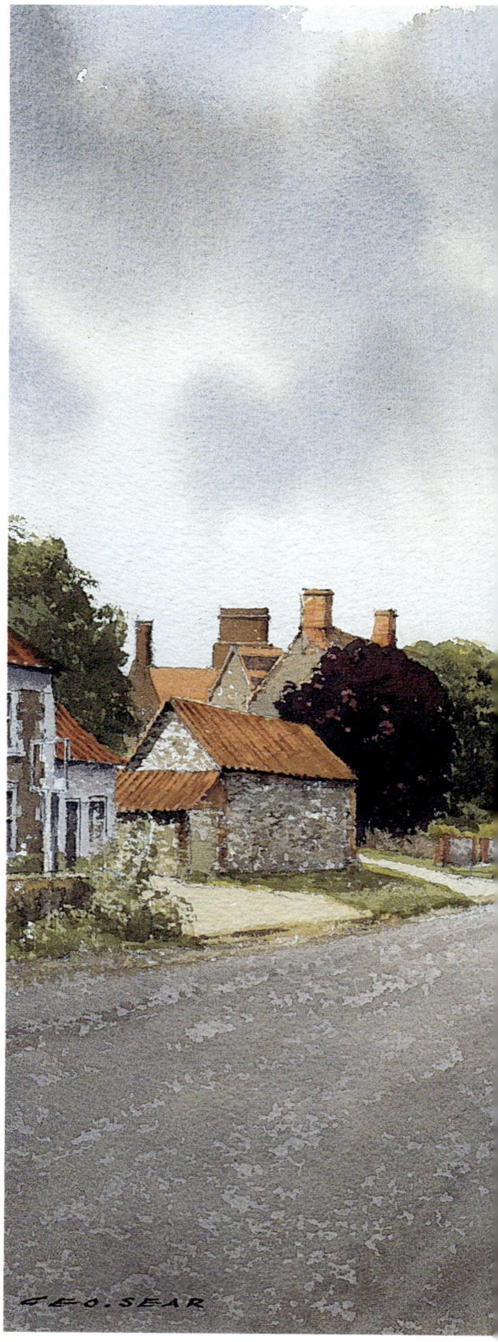

The Street, Binham.

light to come round to the front where it would cast shadows. I passed the time waiting for the light, chatting to an elderly gentleman who was tending his wife's grave. He came from a distance, an act of love and homage every fortnight.

The light came and threw its shadows. The gentleman turned back to the grave.

'It will be wonderful when we're together again,' he said quietly, almost to himself.

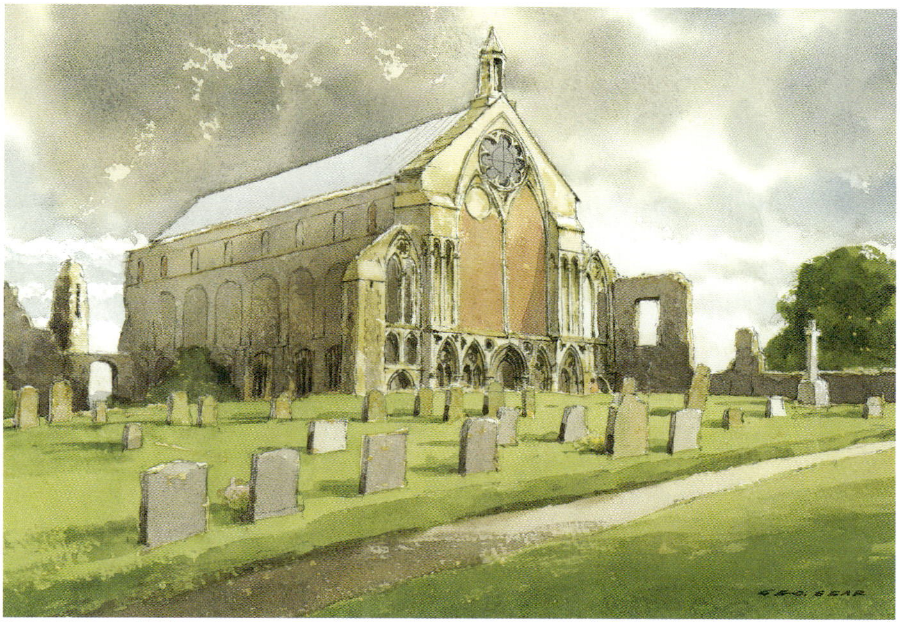

The Priory.

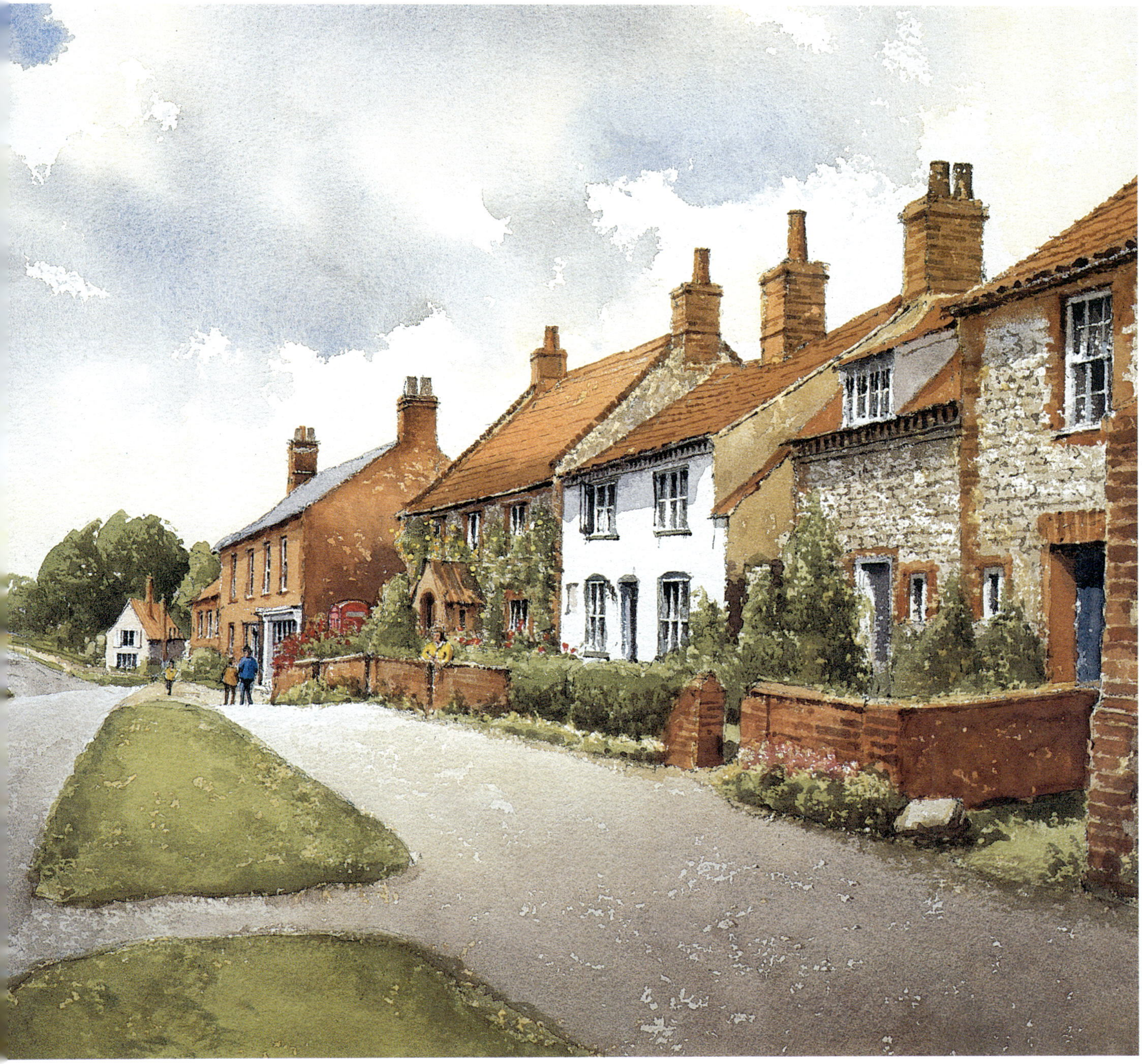

'When you sit amongst its comings and goings...'

Langham

When you paint a village, when you sit amongst its comings and goings, the smells that come to you through its kitchen windows, the meanderings of its dogs, the pounce of cats, you live that moment in its history. It is a moment, a few hours, that is different from the few hours before and as different again from the hours that will follow. You catch it as a fly was caught in amber. You record its moment with the eye God gave you. And your eye is unique, not that of another. Your eye, indeed, is the truth of that moment in the history of that village's being. It is a responsibility and an honour.

Langham, that day, was just sorting itself out. The morning, when I set myself opposite 'The Bluebell' pub with my board and brushes and 2B's, promised a good day, its haze had that quality, it soothed, it did not smother.

As I set about drawing outlines I was conscious of a deadline by which I wanted to get the majority of the work finished. This deadline was about a quarter to four when the school bus returned and deposited the local children, hell bent as they would be on rushing around the village after the restrictions of the day. I tell you now, it is difficult to draw and paint well amongst the racket of a noise and the hubbub of people. They distract. They break concentration. They get on the nerves.

The drawing complete I was preparing and mixing my washes. Things were shaping up nicely and all was well with my world. I caught myself humming 'Oh What a Beautiful Morning'.

To my dismay at that moment, even as I was applying the first wash, a huge brewer's lorry drew up outside the pub completely masking it from view. I could not move my position, obviously. Two burly men began to throw down from the sides of the lorry great metal casks which rang out mightily as they hit the ground. These were rolled onto a barrow and trundled round the side of the building over cobbles. The noise was horrific. Then they started to throw down crates of jangling chinking bottles. On and on they went vandalising the tranquillity of the morning. The amount delivered would have done justice to a street party.

As if to calm my shattered nerves and as, literally, a peace offering as the lorry drove off Myrtle, the landlady of the pub, crossed the road to me bearing a pint of ale. We mardled together enjoyably, for she is a charming and amusing lady.

After the cacophony of the brewer's delivery the village was returning to itself, the gentle hum and rhythm of its daily life. People passed on their way to the village shop and passed again on their return. People encountered each other and passed the time of day. All the while my painting was progressing, bringing it all to life.

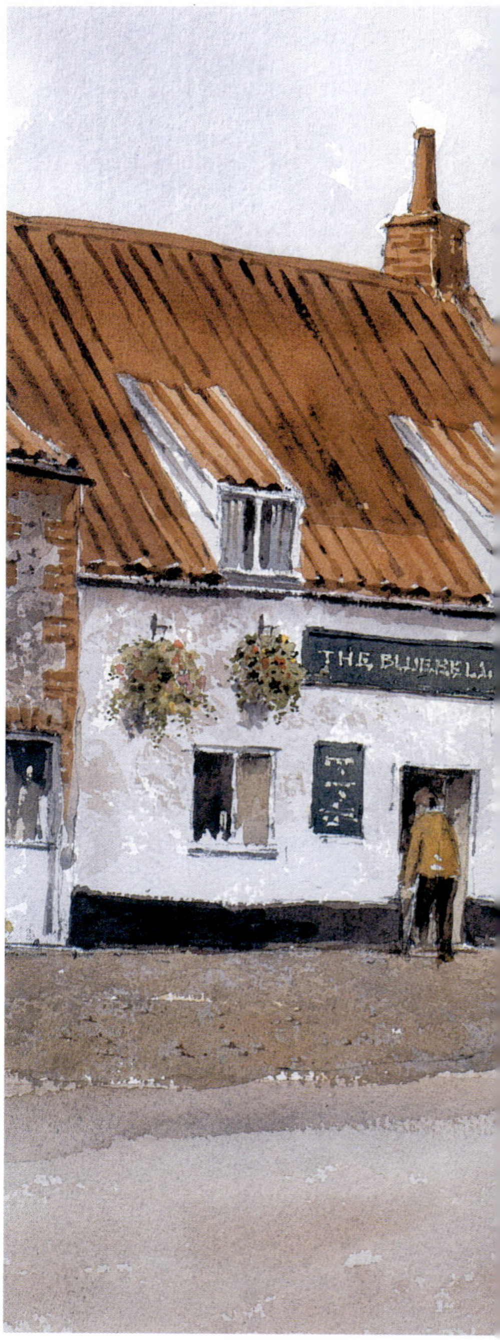

The Bluebell, Langham.

A group of cyclists, tourists, rode past with waves of friendly greeting. An old gentleman walking his black labrador stopped to see what I was doing. As we exchanged a few words the dog cocked his leg above my palette, which is a tin plate, and made as if to water down its contents. The old chap managed to pull it away just in time. The incidents in the day of the village strung together like the beads of a necklace, the murmurings of a rosary.

Again and suddenly, rudely, the peace was shattered by yet another delivery lorry, this time of meat with its refrigeration unit. This became a mind-altering clamour with its throb, throb, throbbing. It seemed to go on incessantly and I realised the deliveryman had decided to stop for a jar and a sandwich. Half an hour later my head ached.

By the time the wretched lorry had driven off there was only half an hour or so before the dreaded school bus was due. As it happened the bus was early and the horde descended running amok like Vikings through the sleeping village. However, the painting was in an advanced state that I could safely complete in my studio. I could pack up before I got pillaged.

There was one detail I had to get right; the pub sign. It was missing. I returned my glass to Myrtle and asked her about it. She explained that it had been removed for refurbishment, as she quaintly put it. But she assured me that it would be the same sign when it was returned. So, in the studio, I painted the original sign as I had earlier photographed it.

A couple of weeks later I returned to the village. The pub sign, freshly painted, had been reinstated on its post surrounded by its decorative ironwork. It was completely different.

So it is that a painting of a village is a minute fraction of its ever-changing history caught in that moment in time. Nothing stays the same, all changes, everything evolves.

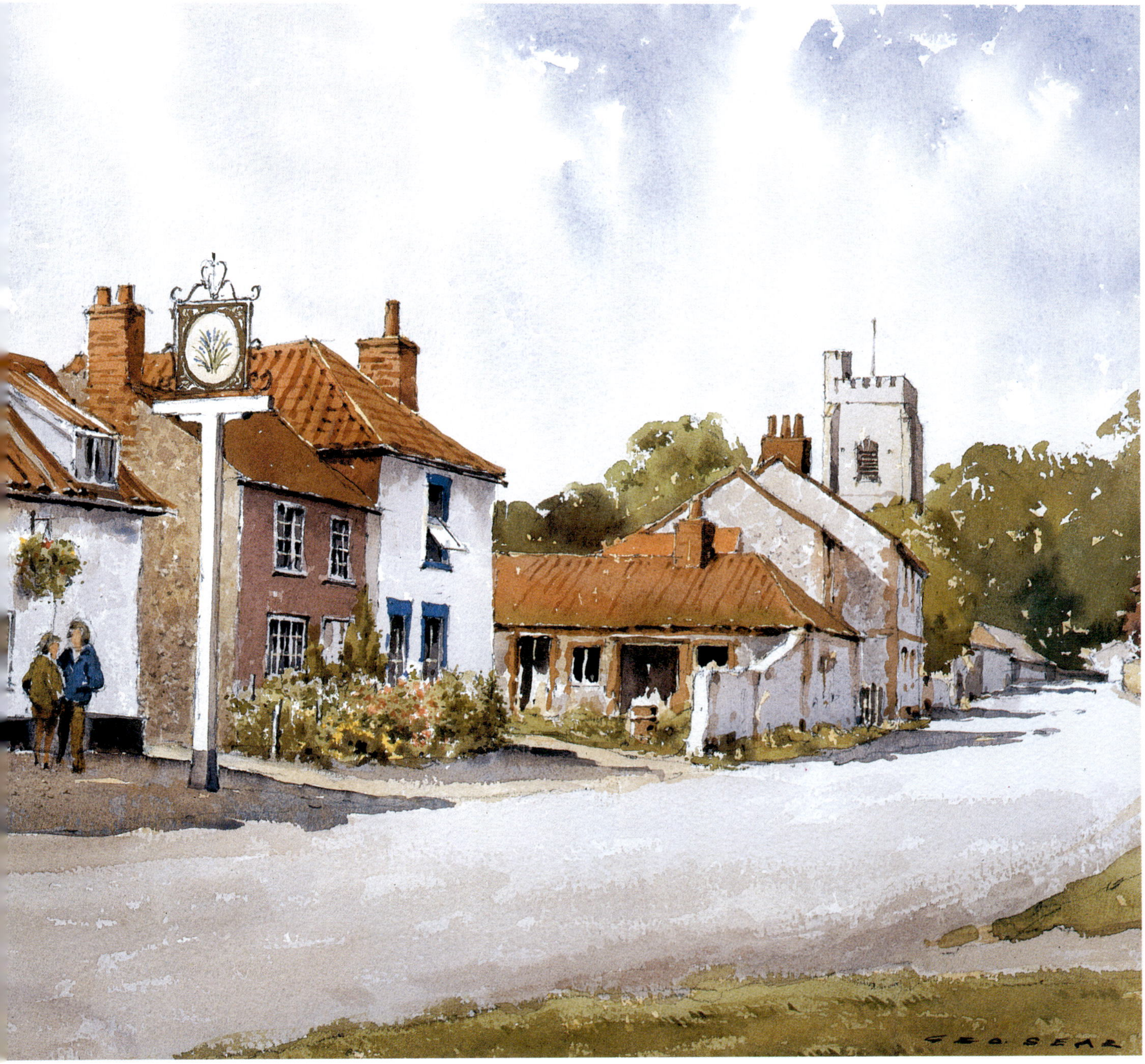

'Preserving in paint and water a flower border...'

Stiffkey Old Hall

The invitation was not a commission in any sense. It was simply and delightfully an invitation to set up my easel, to plonk my rear on my seat anywhere within the grounds of Stiffkey Old Hall. Those who do not paint for a livelihood surely cannot imagine, as we who do, the sense of privilege we feel at being invited onto private property to catch a sky or imprison an atmosphere of such beauty and mesmerising antiquity. My usual realm is public. But here was a privacy of family memories, a haunt of gauntly built flinted ruins. A flight of steps upwards to nowhere. A gaping window you look in to, not out of anymore. All was as muffled in peace as a mouse's footfall the morning I accepted the invitation.

Something had been mentioned about preserving in paint and water a flower border made by a lady who gardened passionately here, but who had died. The fear was that her border would be lost to all but memory under the colonising valerian that, beyond the hall's gates, huddles at the edges of the village streets. Charming as the plant is, as a crowd it smothers, takes over by seeding itself prolifically. I promised to preserve if not each flower in the border then an atmosphere, the skein of a soul that remained.

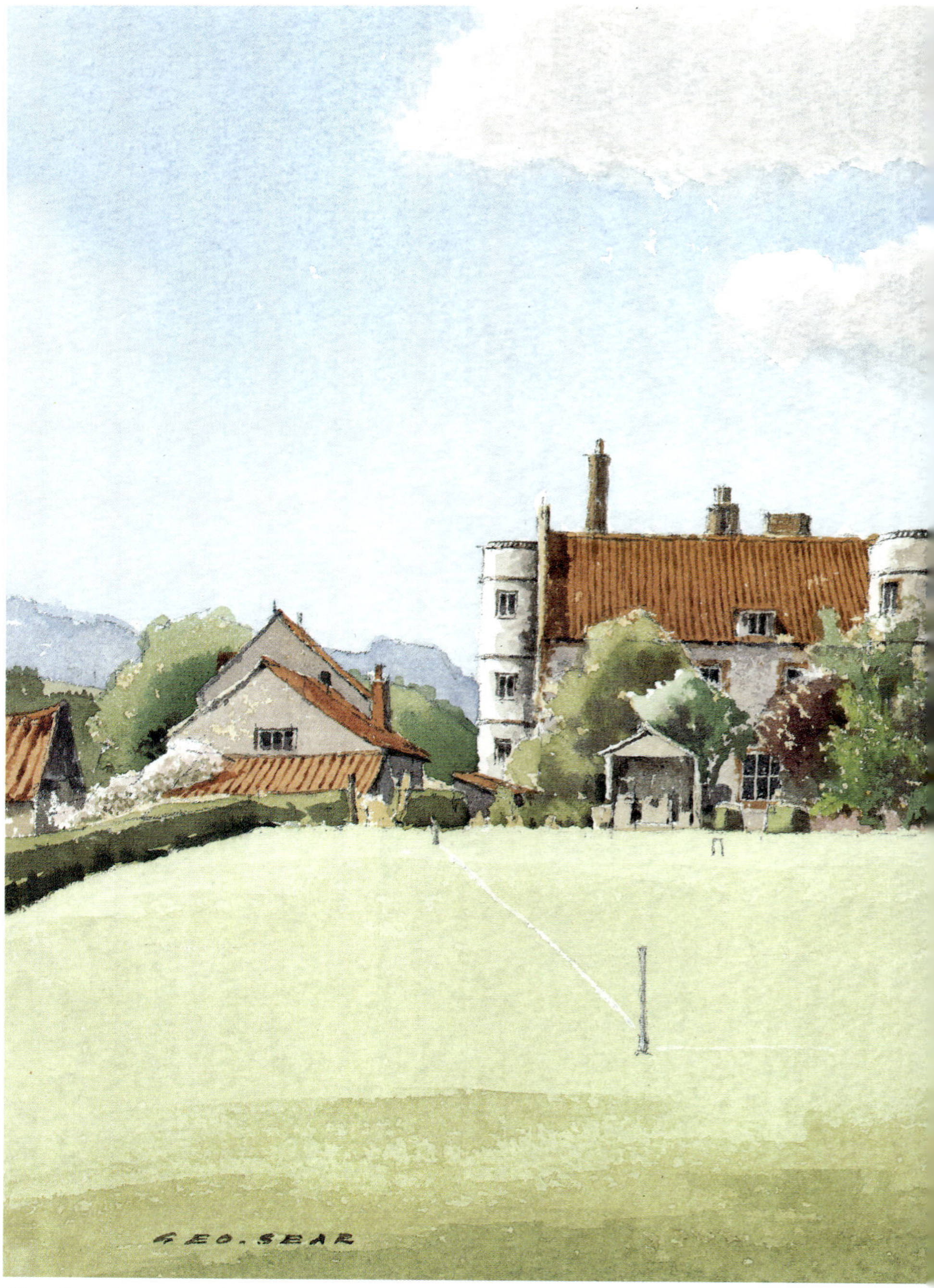

View from the croquet lawn.

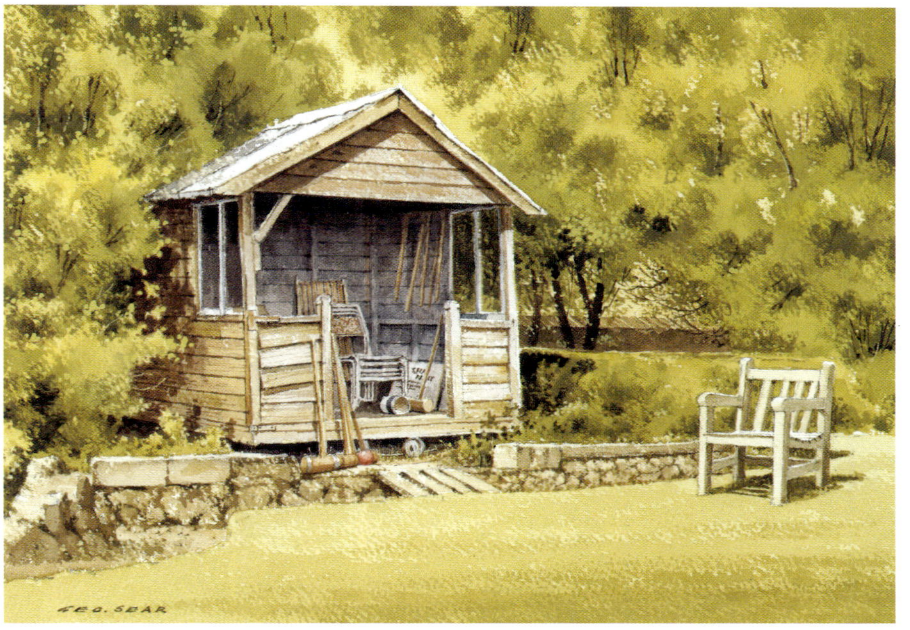

'Game over'

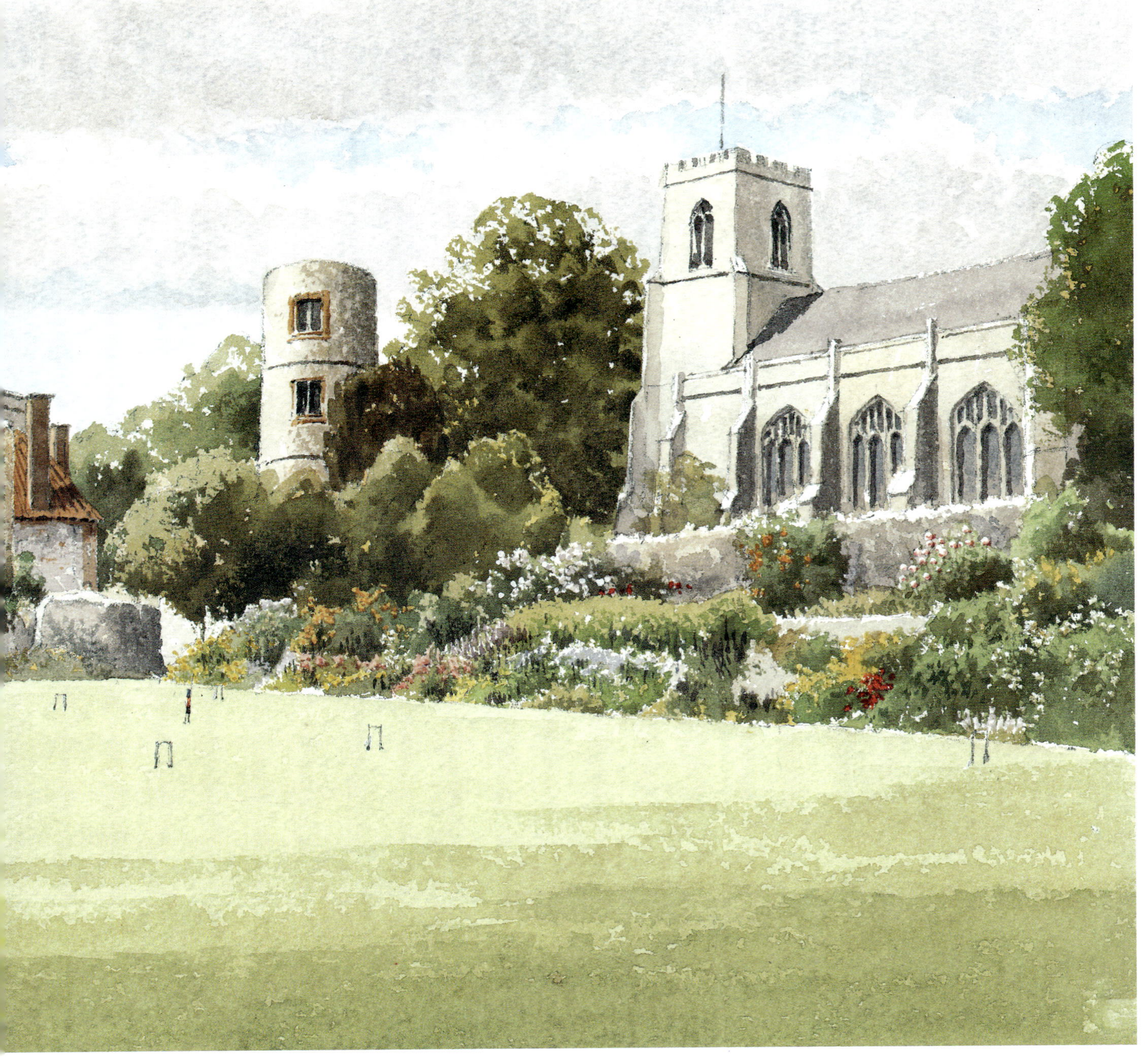

When I started to work I became aware of the difference there is between painting in a public place and, as here, in a secret, private place. Out there in the open public arena there is no sense of invasion by your brush or pigments. No theft. But here within the walls of this lovely place with one shoulder to the church and the other towards the bluff against the sea, I almost shamefully foraged for the picturesque, the personal, the intimate soul of this great but long-doomed house, the building of which started in 1573 and was virtually abandoned in 1791.

Just as the photographer can snatch an image and then manipulate its atmosphere in the dark room and the tray of liquid, as it is brought to life, a softer mass there or a sharper edge here, so the painter grabs what he can, but for him it is once only, the first impression that will stay on the paper for ever after.

My days at The Old Hall at Stiffkey were crowded with the incidents of atmosphere. The lady's border edged the croquet lawn, a haze of colours, a long web of near blues and off-whites and a mumble of pinks and lavenders. And oh a-tumbling fell the purpled aubretia over the edges of ancient stone. And ah a swoop of snowy roses

It was like a candystick laid lengthwise against the emerald sweep of new mown grass. How many chocks had it heard on the humming air of afternoons in summers long gone? How many riddles of childrens' laughter?

Sneaking into my consciousness as I sat stealing the view, came the sound of glasses tinkling musically together. The gentleman owner was advancing across the lawn holding them with a green bottle of sherry. I was beckoned to join him in the little rustic hut where the mallets and balls and hoops higgledy-piggledied over the floor amongst the folded away chairs.

Later, the tangy taste of the sherry on the tastebuds, the distant sibilance of the sea from behind the bluff, we sat wallowing in it all. I, a thief at his side, was aware that all he surveyed was in his gift. Even the day-blanched moon that swung into the opal blue canopy of the late afternoon sky was his for giving. I felt grateful to him for sharing so easily all the somnolent beauty.

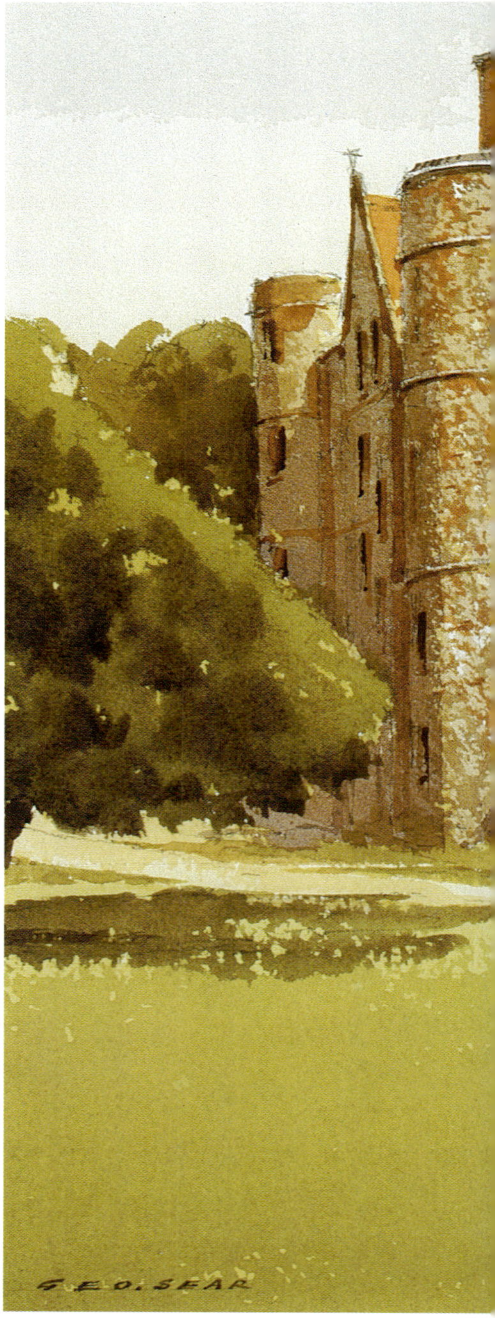

Stiffkey Old Hall.

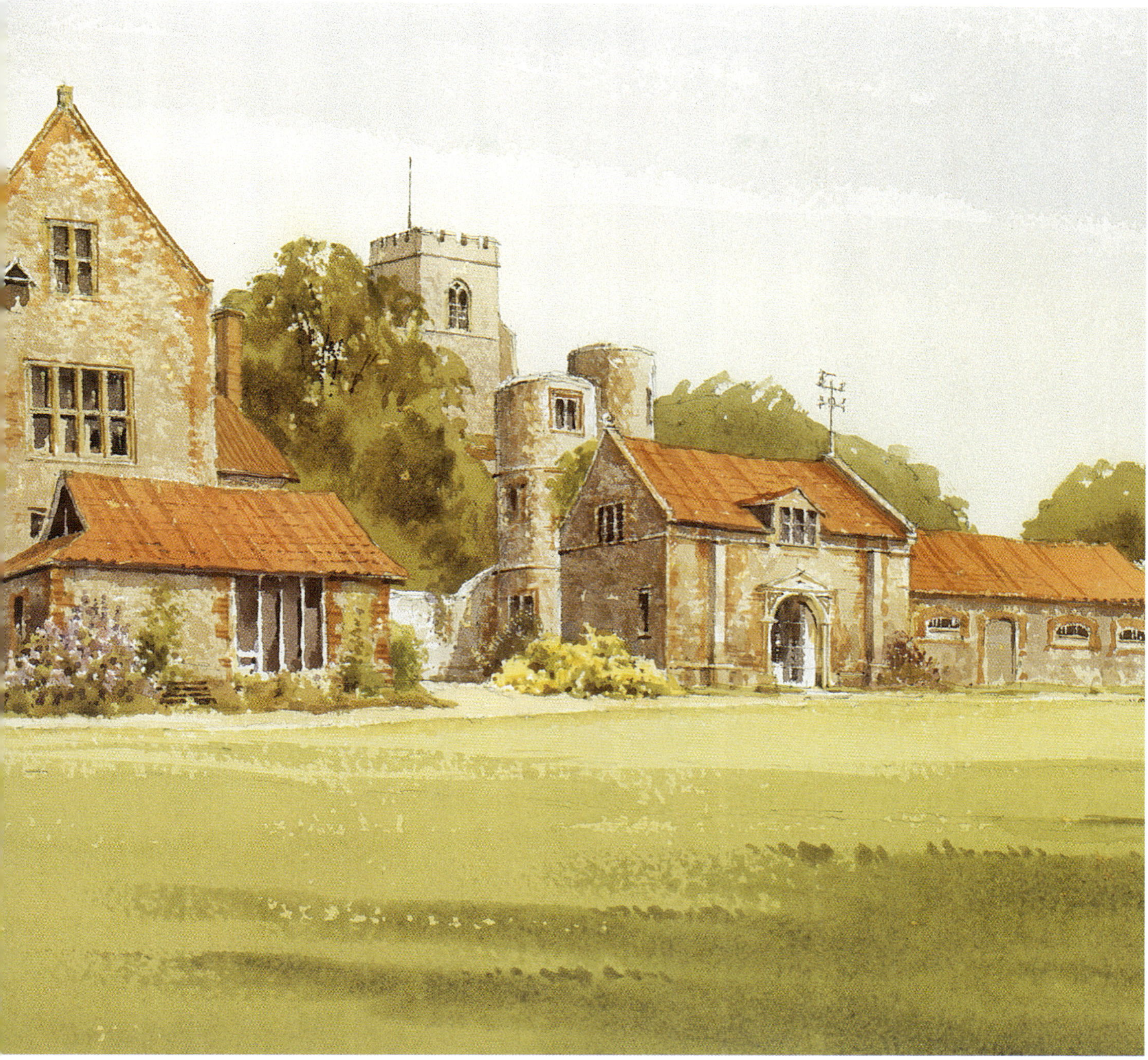

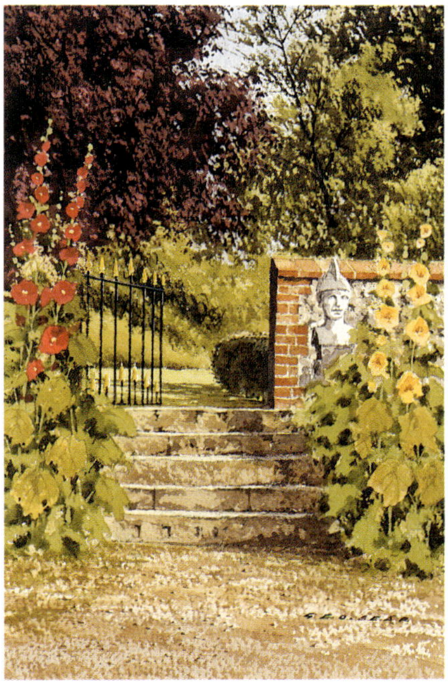

The open gate.

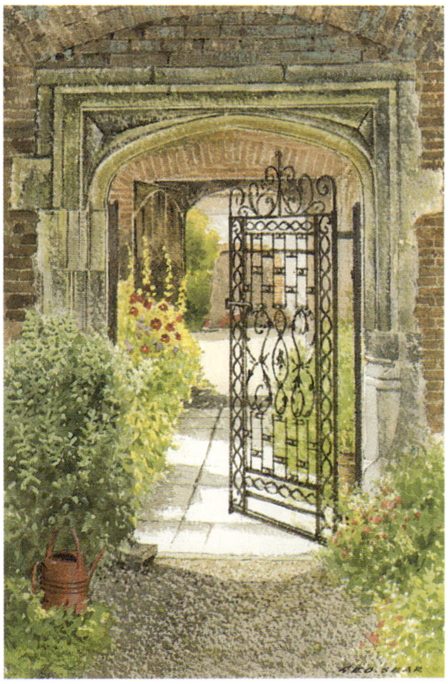

The red watering can.

'Winter's mantle'

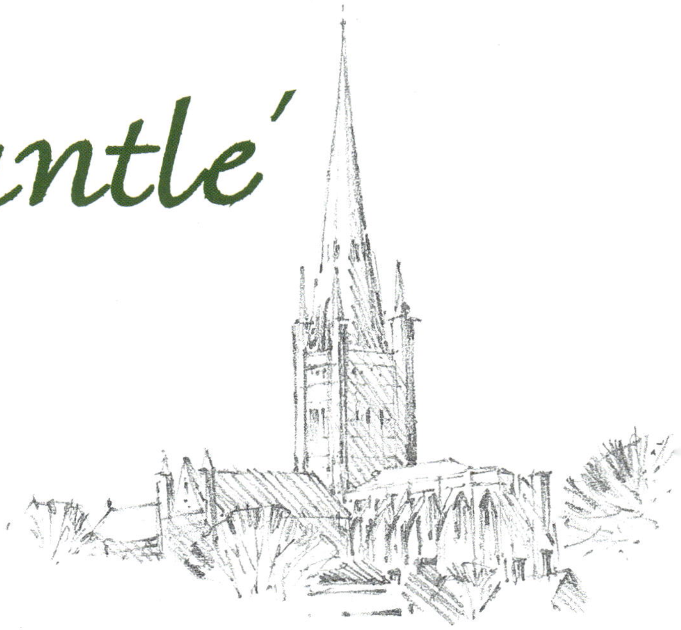

Norwich

You need imagination to paint a traditional Christmas card at the zenith of summer. It was a hot August afternoon in front of Pull's Ferry. Across the river a gentleman was sun-bathing and along the river chugged a holiday craft, its decks a wonderment of bikini-clad girls. They shouted out for me to 'put us in your picture, love'.

Of course needs must that I am amongst the countryside painting it, even in the depths of winter. Suddenly a magic will happen such as when the sky watercolour washes are applied to the paper and they suddenly freeze into beautiful feathered patterns.

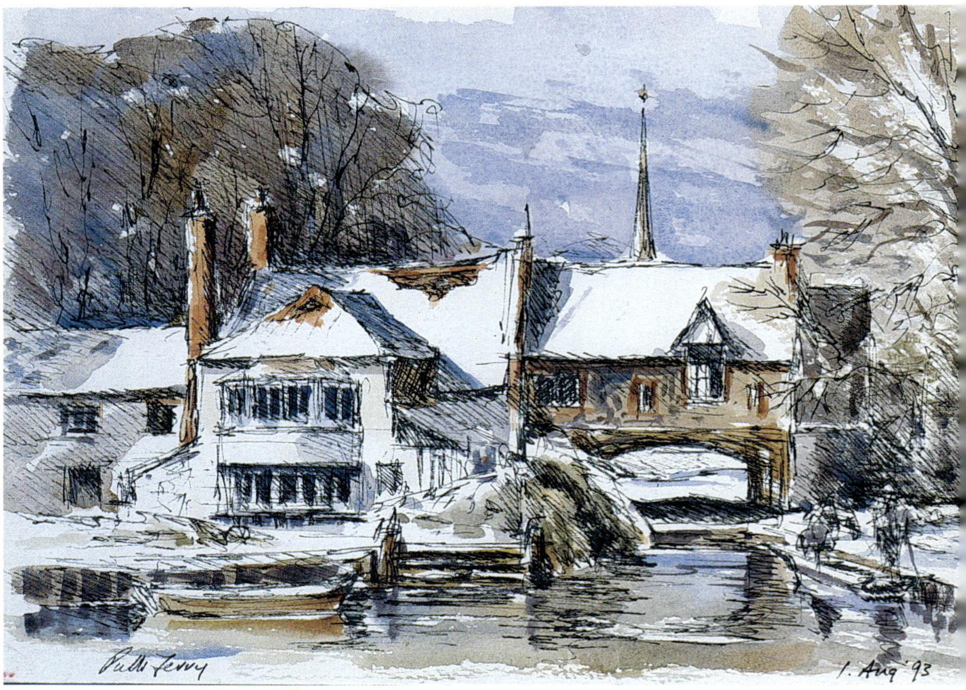

A spread from my sketch book.

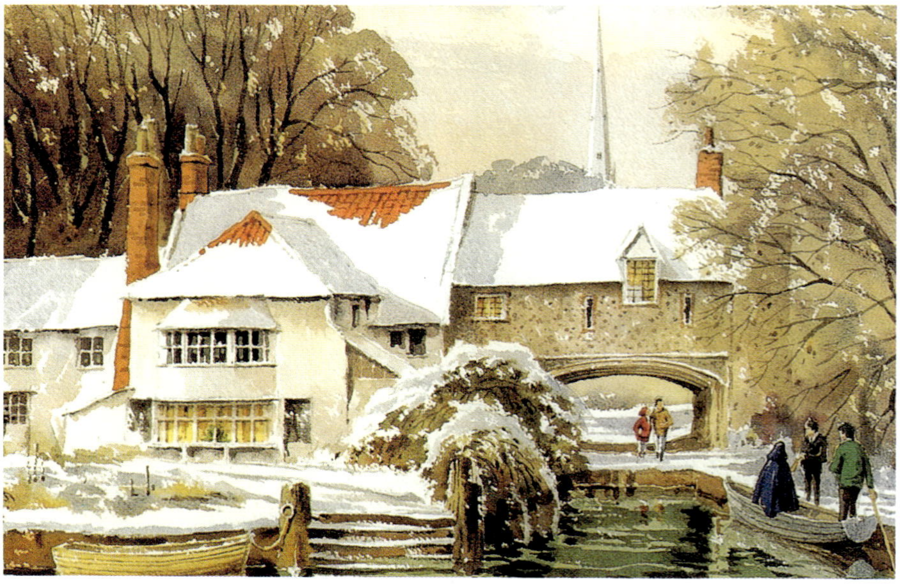

Pull's Ferry.

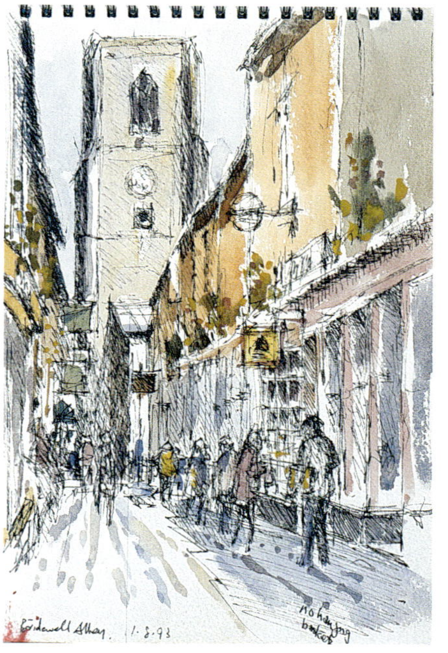

My sketch of Bridewell Alley (above) was actually executed on the first day of August. Obviously there was no mantle of winter. Indeed it was a hot and dusty and the hanging baskets trailed colourful geraniums and lobelia. But with a Christmas card in my imagination and the royalties it would generate the hanging baskets were easily transformed into Christmas trees decorated with colourful lights. The scorched pavement was deep in slushed snow at the flick of a brush and the glint of a pound coin.

Bishop's Bridge was done on the same August day. The deep, lush foliage of the trees disappeared leaving skeletons. The warm stone hardened white with snow. Sleigh bells merried the air, not the slow, languid rhythm of a near-by lawn mower. The short-sleeved shirts and the light cotton frocks vanished under a muffle of velvet and tweed, leather and corduroy. It was no longer the airless gravity of a heatwave but the hollow stillness of a freeze.

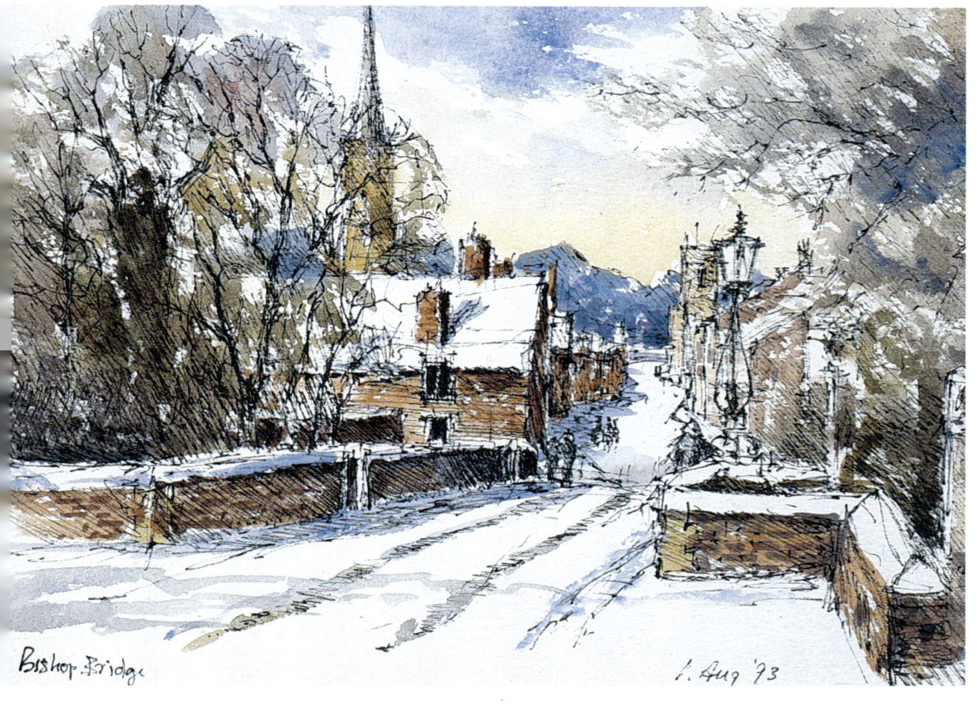

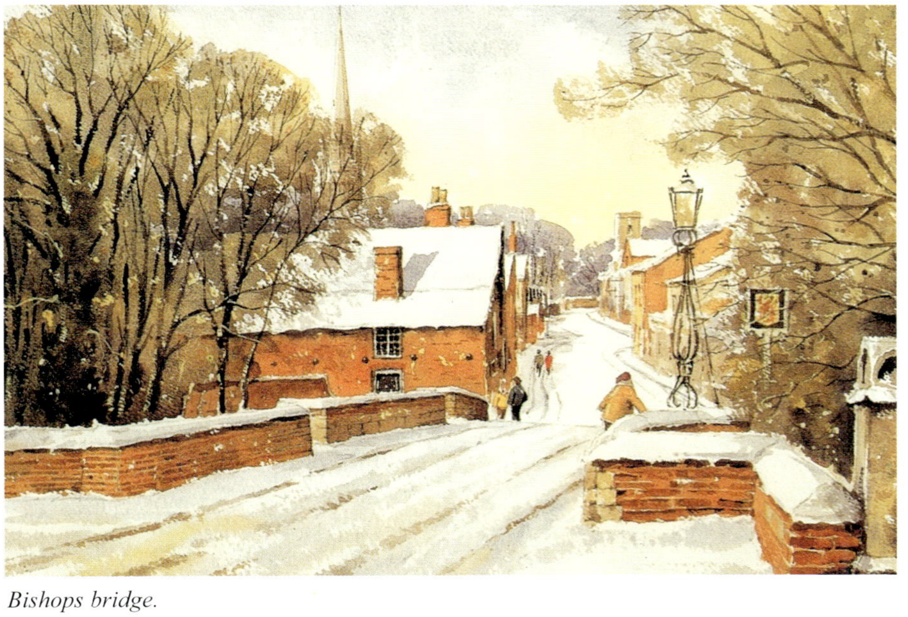

Bishops bridge.

Norwich Cathedral

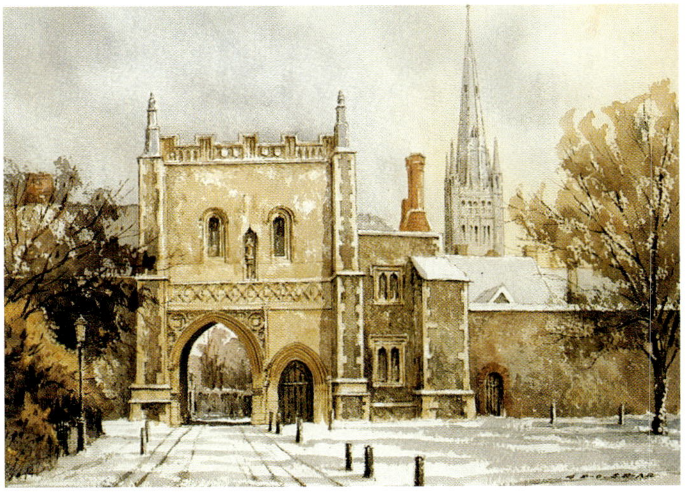

Bishop's Palace Gateway.

One of the many joys for the artist confronted by Norwich Cathedral is its sublime simplicity. It is the purity of a boy chorister's voice as it achieves the highest notes. It is a filigreed architectural hymn of praise. It is light, weightless, airy. The spire is as the spine of a feather. The body of its mass ephemeral.

Yet there was something else, something said to me when I began my painting.Portraits of the Cathedral, they had said casually in conversation, sell best as cards in the gift shop if they are snow scenes.

Snow scenes. The still frozen light of winter. The poignant brevity of daylight. The way snow becomes a rime on stone like icing sugar. Summer suns do not reflect from stone, their heat is radiated in a glow. But the ice of winter chimes when it is snow on stone.

And as I sat wrapped against the unforgiving cold the Cathedral did indeed wear winter's mantle majestically.

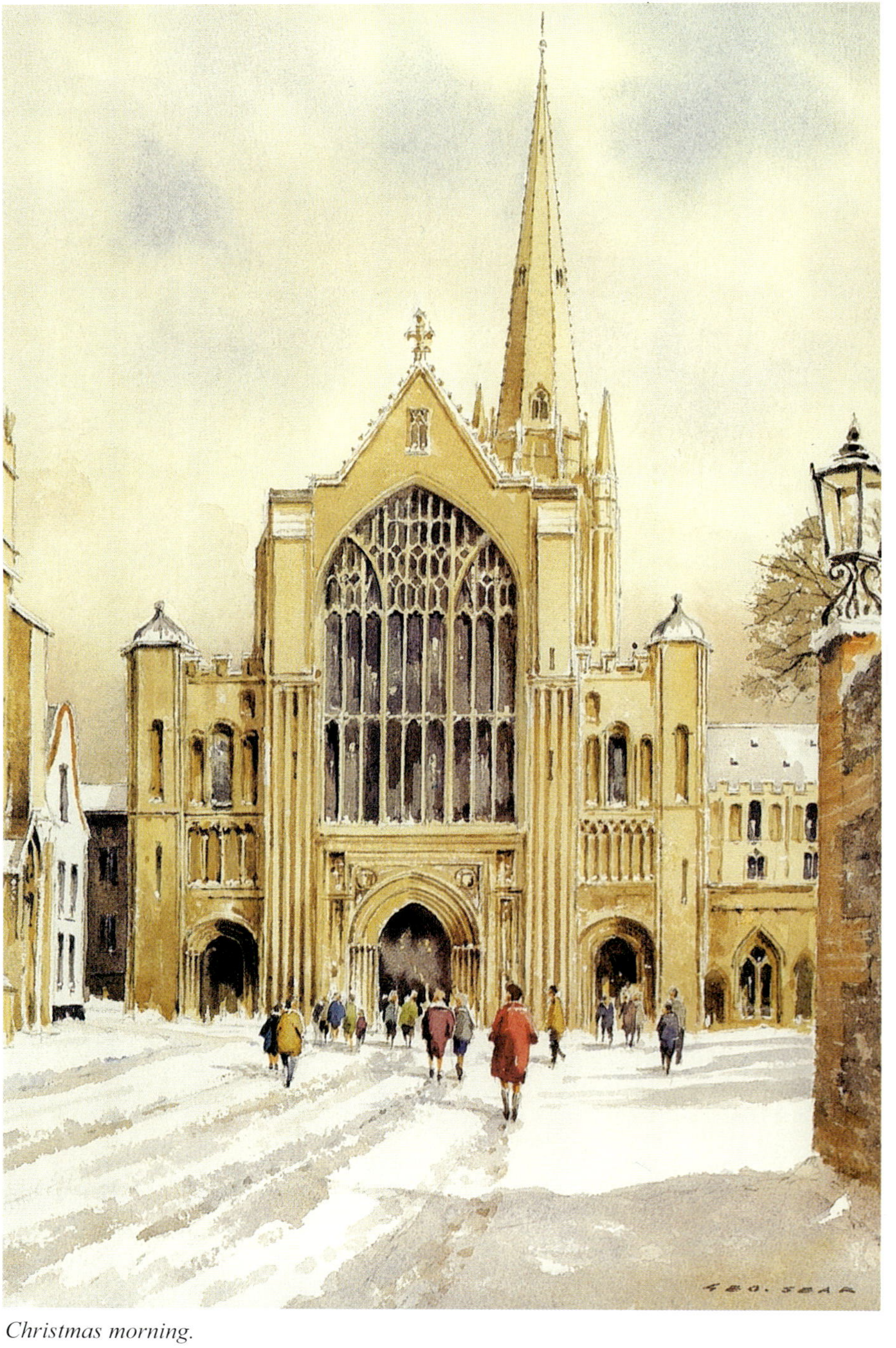

Christmas morning.

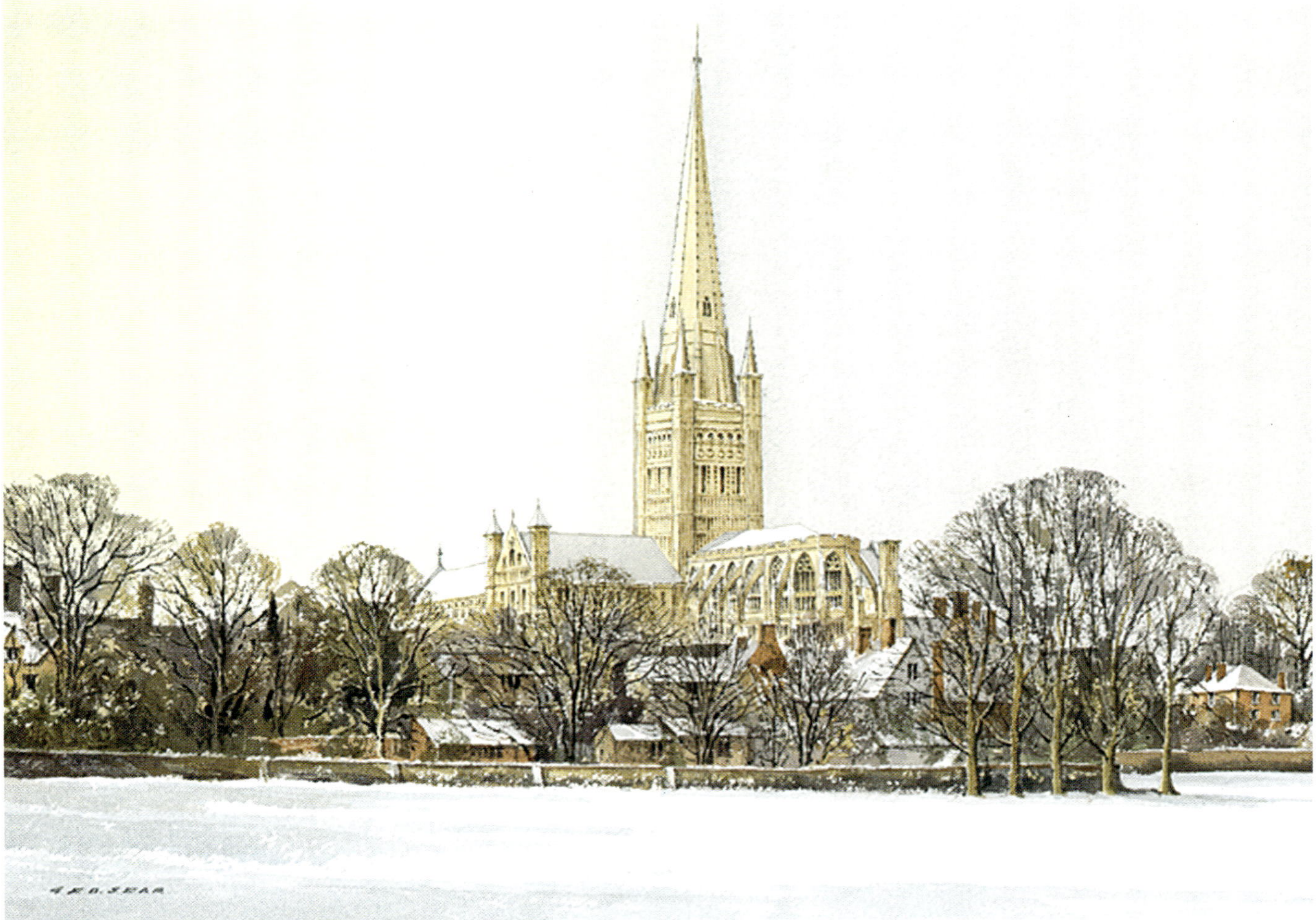

The Cathedral Norwich.

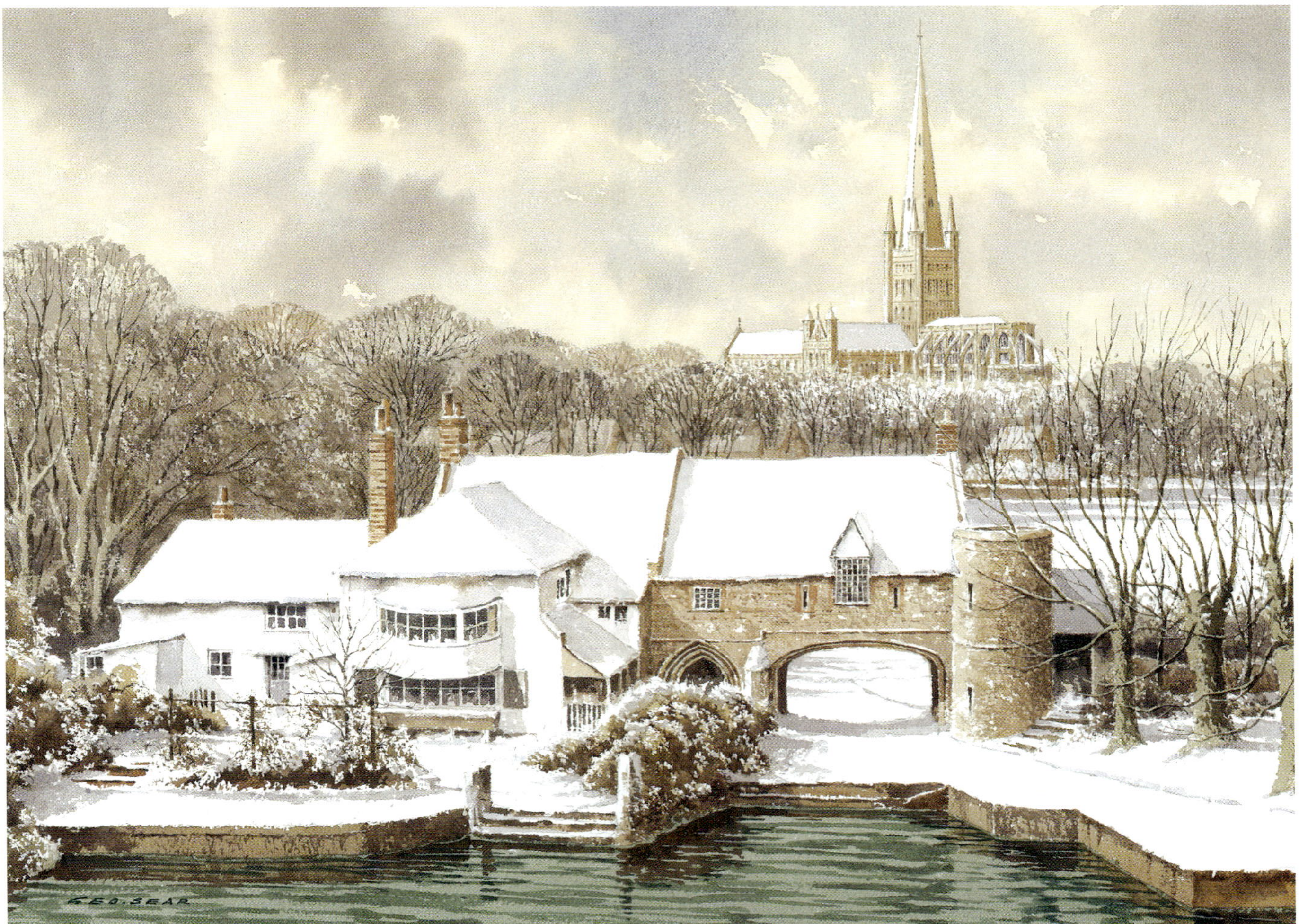

Winter at Pull's Ferry.

'The Art of having fun'

Exhibitions at Picturecraft, Holt

Six times a year an extraordinary phenomena happens outside Picturecraft Gallery in Holt, Norfolk. At about a quarter to seven on a Friday evening - it is always Fridays - a queue begins to form. As the minutes begin to tick away it grows. By seven o'clock about eighty people are waiting in line, the spirit of camaraderie alive amongst them, laughter, shared memories, hugged reunions. By twenty past the queue is 200 yards long stretching across the car park and snaking into the centre of the town. The sense of anticipation is palpable. The air electric. Those at the end envying those at the front. Those lucky ones at the front pressing their noses against the glass of the door.

Inside, the other side of the door, the wine, red and white, is already poured into countless rows of glasses on the long counter of the Framing Department. So is the fruit juice. The owner looks scrubbed in his best suit, his wife in her starchly special frock. The artist hovers nervously with his name printed on the badge he wears in his lapel. His wife dithers elsewhere, not to shade her husband's yearly lime-light. Staff, having worked their guts out for two days preparing for this jolly occasion, are at the ready, their smiles primed. This is art. This is the Preview of a one-man exhibition. The crowd is having fun and long to spend their money. This may be an imposing, cavernous art gallery but there is no reverential hush or awed respectful whisperings.

Instead there is a mad scramble to be first in when the door opens at seven-thirty. Many ignore the proffered wine and dash to get to the pictures. Ceremony is not stood upon for there is none to stand on. The hundreds that flock here only come to look at the new paintings. They do not hold glasses and hold forth. They simply love the work this artist produces and are amazed he can make eighty or so in a year. How can he do it? His one-man shows are important annual events in their lives, not something to attend or to be seen at. And a large proportion of them buy and take home with them - after the five-day exhibition is over, of course - paintings like trophies.

The artist is a sensitive man. In order to satisfy the hopes and aspirations of his admirers he has painted two dozen charmingly small, almost miniature, paintings of letter-boxes that are affordable in two figures. These are immediately pounced upon and there is a flurry of cheque books at the tables where two young ladies arrange the sale of paintings, naming and addressing meticulously.

It is a quarter to eight and the

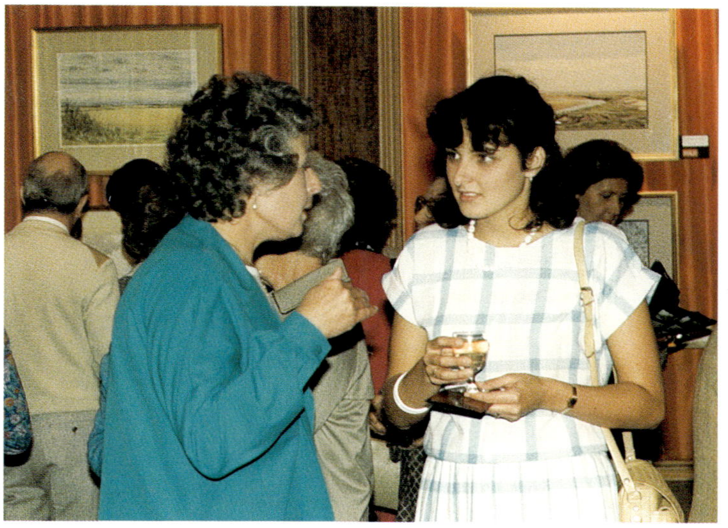

Maureen and our daughter Denise.

gallery is hopping. Old friends meet, a quadrille of admirers dance before the eighty or so paintings hung against the curtains round the walls. The choreography is instinctive, there is much excusing and excused, sliding sideways, bobbing, jigging forwards and backwards. Wine is slurped, shoulders slapped or hugged, hands pumped, cheeks kissed with a theatre of mmmwhahs. Everyone is a darling, my dear. The artist stands chatting amiably in the middle of it all, a king bee, a magnet for those who would touch and talk to celebrity.

The paintings hang seemingly without support, suspended by their own will upon the curtains that cover the bays. The gathered throng at this Preview may not realise, however, that behind these curtains hang other paintings by nineteen other artists, hidden for the five-day duration of this one-man show. These obscured artists have been suspended of their three weekly hanging fee. For they pay only rent to be exhibited at Picturecraft. And when they sell a painting they get what it was sold for. This gallery is unique in that it takes no commission. Not one penny. Other galleries often charge as much as 50%. Not here.

It is twenty past eight and the Preview progresses. The red stickers that indicate paintings sold proliferate. A rash of measles has broken out on the walls. More people gather round the artist as he explains his philosophy for the umpteenth time. His wife moves in as support and protection.The gallery owner and his wife circulate. A wraith-like widow who already has ‘hundreds’ of paintings by the artist from previous shows take the plunge and buys another, a view of Cley Mill. She then wonders to her friends where on earth will she hang it? Her sitting room is already an art gallery in itself. Perhaps, she ponders, something can go up to the spare bedroom to make room? Or maybe - and this could be the wine talking - she could hang things lower, at hip-height? She’ll work that out later. Meanwhile she has a new painting by her favourite artist and all her friends admire it through the green of their envy.

Nine o’clock has been and gone and the evening grows jaded. The die-hards are on their third or even fourth glass and are getting maudlin. Finally and inevitably the art, having been digested and soaked up, becomes a back-drop to conversations that grow louder and more raucous as they lack substance. The bonhomie turns its corner into mawkishness. The artist, game to the last, stifles a yawn. It has been a long day for him and his doughty wife, who even now smiles like a bemused girl and laughs at nothing at all.

The gallery owner signals to a member of staff to start collecting glasses, the bar closed half an hour ago. The art of guiding reluctant elbows towards the door was perfected many, many one-man shows ago.

At last Michael and Teresa Hill turn the key in the lock of their gallery door. They wish George Sear and Maureen his wife good-night. Of course it has been a success. It always is, and not only for George Sear. Every artist’s one-man exhibition is the same; people queuing round the block, laughter, memories reunioned, red stickers all over the place, hangers on hard to move at the end. But that’s the fun of art the Picturecraft way.

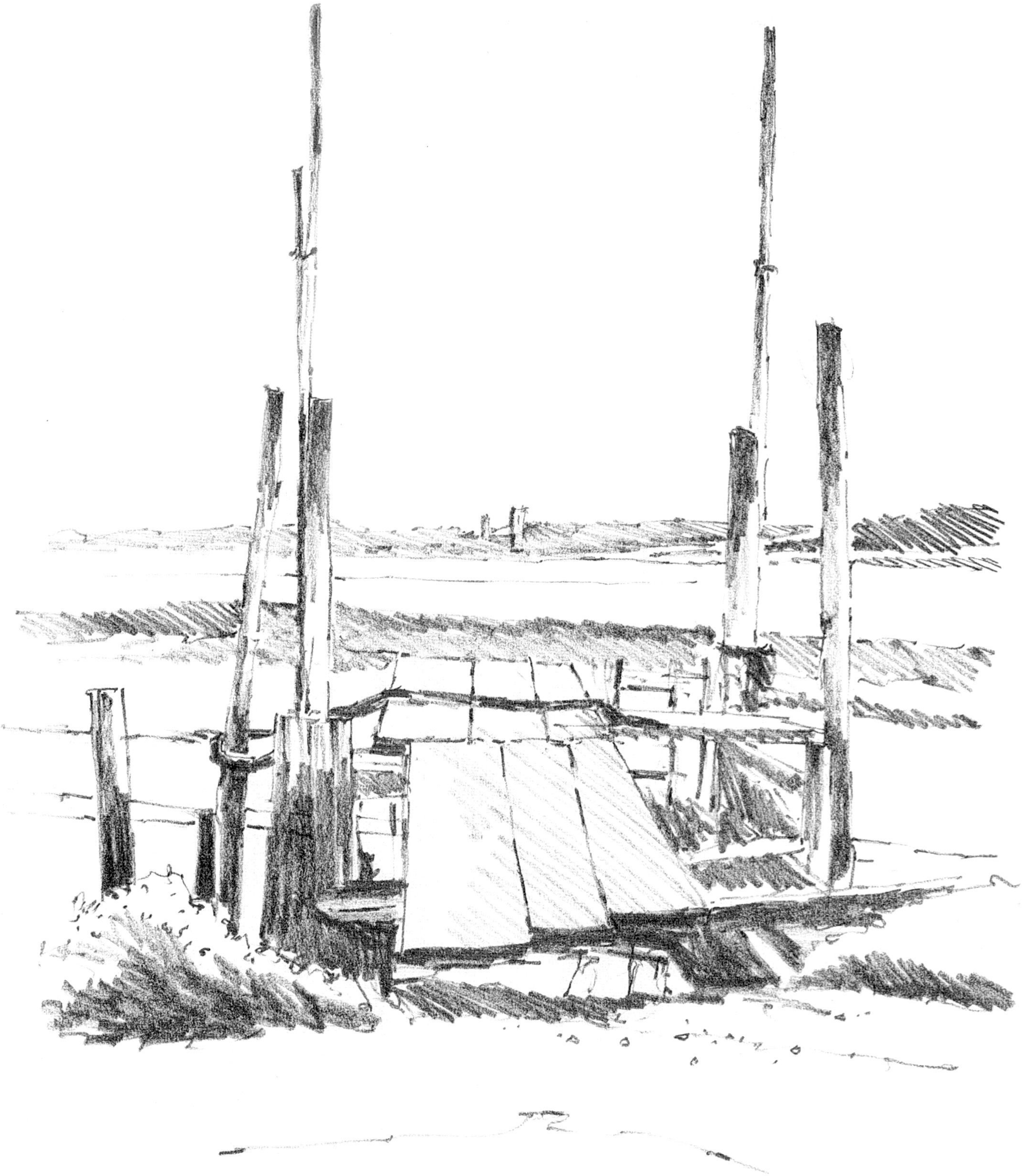

'At home with my paintings'

In the Studios

While the majority of my paintings are executed where and when possible on-site, the sanctuary and peace of my studios in Holt and my home in Hertfordshire is vitally important.

My home in the Chilterns has a large 'Back to Nature' garden, and joins the National Trust estate of Ashridge, so when working there, completing a painting started on site, I can relive the natural surroundings. I also surround myself with sketches and photos of poppies/boats/marshes and sunsets, whatever I need. So what you need is bags of reference to help you.

I do not have a philosophy concerning my work for that is too grand a word. Mine is an attitude towards it, which is fundamentally to always be positive. A glass for the artist should always be half full, just as each painting is not half bad but half good. And yet if it is only half good there must be something you have still to learn, else it would be all good. The only way to learn painting, as in life itself, is from your mistakes. The more mistakes you overcome the more enjoyable becomes the painting, and it communicates your pleasure to those who see it. It's as simple as that.

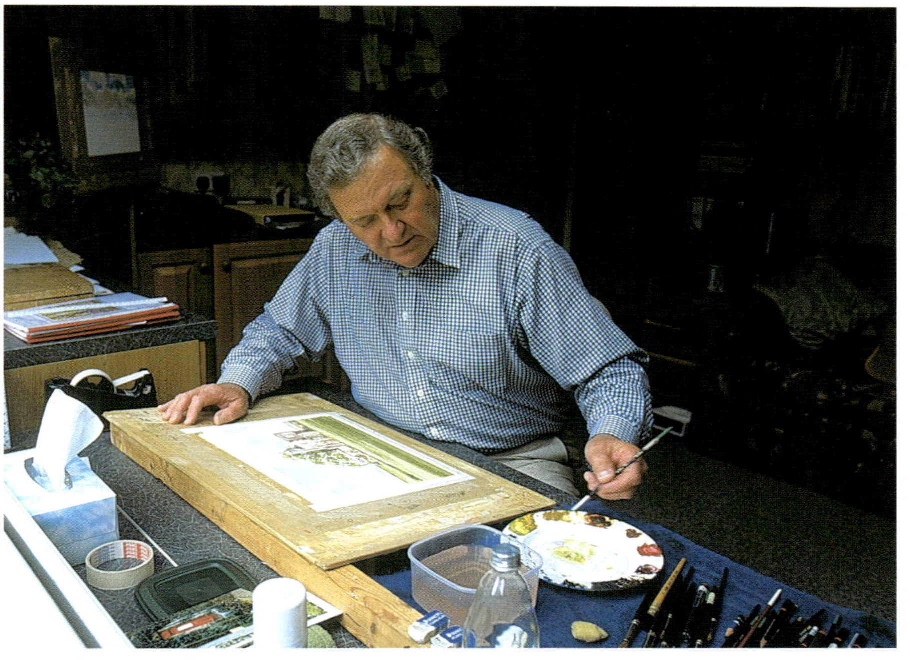

At work in my studio.

'Painting on and off location'

Materials and Equipment

I did not intend this book to become an 'How to paint book'. For those painters who are interested in the materials I use, and the way I am painting at present, a few notes may be of help.

Materials & Equipment

In this part of the book I will mention the various items I use when painting my water-colours. Every artist has his or her preferences, these are mine.

Sketching

My sketch pads are 'The Langton' made by Daler Rowney, 10in x 7in, 140lb water-colour paper, spiral bound.

I draw with Edding 1800 0.7 profipens, these are waterproof and ideal if later you wish to wash with colour. When I sketch with pencils 2B, 4B and 6B, I must fix it with Winsor & Newton fixative spray to stop the drawing from smudging. A ten minute sketch is invaluable; you can work from these in the studio if the weather turns bad whilst painting.

Eraser

The one I use is a Staedtler for paper, you should not need it often, as a sketch, is a sketch.

Paints & Palette

Winsor & Newton Artist Water Colour (Tubes to replenish my palette)

1. Prussian Blue.
2. Winsor Blue.
3. Cobalt Blue.
4. French Ultramarine
5. Paynes Grey.
6. Cadmium Lemon.
7. Cadmium Yellow.
8. Raw Sienna
9. Burnt Sienna
10. Light Red.
11. Alizarin Crimson
12. Burnt Umber

I also carry Winsor Red and Rose Madder.

My palette is a 9' enamel plate, with the colours on the rim, and the central area for mixing. I know this has its limitations, but it suits me.

I made a carry box, and a friend supplied the round sponge in the lid to stop it rattling. I couldn't get a 'Roundtoit'.

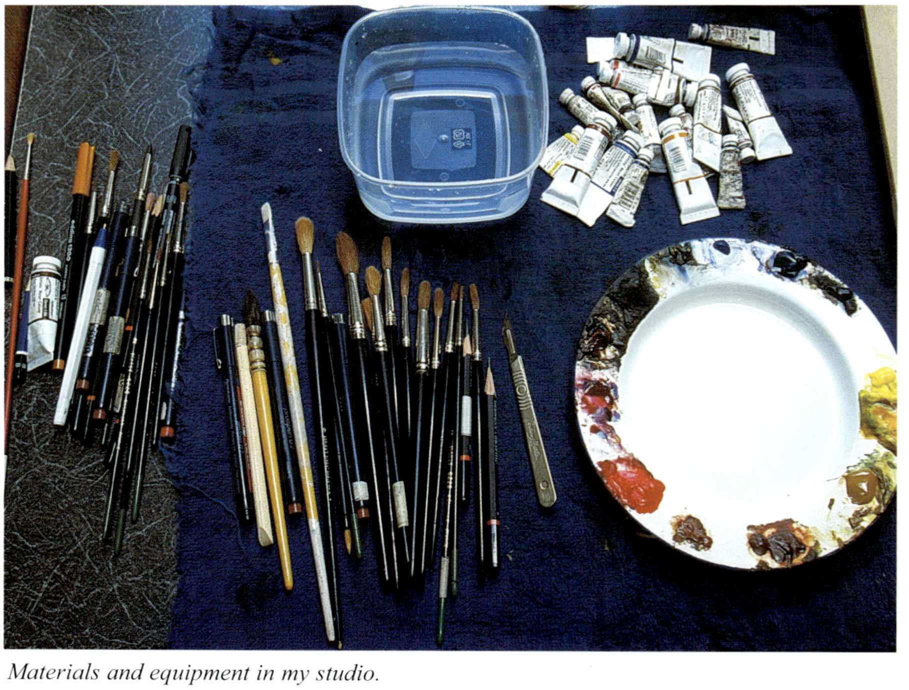

Materials and equipment in my studio.

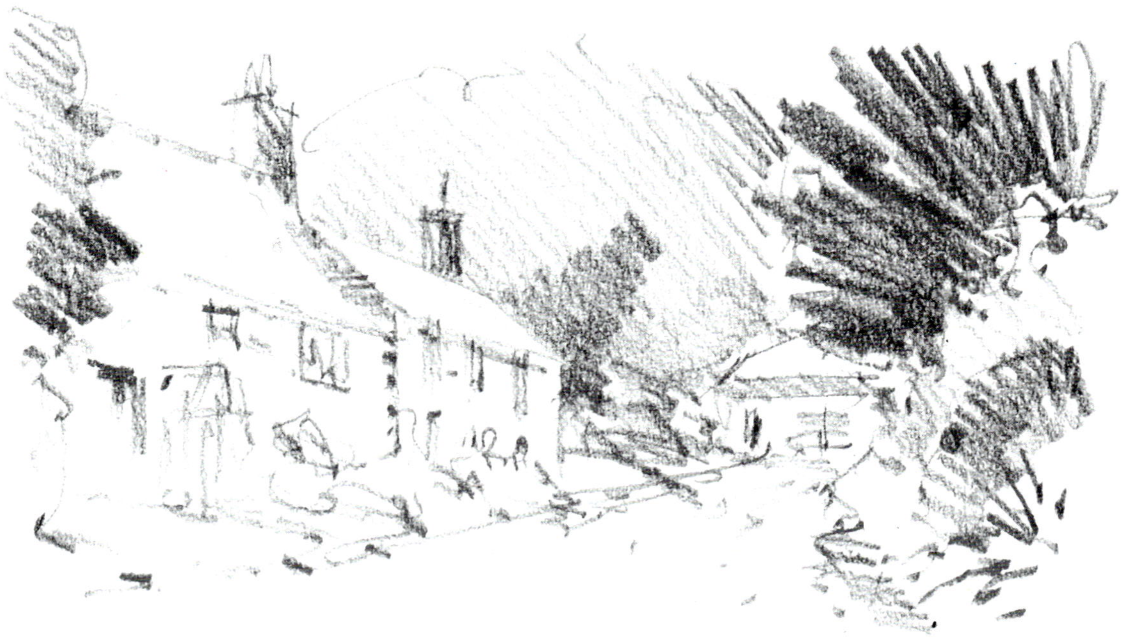

Paper

I use Arches 300lb Rough, and Not, also Whatman 200lb Rough. Taped on to a plywood board capable of fitting a 1/2 imperial sheet. I tend to stretch the Whatman, but not the Arches as this is thicker.

Brushes

Sizes 2.6.9.12.14. I use sable brushes but these are expensive. Beginners can quite adequately use a range of 2,4,8,12, the larger can be a synthetic mixture.

Stool or chair

The one I favour is Phillips of Axminster, light and easy to carry, with seat 14 inches high, enabling me to put my paints and equipment on a towel on the ground.

Water

A square Tupperware box, to carry my tubes of paint in, as this doubles as a water container and can not fall over easily. I carry the water in an old Schweppes bottle.

Carrying Bag

Canvas with waterproof lining. 13' x 10' x 5' with 3 pockets and a zip pocket at the front, with a shoulder strap. I can easily fit everything in, except my art board and stool.

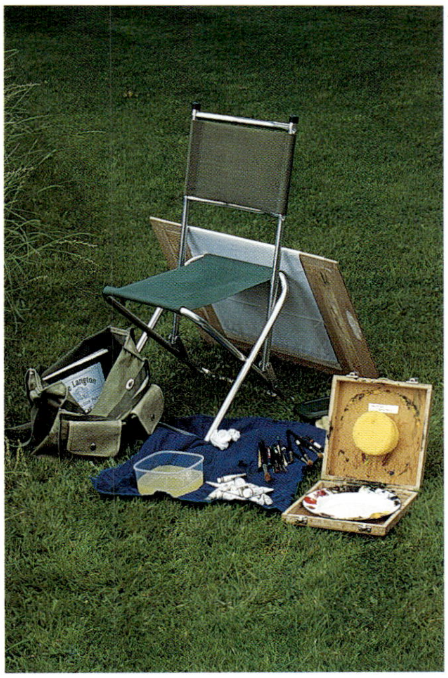

My palette in it's box.

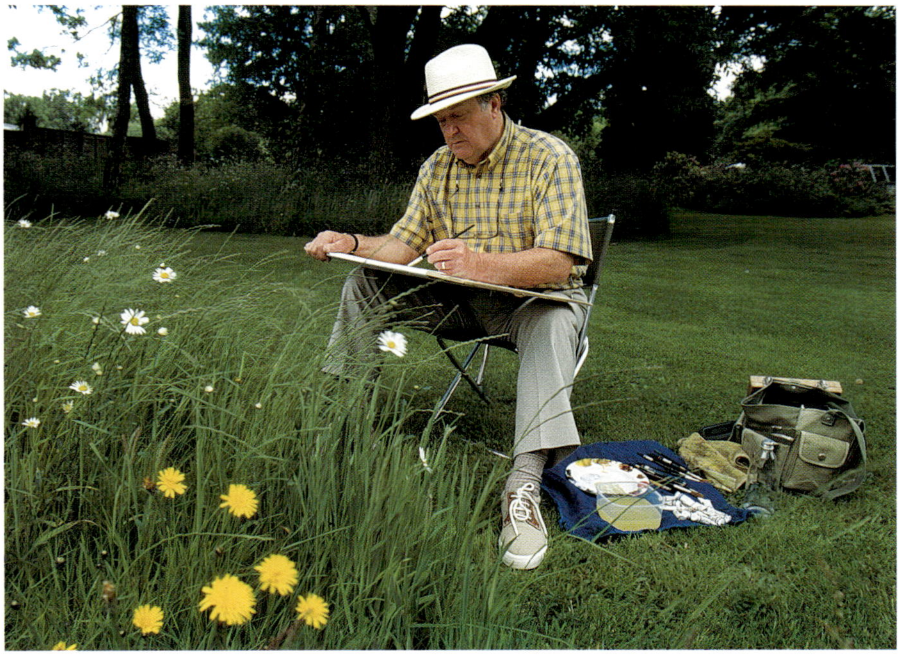

Painting in my 'Back to nature' garden.

On Site

One of the advantages of painting on site is the contact with nature one gets, you feel and are at one with the subject.

Paint in small groups, two or three friends together, it takes a little time to adjust after working from the comfort of your studio at home, but the effort after the initial shock will be a rewarding one.

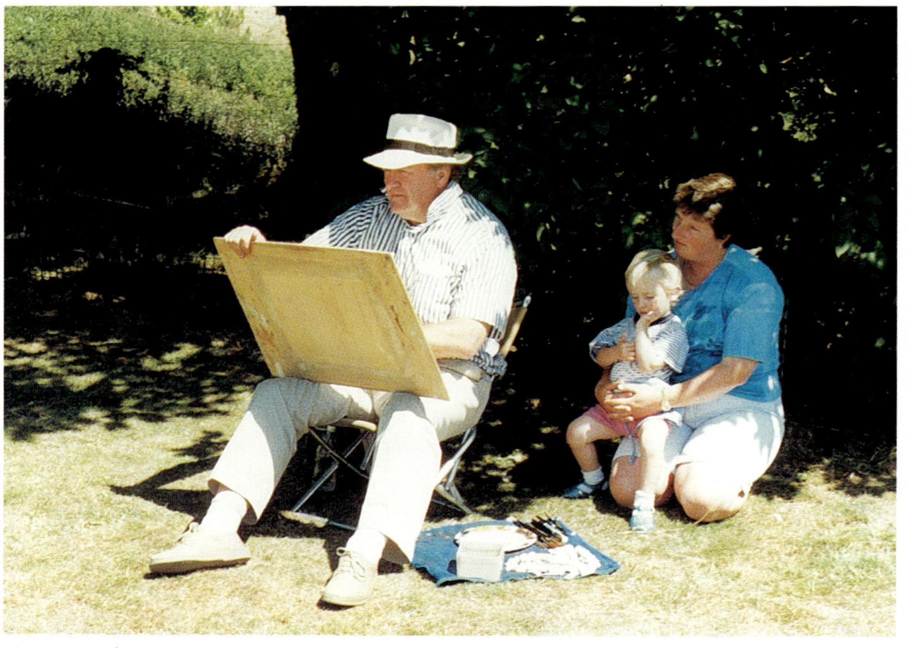

A young admirer.

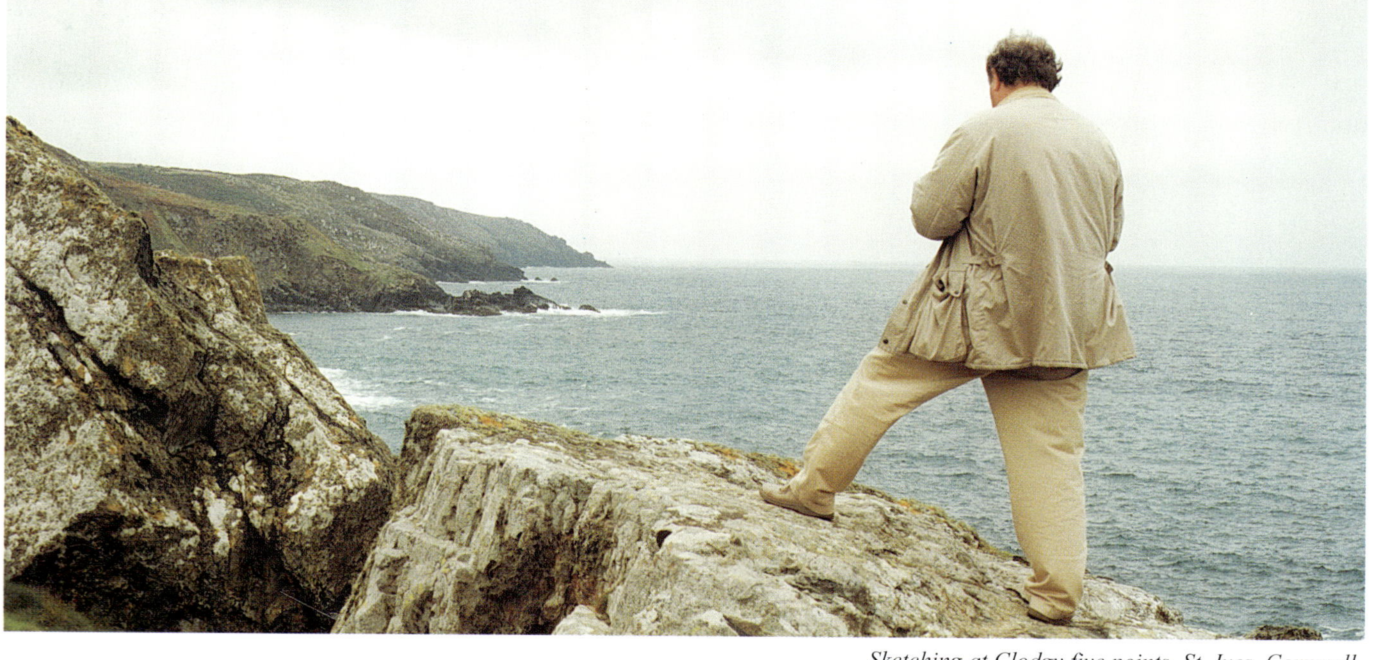

Sketching at Clodgy five points, St. Ives, Cornwall.

'From the Gallery walls...'

A Journey in Water Colour

Norfolk, for me, has been a real find, and has been almost enough. But to complement my Norfolk scenes I do paint in other locations and other counties.

Let me take you on a journey in Water Colour. We start from Norfolk, Holt in fact.

We start from Norfolk with its vast expanses of sky, sea and air; its marshes and estuaries and it's tranquil rivers; contrasting so sharply with the bustling life of its city streets.

We travel on to the busy market towns and rural villages of the Shires and the Wolds, and so on to lakeland's grandeur of mountains and lakes. We soon cross the border into Scotland with its misty mountains and lochs of myth and legend.

We see the sun setting over Skye and the Western Isles, we move eastward to St. Andrews, the home of golf. We now turn southwards to Peaks and Dales of Yorkshire and York itself, with its cobbled streets and snickleways. A brief pause in the groves of Academe of Cambridge. We end our journey in East Anglia where it began.

Many a mile have we travelled and much of beauty and interest have we seen, through our contemplation of the pictures on the 'Gallery Wall'.

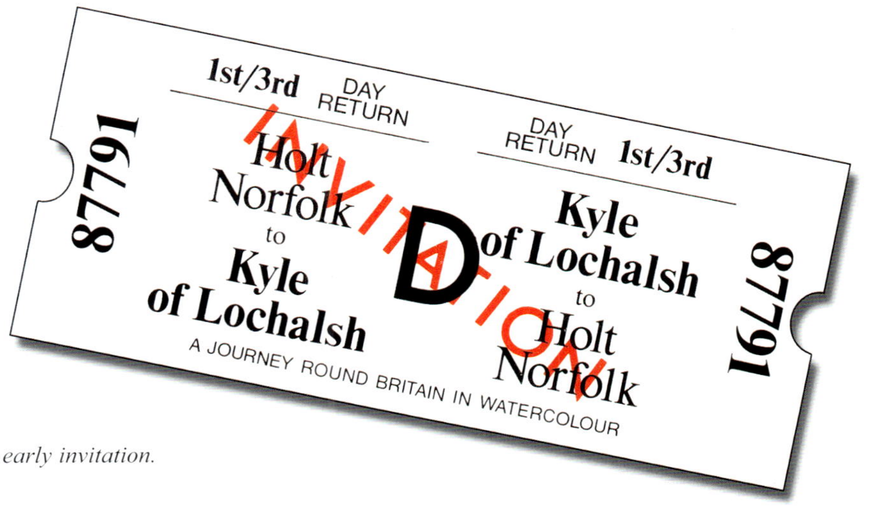

An early invitation.

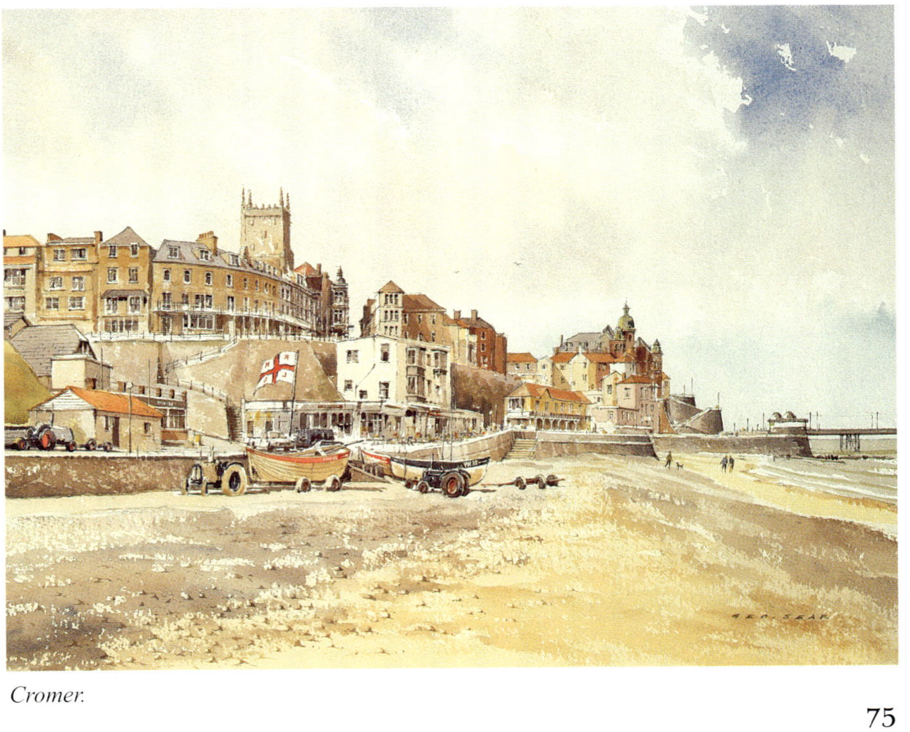

Cromer.

1. *Staithes, N. Yorkshire*
2. *The Old Mill at Corpusty*
3. *A Norfolk lane*
4. *Misty morning, Woodbridge*

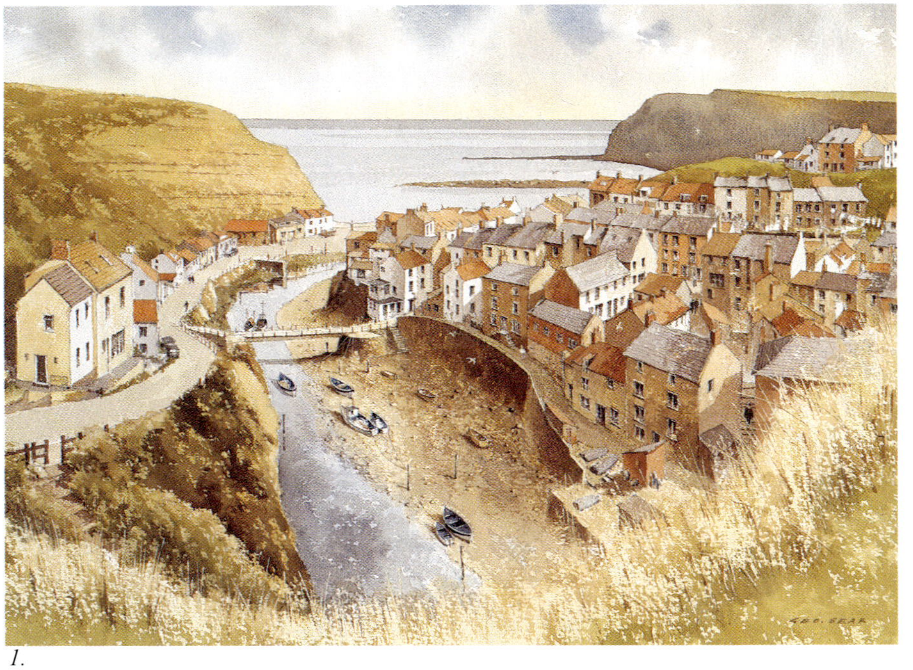

1.

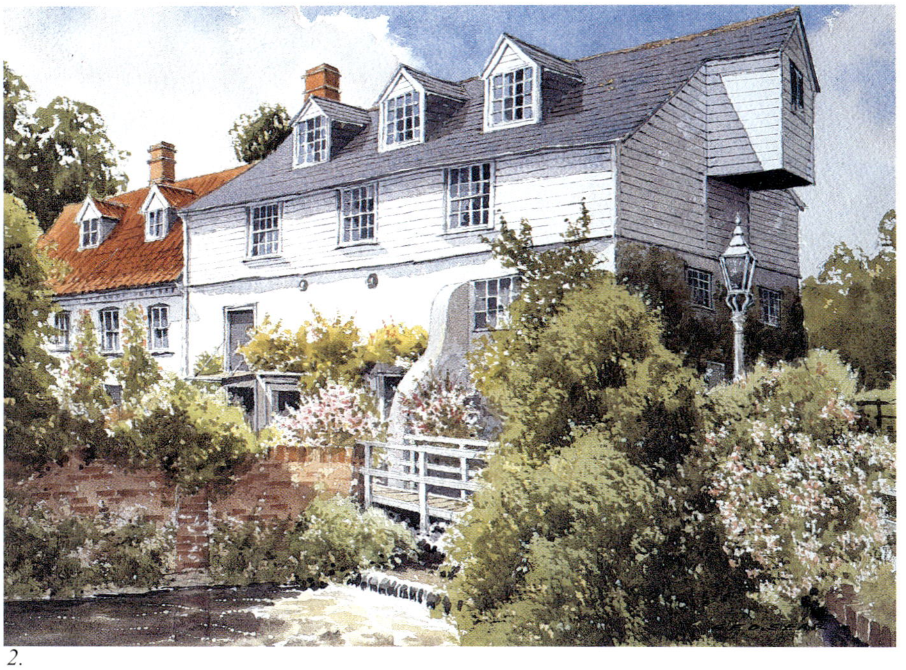

2.

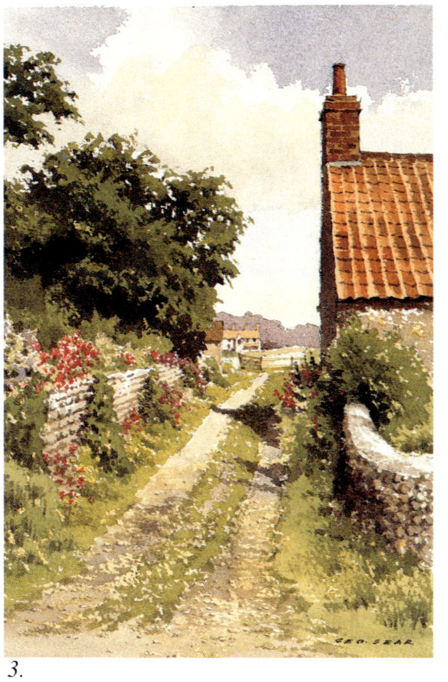

3.

Having passed the Old Mill at Corpusty many times on my journeys around Norfolk; instinctively knowing there must be a great picture here if only I could find it.

One sunny afternoon I took time out to find the ideal angle, unfortunately it meant standing on the bridge railings on the opposite side of the road, to take photographs and more importantly, sketching the mill into my sketch book by transferring details from 'life' onto the paper. This is infinitely better than searching the dark reccesses of a snap shot at home in the studio.

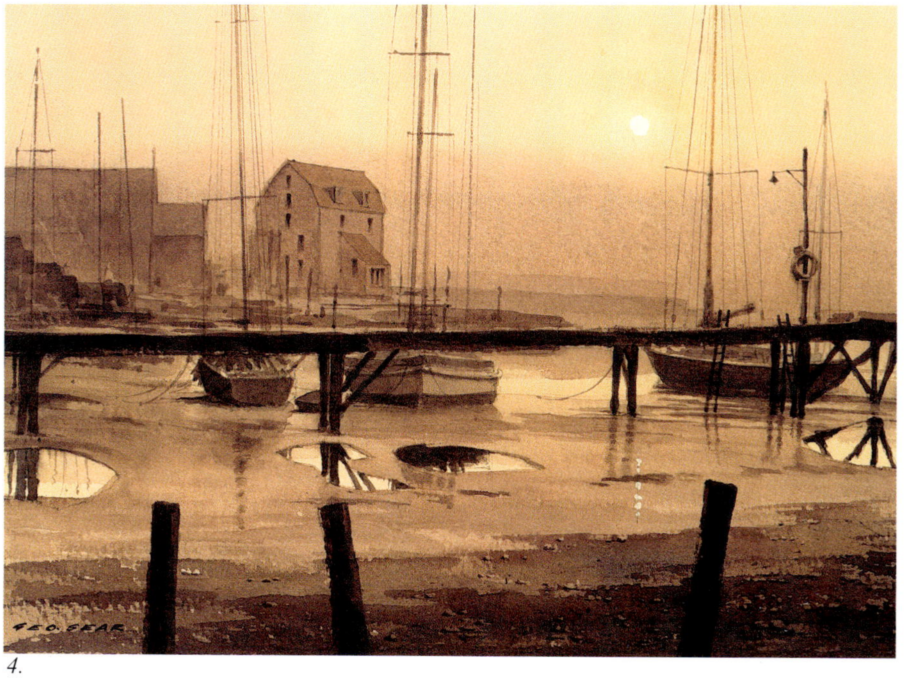

4.

An added bonus was in fact, that two of my regular buyers from Peterborough happened by, they stopped, just in case I was about to jump into the river, saw what I was doing and subsequently, at my exhibition, bought the picture for their collection.

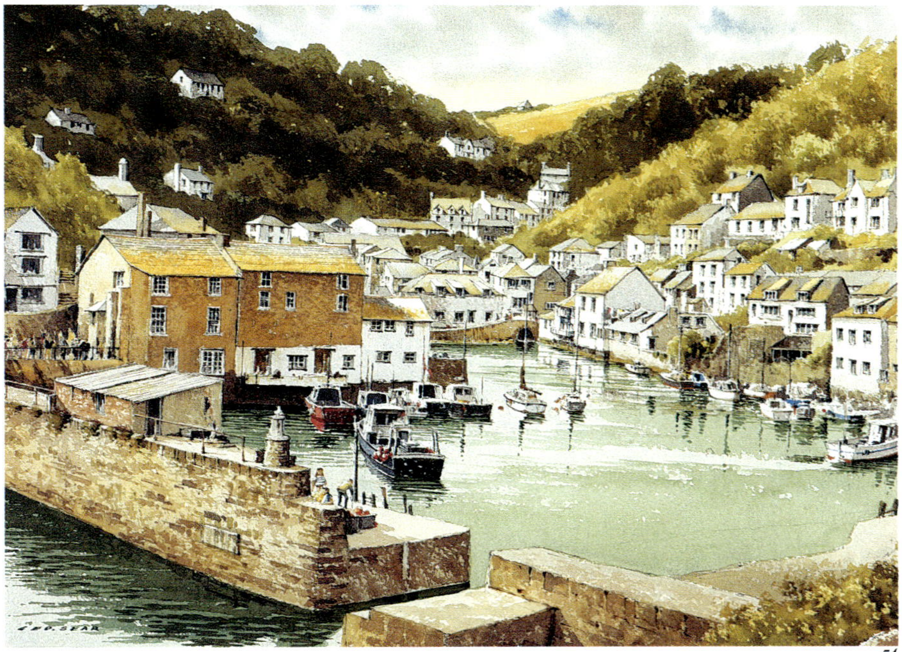

5.

5. Polperro, Cornwall
6. Canterbury
7. The Hythe, Maldon
8. Berkhamsted, Hertfordshire

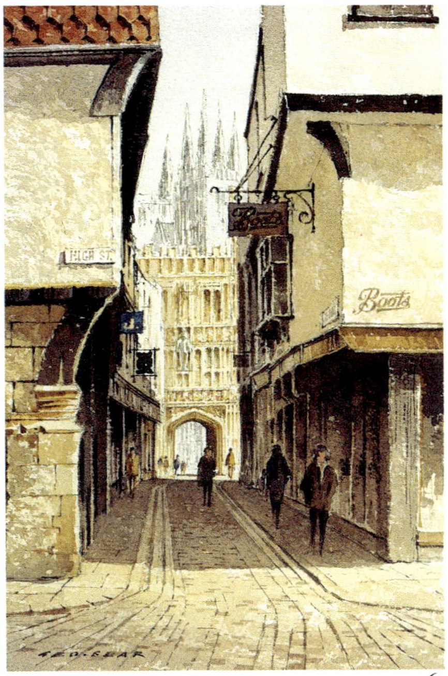

6.

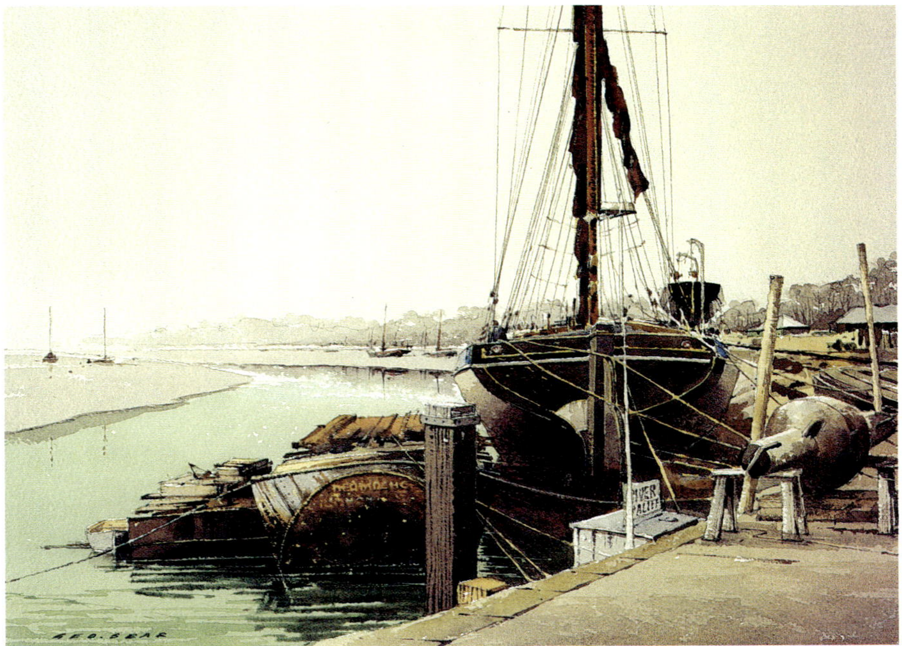

7.

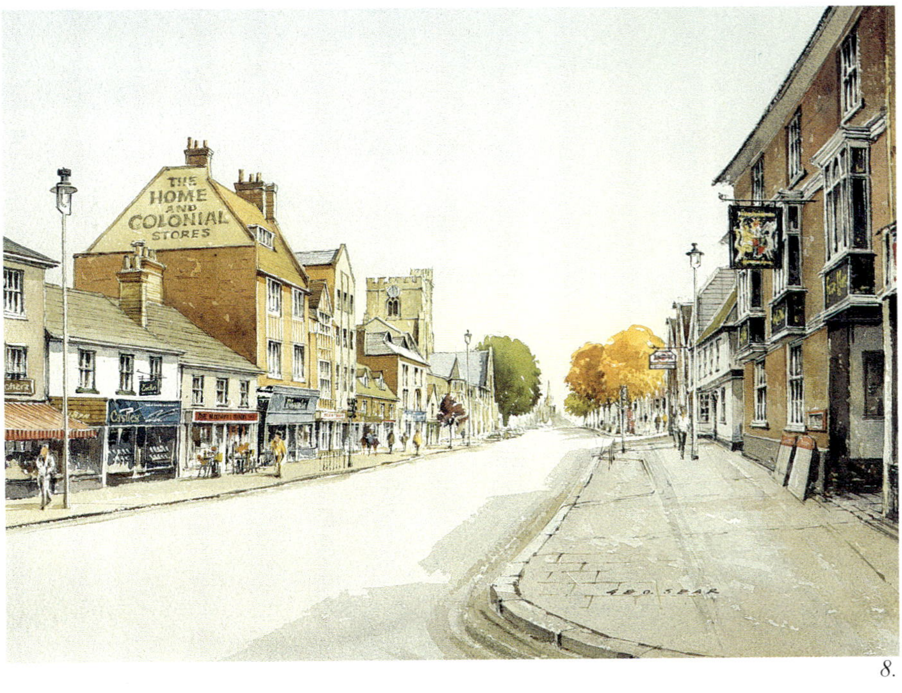

8.

Fact File

A Limited Palette

It was a misty morning when we arrived at the Hythe at Maldon in Essex. Having made the decision today that this was the spot, I drew in the Thames Barge that was under repair and with masking fluid, drew in the moorings.

With no obvious improvement in the weather, I started to paint with mixtures of French Ultramarine, Burnt Umber and Alizarin Crimson.

On nearing completion, I just added Raw Sienna with a touch of Payne's Grey for the water and mooring ropes to complete the picture. Sometimes the fewer colours, the better.

9. Lincoln Cathedral
10. High Water, Alfriston, Sussex
11. Langdale footpath
12. A Chiltern bluebell wood

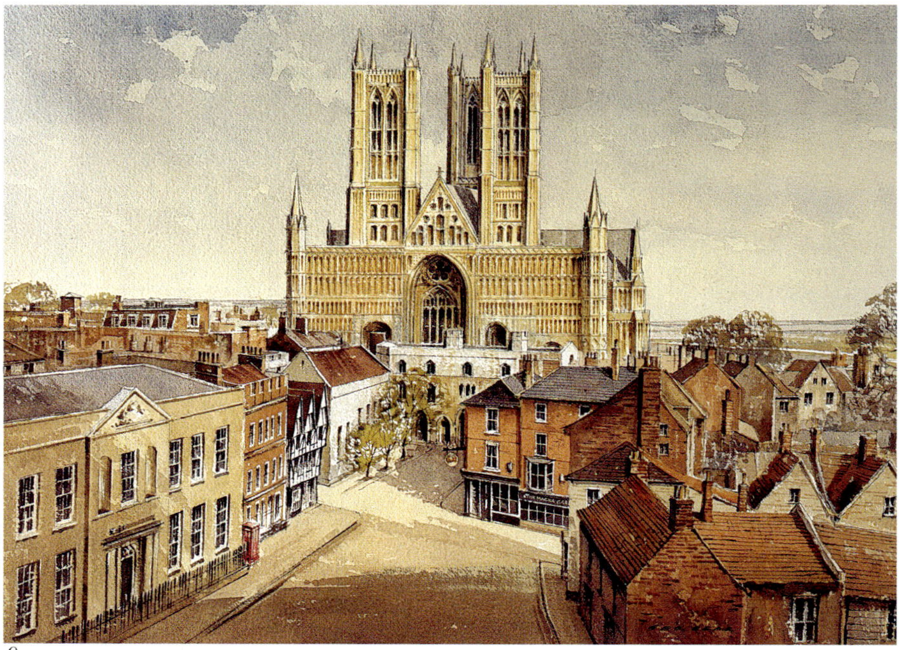
9.

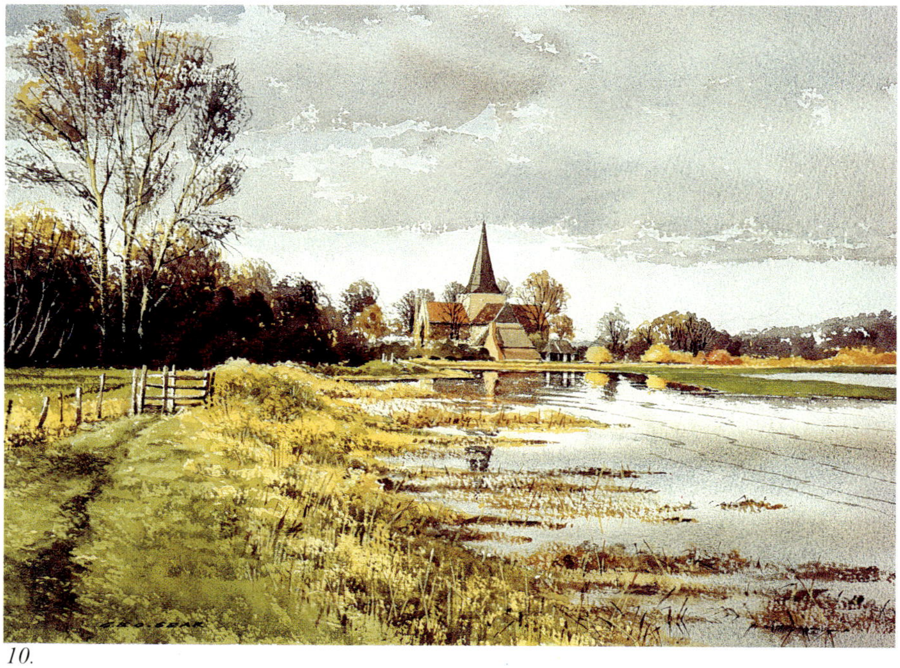
10.

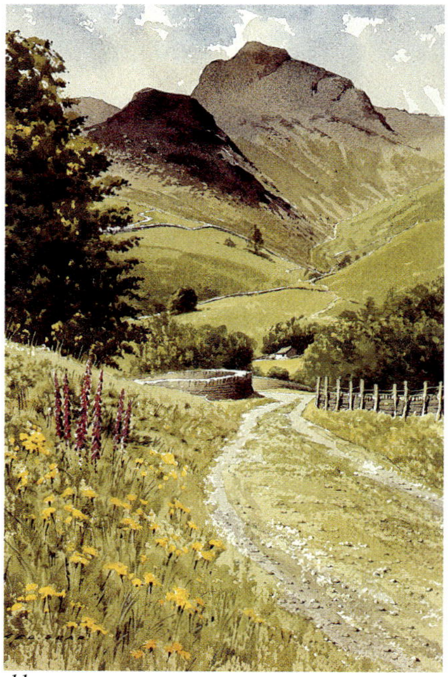
11.

The South Downs, and the Cuckmere Valley with the river flowing to the sea at Seven Sisters near by and Alfriston at the heart of it all, makes this such a paintable area.

I do not get to this area nearly enough. When I do, the paintings I have done can usually be found at Alfriston Gallery in the High Street.

This is a charming place, with a high standard of work of local scenes by professional artists.

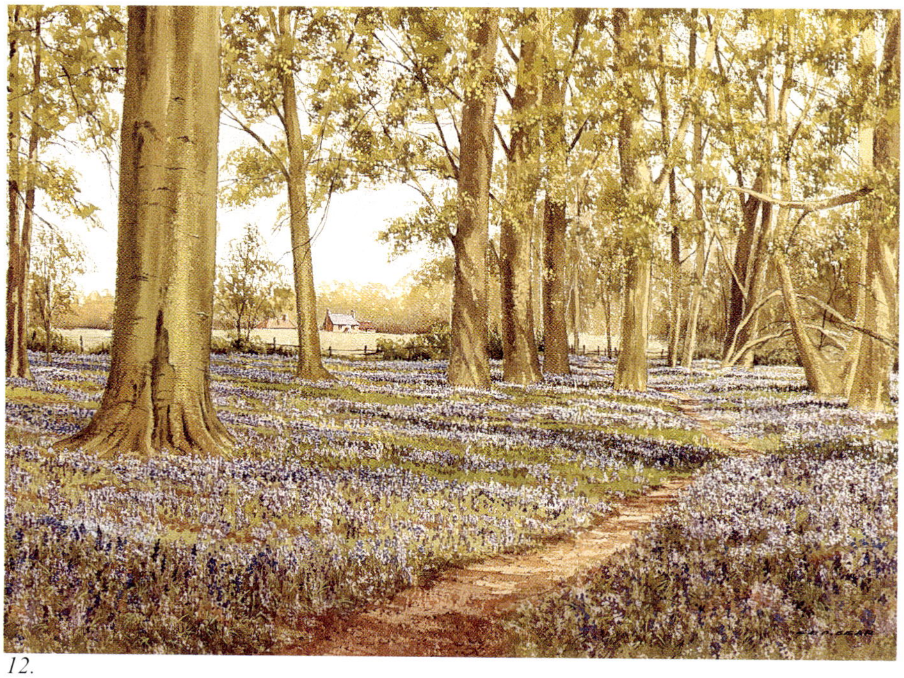
12.

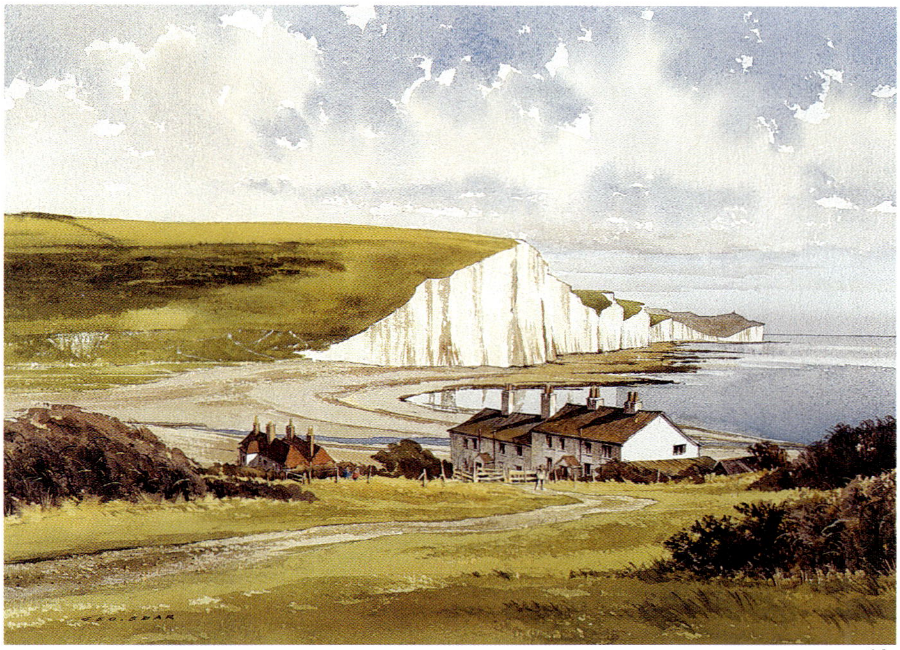

13.

13. The Seven Sisters, Sussex
14. 'Repertor' Maldon
15. The Hythe, Maldon, Essex
16. Northchurch, Hertfordshire

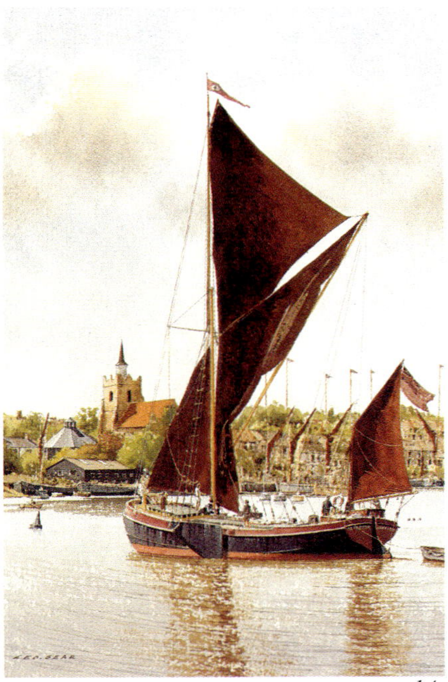

14.

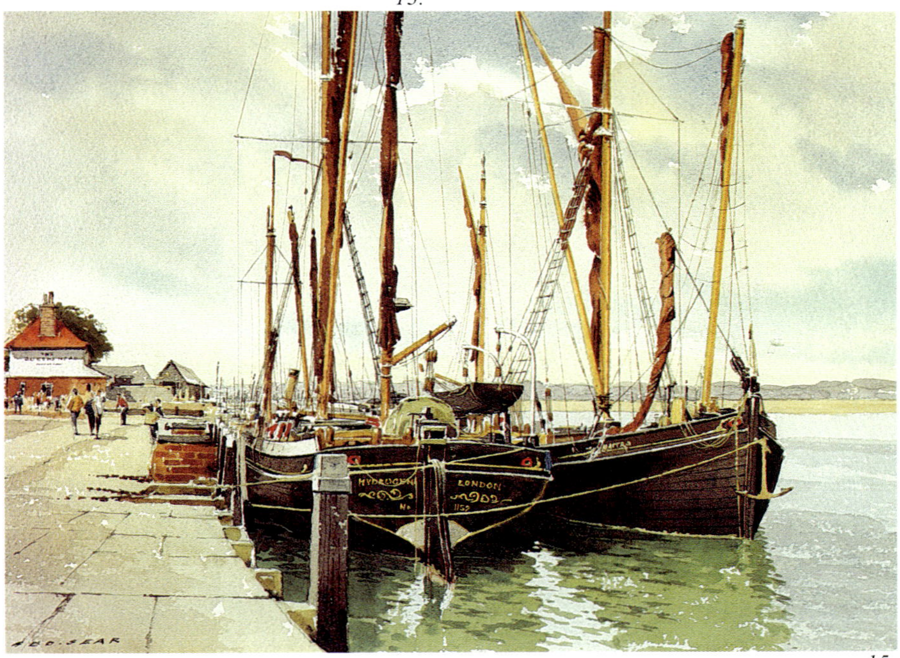

15.

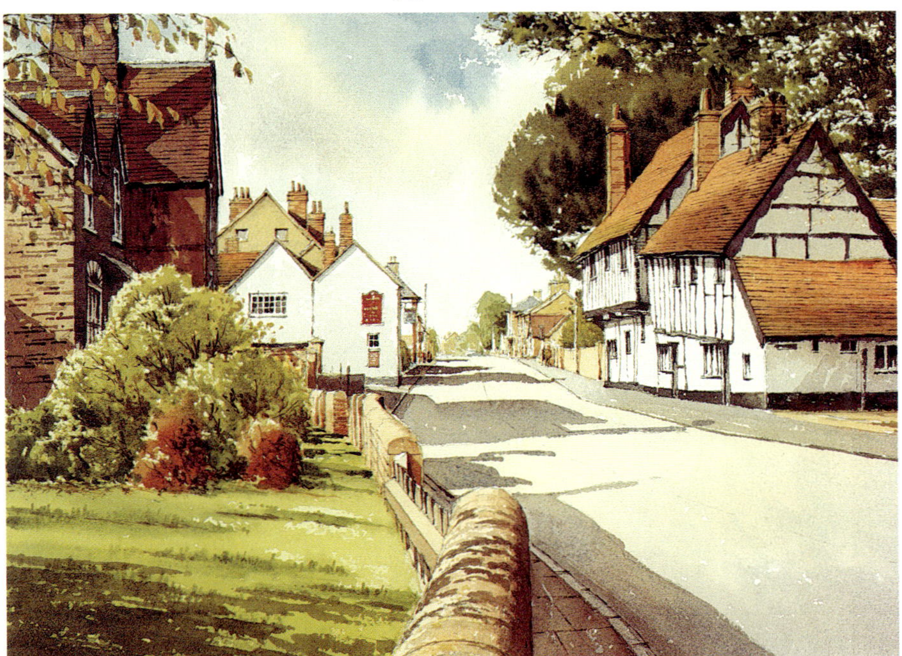

16.

Fact File

Don't get into a rut, variety is the spice of life.
As you can see over the last few pages, I like to stretch my imagination and subject matter. It keeps my mind fresh and alert, able to tackle new challenges, from a simple spontaneous picture, or a complex one.
Townscapes, Landscapes, Marine and Flower subjects all have their own separate challenges.

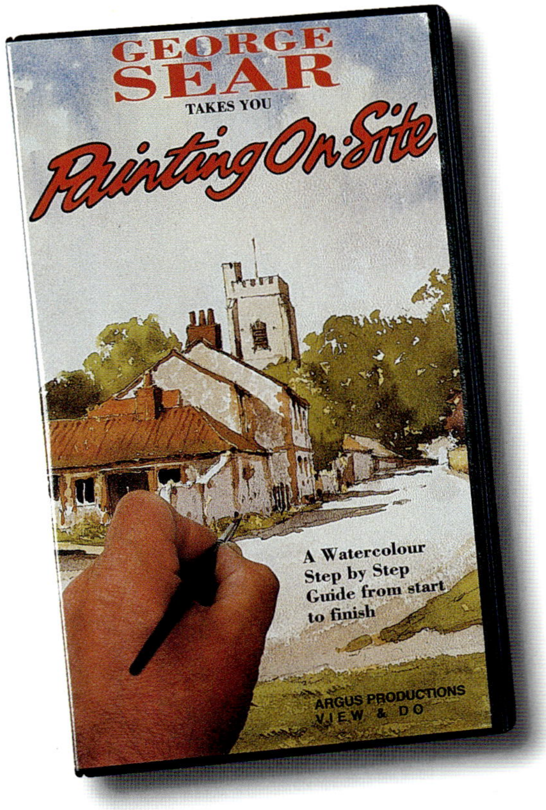

George Sear

takes you

'Painting on Site'

A Water-colour step by step guide from start to finish,
in the attractive village of Langham, Norfolk.
Produced by Argus Productions, Briston, the video is priced at £18 each
including postage from the artist at the following address.

'Clodgy'
Northchurch Common,
Berkhamsted,
Hertfordshire,
HP4 1LR.